FROM VIENNA TO 14th STREET

FROM VIENNA TO 14th STREET

A Memoir

Brigitte Angel

Copyright © 2005 by Brigitte Angel.
Cover Photo by: David Sweitzer

Library of Congress Number: 2005904223
ISBN :   Hardcover   1-4134-9553-2
            Softcover   1-4134-9552-4

All rights reserved. No part of this book may be reproduced or transmitted in any form or by any means, electronic or mechanical, including photocopying, recording, or by any information storage and retrieval system, without permission in writing from the copyright owner.

This book was printed in the United States of America.

To order additional copies of this book, contact:
Xlibris Corporation
1-888-795-4274
www.Xlibris.com
Orders@Xlibris.com
28943

Contents

Foreword		11
Introduction		13
Chapter I	Childhood	15
Chapter II	Austria Invaded (Hitler)	32
Chapter III	Paris	39
Chapter IV	England	44
Chapter V	Boarding School	47
Chapter VI	After Boarding School/Mac	51
Chapter VII	Cambridge	58
Chapter VIII	New York	69
Chapter IX	Aunt Minka	77
Chapter X	95th Street and Environments	80
Chapter XI	My Social Life in New York/Central Park	85
Chapter XII	Marriage and 53rd Street	89
Chapter XIII	Final Divorce	109
Chapter XIV	A New Life	114
Chapter XV	Fire Island/Greece	119
Chapter XVI	Puerto Rico	126
Chapter XVII	Sary/Key West	130
Chapter XVIII	Max's Kansas City/SoHo	134
Chapter XIX	Dr John	141
Chapter XX	Randall	144
Chapter XXI	Martinique	147
Chapter XXII	Mexico	152
Chapter XXIII	End of My Soho Days Tour Guide Through S. America	160
Chapter XXIV	Gaït	164
Chapter XXV	Corsica/Avignon	169

Chapter XXVI	Cadaquès	175
Chapter XXVII	Deya, Mallorca, Spain, Jean-Claude	179
Chapter XXVIIA	Jean-Claude Epilogue	182
Chapter XXVIII	Montserrat/Mont	185
Chapter XXIX	More Cadaquès/Barcelona	189
Chapter XXX	PR Department in a NY University	192
Chapter XXXI	My Hospital Jobs	195
Chapter XXXII	Retirement	199
Chapter XXXIII	Zi/Escondido	201
Chapter XXXIV	Billy	208
Chapter XXXV	Spain/Morocco	214
Chapter XXXVI	Prague	219
Chapter XXXVII	Martinique Revisited	222
Chapter XXXVIII	Edinburgh	225
Chapter XXXIX	Reminiscences About Travels	228

Dedication

This book is dedicated to the memory of my parents,
my father Ernest Angel, my mother Dussja Jefroykin,
to my son David and to my grandchildren
Ben and Ethan

To my friends, past and present, who gave me support during my struggle in writing this, but especially to my friend Olivera who gave me many hours in helping me to edit my manuscript. Not to mention my friends Joyce and Leigh who encouraged me.

Foreword

I am sitting on the terrace of the Hotel Santa Fe in Puerto Escondido, Mexico. I try to write. It's not easy to concentrate on such a beautiful day in such beautiful surroundings. I look over the ocean where the sun is shining so brightly that I have to take shelter during the hottest part of the day. The waiter approaches me to take my order: "A lemonade with *aqua purificano y guacomole*,"* I say.

My decision to write a memoir is in part due to a desire to remember more clearly events and moments in life which I have experienced and which, I realized later, I had perhaps chosen to block from my memory due to the pain they had caused me in my early life, as well as a desire to relive those experiences which have sustained me and given me a great deal of pleasure and joy.

---

*   purified water and avacado dip

Introduction

It was the year 1942 in a South Coast seaside town, called Bournemouth in England—the height of World War II. There was hardly a night when we could sleep. The bombing from the Germans continued relentlessly every single night. At dawn we would watch the American Flying Fortresses, U.S. bomber planes, crossing over our small town towards the Channel and into Germany. The P-38's, fighter planes, called Lightning, would follow behind in formation. Sometimes we looked up and tried to count the number of planes as they left in perfect formation and then at night, we would watch them as they were struggling, straggly, no longer in formation and from that we could see that many of the planes were missing. We would feel so sad, never quite knowing whether one of our American friends had been killed or taken prisoner of war if they were forced to parachute. Many, many years later, driving through the North of England, we happened to come across the American cemetery where there was a huge wall with all the names of the boys who fell during this horrible war.

At the time, I was living in a youth hostel in a room I shared with my friend Esmé. During the day I was working in a department store as a cashier, since I had just graduated from boarding school and I was happy to find any kind of a job. Esmé and I ate our evening meal in the hostel and we would then go to our room where we had to put Schillings into the electric heater to keep warm. When we ran out of money, we would crawl into bed. No sooner did we lie down, we would hear the air raid siren warning us that German planes were approaching. Young, and thinking that nothing could hurt us, Esmé and I would stay in bed until the all-clear sounded. One night the bombs must have dropped on the house next door because we were literally thrown out of our beds. We got so scared that from then on, we did reluctantly run down to the shelter with our blankets slung over our shoulders.

On a bright Sunday morning, we took a walk down to the beach. It was one of those rare days in England when it did not rain; the sun was actually shining. On our way home, we walked through the beautiful gardens on this seemingly quiet day towards our hostel for our Sunday dinner. Most townspeople had come from church and had already returned to their homes for their Sunday meal. Since food was so incredibly rationed, and we only got one small portion of meat per week, Sunday dinner was the high point of the week. People saved their meat ration for that day. We were less than two blocks from home when, suddenly, we heard a great roar. As we looked up, we saw a huge swastika staring us in the face and two seconds later, we actually saw the bomb dropping from the belly of the plane. In my confusion, I started to run, not knowing what to do, but Esmé yelled: "down" and dragged me on the sidewalk next to her. The bomb exploded on top of the building across the street, not fifty yards from where we were lying. The blast from the bomb broke the windows of the bank next to us and the shattered glass fell on top of me, Esmé, being closer to the wall was protected, but I had cuts on my arms and legs from the broken glass and was bleeding. The pharmacy around the corner immediately removed the pieces of glass and bandaged my cuts which were only superficial. Thank goodness my face had not been injured.

The whole incident was over in what seemed just split seconds, but at that moment, being so close to death, my whole life flashed in front of me.

BOURNEMOUTH DAILY ECHO, MONDAY, MAY 24, 1943

In the main road of a South Coast town a large departmental store was destroyed by fire after a sneak raid by enemy bombers. Fire brigades from several towns were engaged in extinguishing the flames.

Chapter I

Childhood

I was born in Berlin by accident.

It just so happened that for some reason unbeknownst to me, my parents were visiting Berlin when my mother gave birth. My father was Austrian, born in Vienna, and my mother was Russian. She was actually born in Latvia, but I believe it was part of Russia when she was living there with her mother, my grandmother, her four sisters and her two brothers. Vienna became my parents' permanent home. My father's mother was Hungarian, his father was Czech. Not surprising, since, at the time, Austria was the Austro-Hungarian Empire, ruled by Kaiser Franz Josef. They lived in Vienna, and that's where my father grew up. They were eccentric people, my grandmother being a vegetarian long before her time. My father's sister, Dora, also lived with them. She was an aspiring actress, so I was told. She was very beautiful, and I had the feeling that she was her mother's favorite.

During World War I, my father had served as an officer in the Austrian cavalry. He received all kinds of medals for outstanding bravery while serving at the front. He never talked about that, but often told me how his orderly had mistakenly poured hot water over his leg while washing his horse. He would then show me his scars from the burns. I can't remember how I felt with regard to his story, since I was only six years old at the time. I am also not sure what he did when the war was over, but I do know that he was an intellectual and that he moved in artistic circles.

Vienna was famous for its café life and different cafés catered to a particular clientele, either writers, theatrical people, or other professions. The *Café Central* was the writers' hang-out and I was told that is where my mother met my father after she emigrated from Russia to Vienna. He fell in love with her because she was a Russian beauty, and they soon got married. The marriage lasted a very short time, so my mother told me.

One of my earliest memories is sitting somewhere on a balcony; my mother is showing me her beautiful hands with long fingernails and tells me not to bite my nails if I want to have long fingernails when I grow up. I never did bite my nails again after that.

In another memory flash: I am maybe five years old; my mother is dressing me. "I don't want to wear this dress, I want to wear the one with the two pockets on the side," I say. We are in the park, I win: I am wearing the dress I love, the one with the pockets. I see a baby playing next to me and I go over and play with it. "You love babies," my mother says. Yes, I long for a little brother, I am thinking.

I reflect now, in retrospect, that maybe that's why I played with my Italian doll way past the age of ten.

I believe I was two years old when my parents got divorced. My father got remarried and moved from Vienna to Berlin. I have no memory of him at that time. When I was six years old, my mother put me on the train from Vienna to Berlin, so that I could meet my father for the first time. He was waiting at the station and I was wondering how he would recognize me. Maybe my mother had put a flower in my lapel? He brought me to his apartment where he lived with his second wife, Hannah. Of course, I was determined from the very beginning to dislike her, because I felt that she had taken my father away from my mother who still loved him. I really did hate my father's wife from the moment I set eyes on her. The feeling was mutual, because I felt that she resented my visit; she was horrible to me. In retrospect, we were both jealous of my father's love. She had good reason to feel insecure, because two years later, he divorced her as well.

When I first arrived at the apartment, she was out and I only met her hours later. Their home was a very beautifully furnished big ground floor apartment and it had a large well kept garden; quite a contrast to my home in Vienna where I lived in one furnished room with my mother because she was so poor. My father did not give her any money.

My father made me lunch and afterwards, he lit a cigarette. "Can I have one, too?" I asked him.

"Of course," he said, to my utter amazement.

I immediately fell in love with him then and there. Of course, I coughed myself silly. I thought to myself that my mother would never have agreed to something as outrageous as that.

My month in Berlin was only wonderful when I was able to spend time alone with my father, which was not often enough. Mostly, I spent my days in the garden by myself, my only company being the maid who was nice to me and who, I felt did not like my father's wife either. Hannah slept till noon; often she would scream: "Don't let the child run down the hall outside my room, she wakes me up." I really hated her.

In the mornings, I got up early in order to spend a little time with my father. I would then walk him to the bus stop and if the bus did not come right away, he would hail a taxi. I was already then very frugal and felt that it was a waste of money, so I would hold his hands down trying to stop him from spending money on a taxi. (I have not changed since). In the evenings, he very often went out with his wife, directly after his work in a publishing house. I believe it was called: *Ullstein*. There was a slogan advertised which read: "Brigitte nimm Ullstein Schnitte."[1] That's how I got my name, I was told. Sometimes my father would take me to a coffee house for a big ice cream sundae. Those were the moments when I was in heaven, sitting there with my father like a grown-up with a date.

On Sunday mornings, while Hannah slept, my father and I went for long walks to the *Wannsee*, a large beautiful lake just outside of Berlin. During these times, he would always discuss politics with me. Even though I was only six years old, I found the subject interesting. These conversations must have stayed with me because, to this day, I am active in politics.

I only have one bad memory of my father from those days: it was the day he invited a playmate for me. She was the daughter of a friend who was an actress. I was all excited to perhaps have a friend, but when the girl arrived, I did not like her because she was fat and unattractive. I told my father: "I don't want to play with her, she is too fat."

He was furious with me and told me: "She is your guest and you must be hospitable." He then spanked me and I cried bitterly. I will never forget it; I was humiliated. It was the one and only time that he ever did this or scolded me. I believe that this incident made me want to go back to Vienna and to my mother again.

I then did not see my father until I was ten years old when he moved to Vienna after Hitler had come to power in Germany and he had somehow managed to escape from Sachsenhausen concentration camp. He had been one of the earliest victims, and I wonder whether he may have been involved with political and intellectual dissident groups. He told me years later that a non-Jewish person had helped him to escape. He did not tell me how it came about.

I was too young to fully understand what he must have gone through before he finally left Germany, even though he often spoke about his horrible experience in Sachsenhausen. I do remember that he thought that Hitler would never invade Austria and the rest of Europe, so that he was able to seek refuge in Vienna, his home. Of course, I was thrilled to have my father living in Vienna, in order to get to know him as an adolescent. Despite being long divorced from my mother, they were still on friendly terms with each other, and he would come for dinner to our house about once a week. At the time my mother and I shared a furnished

---

[1] Translation: Brigitte—buy sewing patterns from Publishing House: Ullstein.

room where we had kitchen privileges. Because there was no bathroom, my mother would have to heat three kettles of water in the kitchen and bring them to our room, empty them into a wash basin, so that I could get washed; a complicated process.

Mother and I mostly lived in furnished rooms, moving frequently like when, one time, we found out only after moving in that the beds had bed bugs. We moved out the next day. I always felt very poor and ashamed, knowing that my school friends had two parents and lived in nice apartments, and some even had maids. Since my father did not support us and my mother did not work, it was my mother's kind and generous brother who was our only support; he sent us money from Paris where he owned a travel agency. Once in a while, he came to Vienna, and then it felt like Christmas. He would take us out to a fancy restaurant and give my mother money to buy me much needed clothes. He also paid for my dentist since I badly needed braces.

On Sundays, my father sometimes picked me up and took me to a wonderful *Konditerei*[2] where I could choose from an assortment of the most delicious pastries, which Vienna is famous for. The more *Schlag* they had, the more I liked them. At such times, I felt especially happy to be with my beloved father.

When I was little, I remember that my mother often went out visiting friends and I was left alone. I would then put on her high-heeled shoes and dress up in her clothes. I would stand in front of the mirror and pretend to be an actress. It must have been my way to escape from the reality which was so painful. I was never able to invite anyone to our furnished room because I was too ashamed and therefore I was always having to phone my friends, hoping that I could visit them.

Sundays were the worst for me. My mother always made me go to the park. Even though it was a beautiful park, surrounded by blooming lilac trees in the Spring, where the wonderful scents permeated the air, there were no playgrounds and therefore hardly any children to play with. My mother and I would stop in a café where they served yoghurt with fruit; that was my only treat. The French expression *Le Dimanche, les enfants s'ennuyent* (Sundays the children are bored) could not have been more true. As horrible as school was, at least I was with my friends and with other children.

My mother's family, who had moved from Latvia to Berlin, were beginning to feel persecuted by the Nazis and decided to move to Vienna. First, my mother's oldest sister, Mussia, moved to a pension right next to my school. She spoiled me by taking me out for ice cream or buying me candy; of course, as a result, I liked her especially. Some time later, my maternal grandmother also moved to Vienna. She was very short, and looked like a peasant, with a pigtail hanging

---

[2] pastry shop

over her back. I loved my grandmother because she played cards with me and she always let me win. I would end up with a few *Groschen* (pennies) to buy some sweets and later when I got older, I would save up to be able to go to the movies to see Shirley Temple, whom I adored.

Like most children of divorced parents, I was always secretly hoping that my parents would remarry. I was well aware that my father had many girlfriends and I was very afraid that he would remarry again. I was jealous of his women, and I always knew that my mother suffered because she still loved him. Many years after the divorce, she did get involved with a man who wanted to marry her. He was the editor of one of Vienna's most prestigious newspapers.

Sometimes my mother would get all dressed up and go out with him. I remember her looking extremely elegant, wearing a long black lace dress; she was truly a Russian beauty with her black hair and chiselled features. As soon as she was out of the door, I started to read my favorite writer, Karl May, who wrote stories about America's Indians in the West, even though he himself had never been there. He described in all his books how the American Indians got such a raw deal from white people; I was totally on the natives' side and empathized with them. Probably, deep down I felt that I too had gotten a raw deal in life, being poor and having divorced parents. I so loved reading these books that I read far into the night. Only when late at night, I heard my mother's key in the door, did I quickly turn out the light.

After a while, my mother found me out; she would feel the light bulb and scold me: "No wonder you can't get up in the morning and are late for school."

My Gymnasium was very strict and very difficult. At age ten, we already had to learn Latin and French, not to mention Physics, Chemistry and Algebra. Even my intellectual father could not always help me with my homework. I hated school, and as a result got terrible grades. Our whole class felt the same way, and we frequently copied from each other, hoping that our neighbor was smarter. My last year in school I failed my Physics examination because I did not understand how the telephone worked (I still don't), and had to repeat a year. I never felt as humiliated in my life, but in the end it turned out for the best because that's how I became such good friends with Janet—a friendship that has lasted all our lives.

One day, just before Hitler marched into Austria, my mother said to me: "Sit down, I have something to say to you. How would you feel if I married Uncle Paul?"

I had already met him on Christmas Eve, but could not help comparing him to my father. I kept telling myself that there was no way that anyone could possibly be as wonderful as my father. In my eyes, he was the most handsome and charming man, and I felt no one could possibly replace him. What made him even more glamorous was that, at the time, he was writing for the cinema and he was working as a movie director.

Once he even took me to the movie set. He also had access to large photographs of movie stars, the kind cinemas put in their windows to advertise a film. I became the envy of my schoolmates when I brought in photographs of Greta Garbo (my idol), Clark Gable and Gary Cooper, amongst others. Since divorce was very rare in those days, I lied to my classmates about my parents' divorce and told them: "My father has to travel frequently." The very thought that my mother would remarry was so scary because it meant that my father might not visit us any more. This thought so disturbed me that I told my mother: "No way." Today I ask myself: why would you ask a little girl's opinion about such an important decision? I often wonder now how our lives would have changed had she remarried. Before this incident, Uncle Paul had tried to bribe me with gifts, especially at Christmas time.

Although we were Jewish, almost everyone I knew in Vienna celebrated Christmas. I looked forward to Christmas so much that I would count the days. Every year my mother bought a tree and decorated it with beautiful glass bulbs and real candles. On Christmas Eve, at midnight, I had to leave the room and I knew then that she would call me in after she had lit the candles and put the presents under the tree. I could not have been more excited. It was the only time during the year that I got presents and, in retrospect, I think my mother must have scrimped and saved up knowing how important Christmas was for me. I remember once, when I was younger, there was a doll's bathroom under the tree, where one could put water in the back of the tub, so that I could actually turn on the faucet and water would come out. I adored it above all my other presents, especially even more so because my mother told me later that my father had bought it for me. That made it even more precious.

After opening my presents, we had the traditional meal, consisting of poached carp and, this being Vienna, I am sure there was also a scrumptious dessert. It was a magical evening and afterwards I would go to sleep and have the most wonderful dreams—that's how happy I was.

A few days before Christmas, when I was still very little, I remember asking my mother: "If I am a really good girl, can I have a brother for Christmas?" Everything changed, however, when we eventually had to move to my paternal grandmother's house. I believe we were forced to move because we had no more money to pay for furnished rooms. My poor mother was beside herself because she did not like her ex-mother-in-law. I couldn't blame her. I didn't either.

Grandparents

Their apartment was very big, but very old. The living room was covered with a variety of frayed Turkish carpets, one on top of the other, in order to hide some of the holes. They might have been valuable in their time, but they were very shabby. An old piano and some dilapidated chairs made up this "salon," which must have been as old as my grandparents.

My mother and I moved into a tiny room which, in better days, must have been a maid's room. The only bright spot was a veranda overlooking a garden with some trees. Here my eccentric grandmother served her vegetarian meals. I must say that she was very ahead of her time in that respect. How I hated our meals and how I longed, like all little girls and boys, for a *Wiener Wuerstel* (hot dog), cup cakes, doughnuts and other junk food.

The household consisted of, in addition to my matriarch grandmother, my grandfather, who was hardly ever seen and who did not seem to count; he was retired and a very passive man in this otherwise all-woman household which also included my divorced Aunt Dora and her daughter Hedy.

My cousin, Hedy, was my favorite for many reasons: she was about seven years older than I, but she made me feel as if I were grown-up and her equal. Also she had the cleanest small room which was like an oasis in this old, not well-kept apartment. She was a cleanliness nut and so compulsive about keeping her room spotless that it almost looked like a hospital room. It was probably her way of rebelling since, except for my grandmother, everyone, especially her own mother, my Aunt Dora, totally neglected her. I admired her cleanliness because I shared her feelings that my grandmother's house was dirty. But most importantly, Hedy taught me all about sex. I was absolutely fascinated when she described her sexual adventures. At an early age, I was getting my sex education from her. My mother, who had once told me: "Don't ever let a man touch you down there unless you get married," was very upset because she suspected that Hedy was confiding in me her sexual experiences with men.

I believe it was about a year later that we somehow managed to escape from my grandmother's house which I remember as our unhappiest time. My mother and I again moved into a furnished room, but at least we were on our own and not beholden to my grandmother. My mother insisted, however, that I visit my grandmother once a week after school for lunch. After those dreaded vegetarian lunches, my reward was that I could go to Hedy's room and hear some more sex stories about her latest adventures with the men she was involved with.

My mother, as a young girl, had worked in an office where she made two very good life-long friends. Her friend, Angela, subsequently married a Yugoslavian theater director and moved to Ljubljana in Northern Yugoslavia. During school holidays, we often visited there. I was about eight years old at the time, and remember only that she had a lovely house with a very big garden, full of flowers. Angela had a little boy, by the name of Titus who was younger than I was; we played ping-pong together in the garden and I learned to count in his language.

My mother's other good friend was Maria who lived in Salzburg, Austria, where she owned a very large loft-like apartment right in the middle of the old town.

After having left grandmother's house and having spent a short time in our furnished room, my mother said: "We are going to move to Salzburg and live with 'Aunt' Maria and her daughter Gretl. You will go to school there, which happens to be right next to Maria's apartment." I much enjoyed school in Salzburg. It was a lot easier than my school in Vienna. I loved living in this incredibly beautiful town, famous for its summer music festival since it is Mozart's birthplace. Salzburg has at least one hundred churches and in the evening when all the church bells rang in unison, it sounded like a beautiful concert. The town is surrounded by two mountains with the river Salzach running through the middle of the town, dividing the old part from the new.

After living in Maria's loft for a few weeks, we finally moved to our own apartment on one of the mountain sides of the *Moenchsberg*, next to the Festival Hall. We had to climb up five hundred steps in order to get there. If my mother forgot a lemon or something, I had to go down those steps to go to the market. It certainly kept me in good shape, but I was already a very thin child. In the winter, when it snowed, I had to ski down in order to go to school. My mother would then take two pieces of wood, put galoshes on my feet, and attach them with some string. A far cry from today's state of the art ski equipment! I would ski down the side of the mountain, past the famous Festival House, where the summer tourists gathered from all over the world.

I loved living in the apartment on the mountain slope overlooking this breathtaking city. It gave me a feeling of power being high above everyone else. To this day, I love living high up with a wonderful view (I now live on the top floor—the 12th in my building).

My only regret about moving out from "Aunt" Maria's loft was that I had to leave my two beloved German shepherd dogs behind, Jochen, the father, and Helen, his daughter. I loved those dogs so much that I would lay my head next to them when they were lying on their cushions. One day, there was an article in the local paper praising my beloved dogs. A small child had fallen into the Salzach River and the dogs had rescued the child by carrying it out of the river. I could not have been more proud. How they managed to do this was a mystery to me, but they did it and it made the paper; that's all I cared about.

In the summer, we often went to Salzkammergut, the Lake District near Salzburg, famous for its "White Horse" Inn on the Wolfgangsee. There was a famous song: "In Salzkammergut da kann man . . . gut lustig sein" ("In Salzkammergut one can . . . have fun"—the dots represented a sexual connotation). The closest lake to Salzburg was the *Fuschelsee* and that's where my mother and I would spend our holidays. We rented a room on a farm from a peasant family, a short walking distance from the village. I loved being there, even though our room was very primitively furnished. Having previously spent summers with my friend, Hasi, near a farm, I had learned to milk cows, churn butter and collect eggs. I enjoyed it tremendously.

My most important event of that summer was, however, that I "discovered" boys. Behind the farmhouse, there was a second house which the farmer rented to a family who had two adolescent sons, about two years older than I was at the time. One had dark hair, the other was blonde; they were both handsome. I was very drawn to the blonde boy who did not seem interested in me; I wanted to make him love me. The other boy seemed to be interested in me, but I was not attracted to him. (I feel that this established a pattern that followed throughout my life: I was nearly always attracted to men who showed little interest in me.) Whenever we happened to run into each other, just talking to the boys got me very excited. But what was even more exciting was that my favorite classical stage actor who performed in Salzburg visited Fuschel, since it was the closest lake where he could relax between performances.

My mother's friend, Dagny, was an actress who performed outdoors at the Festival in the play called "Everyman." Dagny's good friend was the actor, Fred Liewehr, who was my matinee idol. One evening, Dagny, my mother and I went to the country "hop" and she introduced me to Fred. I almost fainted when he asked me to dance, and it was one of the most memorable moments of my adolescence. I told him: "I don't know how to dance," obviously seeing that I had a terrific crush on him, he said: "Never mind, I'll teach you."

I remember that I was blushing, but at the same time I was feeling so fantastic. I couldn't help thinking how envious my friends in Vienna would be when they heard about it. Fred was so well known and so idolized because he performed at Vienna's Burg Theater, that the girls, including myself, lined up at the stage door after one of his performances to get a glimpse of him and to get his autograph. In the summer, Salzkammergut was the center of the performing arts, and because of that, many actors worked and visited there. It was, therefore, not surprising that on another day, Marlene Dietrich was sitting in the café in Salzburg where I was with my mother and Erich Kaestner, the famous children's book author who wrote the well-known book "Emil and the Detective," among many others.

"I would like to have Marlene's autograph," I told them; they encouraged me to go over to her. I finally got up enough courage and timidly asked her to please sign my book. To my great embarrassment, she looked up with her long false eyelashes and said: "I never give anyone my autograph." I felt so humiliated that I almost started to cry. Mr. Kaestner was so indignant that he went over to her with my book and spoke to her. I wonder now what he had said to her, because she relented and signed.

That same year, Marlene and Douglas Fairbanks, Jr., who were lovers, moved into the guest house high up overlooking the beautiful Wolfgangsee, where my mother and I had often gone to have lunch on the terrace because it has such a wonderful view. Even though the lake was many Kilometers away, we managed to walk there, admiring the passing cars with their foreign license plates. I learned to recognize their symbols.

One day, the owner of the guest house came over to us and said: "Don't come here any more for lunch next month. I have rented the entire house to an American lady and her friend." We guessed immediately that it was Dietrich and I gave the landlady my autograph book to get her and Douglas Fairbanks to sign it. This time, Dietrich even included a photograph of herself which I still have to this day. Of course, everyone in the village whispered about these famous Hollywood movie stars now vacationing there. They were thrilled and felt honored by their presence.

As beautiful as this lake district is, it is unfortunately a well-known fact that once it begins to rain, called the *Schnuerelregen*, it never stops. After a while, it becomes depressing because one cannot go swimming, sit in the outdoor café, or even go for a walk.

I remember only too well the time when my father arrived unexpectedly to visit us. I was so happy to see my parents together that I secretly hoped that they would stay together forever. Of course, it was totally unrealistic, knowing my father. A few days later, it started to rain and my father said: "If the rain doesn't stop, I am leaving." We were sitting in the café by the lake, and I remember praying that the rain would stop. It was the first time in a long time that I saw my parents together, and I felt it was too good to be true. Nevertheless, my father left, and I don't know who was more unhappy, my mother or I.

By this time, he had already long ago divorced his second wife; his marriage only lasted a couple of years. They were two very different people; she was very bourgeois and also not a very attractive-looking woman. All their friends seemed to be of the opinion that he only married her for her money.

Of course, my father, being a womanizer, immediately found new girlfriends; that he might remarry my mother was only a little girl's dream and not a reality— a dream which was never realized, but which haunted me all through my childhood.

His actions so affected my behavior towards men later on in life that I was unable to form any deep emotional relationships for fear of being abandoned, just as my mother was. I never felt that I could completely trust any man and this might explain my frequent flightiness with men and fear of commitment.

In retrospect, I think I might have suppressed my feelings towards my mother because of my frequent resentment towards her as a child. Unfortunately, I do not remember her as the caring mother which she probably was. She must have had a terrible time bringing up a child alone without a husband who left her when I was two years old, without money for either her or my support—a husband whom she loved regardless. She was solely dependent on her brother, my uncle, who lived in Paris. I only remember that I must have been a difficult child who did not listen to her.

I remember her often beating me. I still hear my cries and remember the scenes; they will stay with me always. I remember walking down the street with her when I was a little girl and falling down. I was such a skinny child and always fell over my own legs. Instead of comforting me, she would spank me. "You never look where you are walking," she would say.

"Isn't it bad enough that I hurt myself, that my knees were bleeding; why did she spank me as well?" I thought. That's when I began to feel that life was not fair and that's where I told myself that I want to be a lawyer when I grow up, since I thought then that lawyers are supposed to be fair. (Of course, in retrospect, that's a joke.)

I must have been so angry with her, because I remember one incident in Yugoslavia at her friend Angela's house. She was sitting in the garden and for some reason, she got up. Unbeknownst to her, I pulled the chair from under her, and she fell to the ground. "You are a very bad, vicious little girl," I was told. I will never forget how badly I felt.

I also remember vividly how depressed she was when later on in Vienna, my father was supposed to come for dinner and either showed up late or, sometimes, did not show up at all. We had no telephone, but that was no excuse. Her depressions affect me to this very day; it has had a lasting effect on me: I can't bear to wait for someone when I have an appointment or to wait for a telephone call. I feel that abandonment over and over again.

Is it any wonder then, since my father was so distance that I turned to my friends for comfort and love? That my friend Hasi was like a sister to me; someone I spoke to and visited every day. That I spent many of my summer vacations with her and her parents. That I was always at her parents' house. That later on when the Nazis occupied Vienna, that I spent my time with Janet at her house?

It also explains why, when I was a young girl, my first lover was eighteen years older than I was; that at first I was drawn to older men who I felt would take care of me, but later found out that they too were not to be counted on, and then began to look for younger men from whom I expected little and therefore would not suffer from another disappointment.

I have no doubt that my mother truly loved me, but her own miserable existence made it difficult for her to be the kind of mother that I needed, especially since I had no father to make me feel loved.

My mother, ca. 1920

My father about 10 years old with his father

My father, ca. 1933

My father directing a documentary in Vienna

With my mother in Italy, author, about 2 years old

Author about 5 years old

Author 10 years old with paternal grand-father

House on top of a mountain in Austria where author spent holidays with best friend, Hasi, 8-10 years old

With Hasi after school skiing trip

Fred Liewehr, famous theater actor, my first adolescent love

Last school photograph before German invasion

Chapter II

Austria Invaded (Hitler)

I was thirteen years old before I realized that I was Jewish. The year was 1938 and Hitler had just occupied Austria. In our High School in Vienna, we all thought of ourselves as Viennese, and even though we, who were of Jewish faith, did study Judaism; it was no different than studying Mathematics, Biology or any other subject, for that matter. All religions were studied separately by other students without any social stigma. We never thought of ourselves as being anything else, but Austrians. We were all very nationalistic and when we had to sing the Austrian National Anthem, it would bring tears to my eyes. Viennese society made us all feel the same and I felt that this was beautiful. Children always long for things being the same and we were all for our "Vaterland," and that there was no difference between us.

It was a very rude awakening when we were suddenly told that some of us had a Jewish grandmother and therefore were not "Aryan," or that some of us were half Jewish and, for that matter, God forbid, all Jewish, which, as we heard from our parents, meant that we were suddenly heading for possible destruction. There were whispers of concentration camps, but thirteen-year olds could not really comprehend the meaning of that, nor do they really care, since they felt that it could never happen to them. But we sure learned to care, when we heard shortly after the "Anschluss" that our friends' parents committed suicide because they did not want to be arrested and taken to concentration camps to die a horrible death. Also by taking their own lives, they thought they could save their children, my friends, since Jewish organizations were sometimes able to manage to get affidavits for orphans.

It was hard for me to hate these good-looking young German boys in their uniforms when I saw them in the street because they were absolutely my physical type: blonde and blue-eyed, or so I felt at the time. My first confrontation with them came when I was having lunch one day at my grandmother's house; the bell rang and I answered it. Two S.S. boys wanted to come in to see if there were any anti-regime books in the house. I presume they were looking for books by Karl Marx or any other political books or books written by Jews.

I don't know now, being so young at the time, how I persuaded them to come back in a couple of hours, nor how I had the presence of mind to realize what was going on, but I must have charmed them somehow because they gave us two hours' grace. Perhaps I flirted with them in my child-like way.

In those two hours my grandparents and I frantically burned all the forbidden books. When they came back, although they did search, they found nothing and went away. It was a miracle that they did not arrest my grandparents then and there. I was much praised for my bravery.

As a result, I felt it was hard to condemn them totally, and after that experience, even less so.

On the other hand, it was true that I was being hidden in my best friend Hasi's house when her cousin's fiancé who was in the S.S. came to visit. Their apartment consisted of three rooms. In addition, they owned the apartment next door which they rented out. Through the kitchen one had access to the other apartment. The toilets in Vienna are separate from the bathrooms and it was in their toilet that my friends' parents hid me. I felt very strange and nervous waiting in that dark place until they came to get me, saying: "It's O.K. now, you can come out, he's gone." I was too young then to realize the dangerous situation I was exposed to. Also, it was dangerous for my friend's parents that they were hiding someone who was Jewish. Of course, I was very shaken about the incident. All the more so, because I realized that I was bound to lose my best friend. Our relationship, which began when we were six years old, could not continue. Up to that time, I had almost spent every summer with Hasi.

Her parents owned a house high up on a mountain. In the beginning of the summer we had to hike up with two month's supplies of food. The house was isolated on a huge meadow surrounded by a forest. Our nearest neighbor was the farmers' house at least two kilometers away; there we went to fetch milk, butter, eggs and fruit in season.

Hasi and I would milk the cows, churn the butter, collect the eggs and bring them back home. We also took the cows to the meadow for grazing; as a reward, the farmer's wife would make us "Zwetschkenknoedeln" (plum dumplings), and we would compete between us as to who could eat more. They were so delicious that I can still taste them to this day.

When we did not take care of the cows, we went into the forest to look for wild strawberries and gather mushrooms. We became experts because her parents gave us a mushroom book which we studied avidly so as to learn to recognize the poisonous ones. "Never pick mushrooms growing on tree trunks," they warned us. Our favorite one was a big mushroom which looks like a parasol and had a ring around the stem. That's how we were sure that it was a non-poisonous one. Her parents prepared it like a breaded "Wiener Schnitzel." That was our favorite meal. In the forest we often saw deer in the distance, but no matter how still we kept, the minute they felt our presence, they would flee. (Not like these days when they are so tame.) We had read the book "Heidi" in school, and we understood why they were afraid of human beings.

One beautiful day, we were climbing on some rocks in an open field, when I suddenly saw a cross on the forehead of a snake between the cracks where my hand was holding on. It was the sign of the most dangerous species of snakes: the "Kreutzotter" against which we had been warned. I was terrified and ran away screaming. Hasi couldn't imagine what had happened to me. I could hardly get my words out to tell her of this horrible experience. From that day on, we were careful and more aware of the dangers that surrounded us in the forest.

I also remember another day when I climbed up a big apple tree in front of our house and fell, landing on my back. I lost my voice temporarily and everyone was fearful that I had hurt myself badly. It must have been caused by the shock because I soon regained my voice.

During those summers—we were probably between the ages of seven and ten, we were very unhappy when we lost our two pets, two rabbits which we loved dearly. They were given to us when they were cute little babies and we took great care of them. When they got older, they started to hide and we had trouble finding and catching them because they started to bite us. At the end of the summer, my last year on the mountain, they suddenly ran away, never to be seen again; we tried to console ourselves with the thought that they would be happier in the forest with the other animals, but nevertheless we were very sad to have lost our pets. In retrospect, these were wonderful happy, carefree days and they will stay with me always.

Apart from spending our summers together, Hasi and I were in the same class in grammar school in Vienna. Neither of us had siblings, and since we lived one block from one another, we saw each other every day and, much to my mother's chagrin, called each other constantly on the phone. "What on earth do you have to tell each other when you just saw each other?" she would ask me.

Despite the political situation, we tried our best to sustain our friendship, but it became increasingly dangerous for all of us. It was whispered that even children reported their own parents when they were in contact with Jewish people.

In 1952, thirteen years later and long after the war, when Vienna was occupied by the Allies, I went back to see Vienna again and to visit Hasi. As is often the case in such instances, my visit was a great disappointment. Our lives had grown into too many different directions, and we were worlds apart, literally.

This time, I remember going to her house in Vienna, walking through the all so familiar courtyard and ringing her bell. It had been a long time, thirteen years, and yet everything seemed the same. She opened the door and I looked at that blonde pretty young woman as if she were a stranger. She must have looked at me with my prematurely white hair and perhaps thought so too. It was an awkward moment after all those years. We sat and drank coffee and talked about old times. I told her about my life, and she confessed to me that she had married a few years ago, a much older man for money. He was Italian and lived in Trieste where her parents came from. It seemed that they had separated and she had moved back to her parents in Vienna. I told her that I, on the contrary, had married a poor man for love.

We arranged to meet the next day to go to a "Heurigen" with her parents; a typical way to spend an evening outside Vienna where the grapes are cultivated and new wine is pressed then and there. The wineries set up tables and everyone brings a picnic. There is music and it is all very gay. I was too young when I left Vienna and had never experienced these festivities.

Hasi had arranged for me to stay in a bed and breakfast nearby and was supposed to call me the next day. She never did.

During my stay in Vienna, I got in touch with an Austrian painter who was my father's friend and whom I had met before in New York. He was thrilled to hear from me and to know that I was in Vienna. We made a date to meet in the Stadtspark. I was sitting there, wondering why I had not heard from Hasi when Franz arrived with a dozen of the most beautiful red roses. It was a great surprise, especially since he was gay! We enjoyed seeing each other again and we arranged to meet for dinner on the next day.

I never felt like calling my friend Hasi back after her silence. My disappointment was so great that I decided to leave Vienna. It was no longer my home. On the day before I was to leave, I called her up just to say good-bye and to tell her that I was leaving for Paris on the 7 a.m. train the next morning.

She must have been extremely guilty, for when I got to the station, there was Hasi waiting for me to see me off. Despite the fact that we promised to write to each other, we never did, nor did we ever see each other again. In my heart I knew then that this was the end of a friendship; that this was the end of a chapter in my life and that I would probably never return to Vienna. It had become too painful and there was no longer anyone there for me.

Leaving Vienna meant leaving my childhood behind for good. These events, however, were far away in the future.

My mother had two brothers; one of them was reluctant to help us escape from the Nazis even though he was in America. The other uncle who owned a travel agency in Paris was the one who came through. My father had already managed to get an affidavit for himself to go to England and he had left with the intention of getting my mother and me to join him there. It was decided that we should go to Paris with the help of my uncle who succeeded in sending us a 24-hour transit visa for Paris and a permanent visa to Uruguay in South America. Of course, we had no intention to settle down in Uruguay; we left for Paris hoping to extend our 24-hour transit visa in order to be able to stay there.

It was terrible for me to have to leave my beloved Vienna. My Vienna—where in the Spring the air was full of the wonderful perfume of lilacs the minute you walked into one of the most beautiful parks, surrounding the city. My Vienna where I knew every street. My own street where I lived and where my mother used to sit in the café opposite the theater of the Josefstadt (our district) where the actors had their own table reserved for them. The city where I went to nursery school, to grammar school and to High School. Where the smell of fresh coffee permeated the streets outside its famous coffee houses. And most of all to leave my friends!

My best friend, Hasi, who was not Jewish, was staying in Vienna. She had no reason to leave, but then came the day when my second best friend, Janet, who was partially Jewish, left for England to join her mother who had managed to receive an affidavit from an English family to work for them as an "au pair."

I will never forget the time when I went to the *Bahnhof* (station) to see her off. It was winter and we were dressed in our woollies. I remember it was very cold. We were huddled together, two little girls alone on the station platform which seemed to be deserted. She is shorter than I am, but she seemed much braver. I am the one who is more sentimental and also the one who was left behind. "Cheer up," she said, "I know we'll see each other again. You will be going to Paris shortly and I envy you—after all, it always rains in England, so my mother writes." The reason that there were not many people on the station that day was that the train was leaving Austria. I did not know then whether we would ever see each other again, and I cried bitterly when I saw the train pulling out of the station. We waved until the train with her looking out of the window, was out of sight. I walked away feeling very sad, lonely and abandoned, and I started to think about our last year together. We ended up in the same class together because I had had to repeat a year, having failed Physics. We had known each other since we were five years old, playing hopscotch in the park and met again later because I was in the same class with her cousin. When Hitler marched into Austria, we were allowed to finish the school year, but were forbidden to continue school after that. As a result, we had a lot of time on our hands. Janet had one "aryan" grandmother, but under the Nazi regime this did not save her from being Jewish. In Vienna, my mother and I lived in a furnished room, as usual, and therefore I never invited my friends, but always went to their house. Janet lived with her parents in a large apartment in a very good neighborhood, and they had a maid. I frequently visited her and the maid would always answer the door. It seemed to me at the time that her mother was always out and her father was working. We would immediately sit down and play Monopoly, which we adored. It made us feel rich to acquire all that elegant property, like "Park Place," "Mayfair," and others.

It was quite a long walk to Janet's house, and I believe I took the tramway home. How I loved those visits to what I then considered a "normal" household. Ironically, I found out much later that her mother was "cheating" on her husband. That's why she was never there when I visited. After my visits, I felt sad having to return to my humble room with only my mother to talk to. She usually scolded me for coming home late, not having done my homework. But in that last school year in Vienna, there was little incentive since some of our teachers had become anti-semitic and they had always been overly strict even before that. I was so discouraged; no matter how hard I tried, my grades remained consistently bad. Curiously enough, when I went to boarding school in England, I became a very good student.

I already began to miss Janet, and she had only just left. Slowly, my other friends who were lucky enough to get out, began to leave Vienna. I experienced this as a terrible loss. All the more so, at that time, because I did not know yet what my own fate was going to be.

That's when I began to hear rumors that children could be saved and be brought out of Austria by organizations in England, if their parents were dead. Then the terrible tragedy occurred when my friend Lola's parents committed suicide. They jumped out of their tenth floor window and left that poor little girl all alone. How could we possibly console Lola—there was nothing we could say or do. It must have been a most horrible trauma for her, and it must have made her feel guilty for the rest of her life.

I was so upset, angry and afraid that the same fate would befall my friend Susan's parents that I remember going to visit them the very next day. She had told me that she overheard her parents also speaking about committing suicide. As young as I was, I got angry with them and told them: "There must be a distant relative somewhere—think hard; maybe in England or perhaps in America." Isn't there a cousin, an uncle or a friend somewhere?" They did rack their brains after my pep talk and came up with a distant relative who, eventually, did send them an affidavit for America; they managed to get out just in time. My friend Susan also got to England, probably through one of these children's organizations. Eventually we all met. It was rather miraculous when I think back now how we did meet and stayed in touch. Later on, Lola also came to the United States. Happily, all my childhood friends managed to escape.

One day, just before we left Vienna, I ran into my father in the street. "Guess what," he said. "Your favorite crazy cousin, Hedy, has just returned from England. She has managed to swindle her way back into Nazi Vienna. She so hated her employers in England, where she was working as an 'au pair,' that she preferred to come back. After being so lucky to get out, it is hard to believe that she would do such a crazy thing."

Then came the day when my mother said: "We must now pack and we can only take the most necessary belongings. We have no idea what's going to happen when we reach Paris. Perhaps we really have to go to South America and the French don't let us stay in Paris." It was a terrible decision. I could not bear to leave my dollhouse behind. But my mother said: "You may take your beloved doll, but most other things will have to be left." Even though I was in tears, I knew she was right. In my dreams, I thought of Paris as the most beautiful city in the world—and so it was.

It seems very strange that I don't actually remember leaving Vienna, I only remember arriving in Paris or just being there.

Chapter III

Paris

Even now, it is extremely painful to remember my first stay in Paris. From the moment my mother and I arrived, we knew that we might not be able to stay there beyond the 24 hours that our visa permitted. The day after we arrived, we immediately took the Metro to the police station in the Latin quarter. It was a large and, to me, frightening building, since I knew our fate would depend on the outcome of this visit. The waiting room was filled with many other immigrants, and after hours of waiting, it was finally our turn. They called our names and we found ourselves standing in front of a gendarme who looked us over.

"Our fate is in his hands," I thought.

After what seemed an interminable time, while he was looking over our papers, he finally said: "You may stay in Paris thirty more days. Report back here." He stamped our transit visa and called: "Next." In spite of our momentary relief, we were beginning to dread our next appointment. We went home afraid that we would have to leave Paris. This must have been even worse for my mother, because I could see that she was getting very nervous and depressed. "Home" was 2 rue Boulard, a run-down residential hotel on a small street off the Boulevard Montparnasse. This was the quarter where artists and writers had lived, and were still living, as well as many expatriates; the café *Dome*, *Le Select*, and the famous restaurant, *La Coupole*, had been favorite places for most creative artists of the past, as well as for the present generation of artists. I imagined Modigliani, Monet, Manet, Matisse having had their drinks in the cafés after they finished painting at the end of the day. Gertrude Stein and Alice B. Toklas had their "salon" in Montparnasse, where artists and writers, like Hemingway, Proust, and Picasso, amidst many others, were frequent visitors.

In contrast to living in this exciting quarter, there was nothing glamorous about our hotel. My mother and I once again lived in a poorly furnished shabby room. The only difference between our last room in Vienna and this one was that my maternal grandmother and three of my mother's sisters also lived there. I do not know when they left Latvia and whether they were it touch with my mother at that time. I only heard that they had to leave Latvia and emigrated to Germany. When Hitler was elected and came to power there, they must have had enough foresight to know that the Jews would be persecuted. This was the time when my Aunt Mussia and my grandmother moved to Vienna. Then with the help of their brother, my uncle, they moved to Paris. I imagine that my uncle must have arranged for all of them to have some sort of permanent permission to live in Paris, where they stayed until Hitler took over Paris. At that time, they fled to the South and were in hiding in Nice.

In the hotel lived my Aunt Mussia, the oldest sister, and Natascha, the youngest, as well as the middle one, called Taissa; she apparently was the last one to arrive since she had no permanent status. I adored my grandmother, who was a tiny, thin Russian peasant-looking woman with a pigtail hanging down to the middle of her back. I enjoyed visiting her because she was gentle and kind to me. When we played cards together, she would always let me win. We played for very small amounts of money. She knew that I loved candy, and I was able to buy some with my winnings.

On the other hand, my three aunts who had no children drove my mother and me crazy. They were always criticizing the way my mother brought me up: "Don't let the child go out alone, don't do this or that. Look how she is dressed." Although Natascha was married, to a much younger man, she acted like an "old maid." It was insinuated that Mussia had had a heavy love affair and that the lover died during World War I. Taissa, however, was truly an old maid. She had been a school teacher in Latvia.

Just to get away from that chaotic household, we often visited yet another sister, Minka, who lived nearby on the rue Daguerre with her husband, Peter. He was a political German refugee and was also ten years younger than my aunt. Together they managed to escape from Berlin, where they had been living until Hitler came to power. I imagine that my kind uncle also helped them to get to Paris, but I am not at all sure how my uncle was able to rescue the entire family. Minka and Peter lived in what I considered to be a "bohemian looking" apartment, minimally furnished, but with many beautiful impressionist paintings on the walls. They were painted by Peter and Minka's friend, Karl Heidenreich, who had been living in Spain for some time and had escaped when Franco took over that country. He fled to Paris, where they were hiding him since he had no legitimate papers to live there.

There must have been some vicious neighbors who wanted to report Karl to the police. I remember that every time the bell would ring, he would hide in a closet. After the gendarmes left, he came out. I found the fact that he had to hide rather exciting; it seemed like a story in a movie. As soon as the police left, he would set up his easel and continue to paint. I enjoyed watching him paint.

My real problem, however, was not to be able to speak French. Although I had studied it in school in Vienna, speaking it presented quite another problem; this is so often the case when studying languages in school. My mother decided that I should enroll at the Alliance Française to learn French conversation; the school was situated on the Boulevard Raspail, walking distance from our hotel. I attended school every day and was put in a class with other students from various countries. The classes were only conducted in French, and you were not taught to translate from your native language. I did not find it easy, and I had a lot of studying to do. It seems strange to me now that I did not form any friendships with a single classmate, perhaps because there was so little time. My classes were given in the morning, and I would spend the afternoons at the Jardin Luxembourg, where I prepared my homework for the next day. Sitting in this beautiful park surrounded by gorgeous flowers, I watched with envy boys and girls talking to each other, friends meeting and kissing each other on both cheeks as is the custom in France. I would then walk home through the Luxembourg Garden and the Boulevard Montparnasse. I loved Paris more than anything in the world. I don't know how I can explain it, but it is always easier for me to love places rather than people. Walking through the beautiful Paris streets made me very happy; it erased the dread of having to go back to my ugly hotel.

Paris has many different facets: there is the glorious *Place de la Concorde* from where one can see the *Arc de Triomphe* in the distance at the other end of the Champs Elysées; that magnificent long elegant boulevard with museums on one side and cafés on the other side. At all times the cafés are crowded with people of all nationalities meeting friends and also people watching. Again, different cafés attract a special clientele and friends always knew in which café they could find each other.

In contrast to the elegant Right Bank where the most luxurious hotels and shops are situated, there is the Left Bank where book stores are set up along the bank of the river Seine. This is where I lived. The river divides the city. Students live in the Latin quarter since the Sorbonne is situated there. To me, however, the most interesting part of Paris was Montmartre with the church of *Sacré Coeur* high up on a hill overlooking its rather seedy streets with cabarets. Many painters set up their easels there and try to sell their paintings to the tourists.

The famous *Follies Bergères*, where the painter Toulouse Lautrec got his inspiration is situated in the streets below. Being a young girl, I was also fascinated to hear whispers that in these streets the prostitutes conducted their nightly business.

Another one of my favorite places was the Place des Vosges, an enclosed intimate square surrounded by historical buildings and little cafés tucked under their columns; it is a very serene place because it is totally cut off from the busy hustle and bustle of the noisy Paris streets.

Because my home life was so depressing and I dreaded going home to my miserable hotel, I spent my next three months roaming through this magical city. The only highlight was when my uncle Peter would take me to a movie on the Champs Elysées or, to one of the cafés in Montparnasse. Sometimes my mother also took me to a café for ice cream and we would then sit and watch the people go by; a favorite pastime in Paris.

One day my mother said: "Uncle Israel and his wife Malka have invited us to their beautiful country house for the weekend. Their chauffeur is going to pick us up; you'll have to wear your best." This was the kind uncle who supported us and, in retrospect, I believe he also supported the rest of the family—the uncle who saved our life by sending my mother and me an affidavit to escape from Nazi Vienna. As promised, the Rolls Royce picked us up and drove us through the magnificent French countryside to their idyllic old house next to a rushing brook—the sound creating a lovely serene atmosphere. I had never seen a house which was so beautifully furnished with antiques. My cousin Jules, who I had once met in Vienna, when I was very little, and his new bride, Nina, were already sitting in deckchairs in the garden. They looked like a young couple right out of a fashion magazine. Nina was working as a fashion designer for Pierre Cardin, and she looked the part. Next to her, I felt very shabbily dressed and altogether poor, but I was in awe of my glamorous surroundings. I remember little about this week-end, except that we were sitting in deck chairs in the garden, sunning ourselves. But what does stand out in my mind and what I will never forget was our trip home on Sunday night. I was sitting in the back of the Rolls Royce when I began to feel terribly nauseated and knew that I had to vomit. "Stop the car," my mother said after I told her how I felt. It was one of the most embarrassing moments I ever experienced.

Time in Paris was ticking on relentlessly. Two more dreaded visits to the Police Station gave us thirty days' grace each time; we were both beginning to hope that we would be in England by the time the next visit was scheduled. My father had already sent me papers to enable me to come to England and he had been successful in enrolling me as a boarder in a posh Public School, where I was to live for the next two years. Once again, my uncle paid for my schooling and had made it possible for me to attend a "finishing" type school. Since my father was only able to get me out at first, it meant leaving my mother behind. However, he promised to send her papers so that she would be able to work as a librarian in my school as soon as I arrived there; this was my only consolation.

In July 1939, I left Paris by train, where the entire family saw me off at the station. I was scared stiff, since I had to travel first by train and then cross the channel by boat all by myself. Knowing I was prone to car sickness, I was sure that I would also be seasick and be embarrassed.

Leaving my family behind on the Gare St. Lazare was a very traumatic experience for a fifteen-year-old. This time, I was the only one who was leaving and waving until I could no longer see my family, as they stood on the platform until the train was out of sight. I never felt so alone in all my life. Leaving the family and, in particular, my mother, behind in Paris made me feel incredibly sad.

I sat down in my compartment with my little suitcase which contained all my worldly belongings. I don't remember who else was in the same compartment, because I could think of nothing else but my fear of becoming train sick. Back in Vienna, whenever I went with my school for a ski week, my mother always gave me extra money in case I would get sick, which happened frequently. In Austrian trains, there were signs posted which read: "In the event of dirtying the compartment, call the conductor and pay a fine of X Schillings." I must have been so scared that I did not get sick on the way to Dieppe.

But I was even more afraid of the boat ride across the channel, which was known to be rough. In addition, it was a long crossing because Dieppe and New Haven are the furthest distance between France and England; Dover-Calais being the shortest. Despite the gloomy weather and a fine drizzle, I opted to stay on deck to breathe in the fresh air. That's what I did for what seemed an interminable time—actually it was only about six hours. Luckily I was fine and arrived in England at long last in one piece.

Chapter IV

England

In New Haven, England, carrying my little suitcase, I had no problem changing to the train which was heading for London. But once sitting in the train, I began to worry that my father would not be waiting for me. My anxiety was so intense that I forgot to be train-sick. It is strange what the mind can do when faced with an emergency.

Seeing my father standing on the platform when I finally arrived in London was the most wonderful sight, and alleviated my worst fear that I would be arriving all by myself in a totally foreign country, without speaking the language. I was so happy to see him that I could not stop hugging and kissing him.

We had to take the tube from London to Putney, a suburb of London, where my father was staying as a guest. "My hostess has kindly invited you to stay there as well for a few days, until you will be leaving for your school in Bournemouth," he told me. On the way there, we had much to tell each other since so much time had passed since I last saw him in Vienna. I told him all about Paris and how much I loved that city, but how sad I was to leave my mother behind. "You will soon be seeing her again, since I have already arranged for her papers to come here," he said, trying to console me.

The house in Putney was typically suburban, but pleasant, with a small garden and beautiful flowers; our hostess was most hospitable. But the thing that stands out in my mind to this day was that when I went to the bathroom to brush my teeth, I saw a glass of dentures staring at me. I had never seen anything like that before, and it disturbed me. When I told my father about it the next day, he just laughed.

That first night in England, I dropped into bed dead tired, but in spite of it, I was too excited to fall asleep, and I spent a long time reliving my journey which brought me there. I finally did fall asleep in my new bed in Putney, and felt secure that my father was sleeping in the adjoining room.

The next morning I was very eager to see London. My father showed me around the city, but I remember being very disappointed by my first visit. London for me had none of the charm that Paris had for me; I missed the outdoor cafés where one can people watch. On the other hand, I felt secure being with my father, and I was very flattered by his attention. I remember that he even took me out one night to see a Shakespeare play performed in Regent Park's open air theater. It was such a treat to be allowed to be out so late, that it felt like a grown-up date.

All the time, I was aware, however, that my days with my father were numbered because he had told me that I had to go to Boarding School before the end of the term. The school had assured him that I would be able to spend my summer vacation with one of the girls' parents somewhere in the countryside. In this way, I could learn enough English and be ready to start school in September. My father had already made plans to leave for America and had promised to send for me as soon as my two years paid for schooling was completed.

All too soon, the dreaded day came when my father and I took the train to Bournemouth, a resort town on the south coast. I remember it as one of the worst days of my life. I knew that soon I would be left alone in a strange school, in totally strange surroundings, without being able to speak the language; that I would be exposed to an environment where I knew not a soul.

The school buildings were built of red brick and they resembled an institution, or a prison. There were, however, lovely woods surrounding the school and a field of heather bordered the grounds which gave it its name, *Talbot Heath*. There were twelve tennis courts, of which four were built of clay, the rest were grass courts. A cricket and hockey field adjoined the actual school building, which was attended by both day and boarding school students. There were three boarding school houses, where we slept and ate. My house was called St. Katherine's. This is where my father and I went on my first day to see Ms. Wilkinson, the House Mistress, who looked like a typically English "old maid." She was short, thin and dried-out looking, with thin lips and a repressed manner. After introducing me to her, she explained to my father: "It is compulsory for your daughter to go to Church twice on Sundays." My father agreed that it might be good for my education to learn all about various religions, even though I was Jewish; he signed some papers agreeing to this. After what seemed to me to be a very short time because I couldn't bear for him to leave, he said: "Now I have to go back to London."

Until this very moment, I was in denial and didn't quite realize that he would leave that soon. I walked out with him towards the gate that separated the real world from where I was going to spend the next two years. My only consolation was that my mother would join me shortly. As I waved good-bye to my father and saw him disappear, I broke down and cried. I will never forget how abandoned I felt at that moment.

I turned back towards my house where Ms. Wilkinson showed me my dorm and the dining room where we were going to have all our meals. It was already dinner time and the gong had been rung. I was assigned to a table where I was introduced to some of the girls in my house and in my class. I could not speak to anyone and I saw them looking at me and whispering. Obviously table manners were very important in my school, and I was holding my fork in my right hand instead of the left hand, while eating, as is the custom in Europe. I was also taught in Vienna to keep my hands under the table; in England one is supposed to keep hands on the table. I asked for the salt without first saying "please" and "thank you." No one responded. I found out later that's why no one passed the salt. In Paris, I had only a few crash courses in English before leaving for England, but I understood enough to know that the girls were making fun of me. I was humiliated and embarrassed. That night when I went to sleep in my dorm, I was a very unhappy little girl, feeling very lonely.

About three days later, school was over. I had already been introduced to Pamela, who seemed a little kinder and had more empathy than the other girls. A few days later, her parents came to fetch her and me. I was to spend my holidays with them. They had a lovely house somewhere in the Cotswolds, an especially beautiful part of England, with quaint old houses and inns, and a luscious countryside with its green pastures and rolling hills where the sheep were grazing. Pamela and her parents were kind, but formal. There was hardly any conversation at the dinner table which surprised me. How different they were from the gregarious Viennese, I thought. In retrospect, I spent the summer trying to learn English; our days were pleasant, but uneventful.

One day, towards the end of the summer, we drove to the nearest village to do some grocery shopping. We were standing in a small country store when I heard an announcement on the radio: "War has been declared between England and Germany." There were shouts of dismay in this small country store. Bad news travels fast. Outside in the street, people already began to gather in groups outraged and horrified. Everyone's life was going to be affected in the worst possible way. Mothers were going to lose their sons who had to go to war; wives were going to lose their husbands and children were going to be deprived of their fathers. Who knew what was going to happen; what the future would bring with that madman Hitler who was trying to take all of Europe. The horrible realization came to me, that my mother would never be able to leave Paris, since all borders were obviously going to be shut; that I was going to be totally cut off from both my parents, since my father was momentarily leaving for America.

At that moment, I had no idea what real repercussions the declaration of war would have on my future.

Chapter V

Boarding School

A few days after we found out that England was at war, we immediately left the country and returned to our school in Bournemouth because the new term was about to begin. Up to this time, no radical changes were noticeable other than the fact that food was immediately rationed. Upon returning to school, the first thing I had to do was to get my uniform. This consisted of a navy blue tunic, several white shirts, a striped tie and a hat with our Talbot Health emblem on it. The very first morning, while I was trying to tie my tie, I found that I was unable to do so. The wrong end was always too long, and I finally faked it by just swirling it around and rushed downstairs in time for breakfast.

"Go upstairs and tie your tie properly," the matron said. Back in the dorm, I luckily found someone else who was as late as I was and who helped me. The next morning, I had done something else wrong. Again I was scolded: "Go back to the dorm and fix your bed properly. You didn't make hospital corners, like you are supposed to," the matron said.

The discipline was beginning to get to me. I soon found out that life in an English Boarding School was not easy and, I felt as though this must be what life might be like in either the army or in a prison.

My very first school day was another new experience. We had to walk single file, without talking, through a courtyard which was surrounded by beautiful flower beds until we reached the Auditorium for our morning "welcome" and our prayers. The headmistress made a speech in which she pointed out our responsibilities regarding our behavior to the outside world and stressed that we would be considered products of this very highly regarded scholastic institution; we would have to act accordingly. After a few religious hymns and the Lord's prayer, we were dismissed and assigned to our various classrooms. My curriculum consisted of German, French, Biology, Geography, English Grammar and English Literature. This was in preparation for the *Oxford School Certificate* which we were hopefully able to pass at the end of the Spring term. To me, this seemed like an impossible task, since I was still not able to speak English too well. French and German would not be a problem for me, but worst of all, we were going to be tested on Shakespeare's play *Macbeth*. How was I ever able to read and understand this complicated play in difficult Elizabethan English. Luckily, I had a brilliant English teacher who read the play out loud to us in class, as if she were acting in it. It felt like actually seeing the play in a theater. I began to understand it. I made up my mind to memorize the entire play, since I felt that this was the only way that I would be able to pass the examination. Since I was still unable to compose a good essay, I would simply write: "Lady Macbeth said to Macbeth: quote, quote . . . He answered her: quote, quote . . ." Since I was very busy with school during the day, I knew that the only way to accomplish this was to study at night under the covers with a flashlight. Most nights, I got away with it, but occasionally the matron caught me doing this and would then confiscate my flashlight. I did poorly in Mathematics, but I knew that my real strength would lie in languages, for which I had talent. Managing to get a B in Biology because I was interested in that subject, and on the strength of my excellent new language skills, as well as remembering the lines from *Macbeth*! I was thrilled to pass my examination. After only three terms, I received my Oxford School Certificate; this gave me a lot of self-confidence which I so badly needed. I had a low self-esteem because I always felt like an outsider. After that, I would have had to spend two more years of schooling to receive a Higher School Certificate in order to enter an English University. There was no more money left in order to finish my studies. Interestingly enough, later on in New York when I applied to Hunter College to continue my education, I was told that they would give me two years credit for my English education. However, I became pregnant and even though I had already completed two courses there, I was not allowed to enroll for the following term. How times have changed.

As the war was progressing, a big change occurred: the bombing began. Since we were living on the south coast of England, we had to carry our gasmasks at all times. In addition, without our parents' consent, we were no longer allowed to sleep in the dorm. Since I had no parents in England, I had to sleep in the shelters which had been dug out below our school grounds. Every night we carried our straw mattresses to the shelter and placed them on a wooden bench. It became such a routine that we didn't even think of the danger that a bomb might hit us. We slept with all our clothes on, and I would wake up in the morning hurting all over. Now I wonder how we were able to sleep at all. I continued to sleep in the shelter night after night. It was a nightmare; it was so damp that we could see drops of water running down the wall surrounding the shelter. I was afraid to get sick, but those of us who didn't have our parents' permission didn't complain, knowing that it was for our own safety. It was a horrible ordeal and we just wanted to get it over with, hoping that the war would soon end.

One morning, we woke up and saw that our entire grounds were covered with small incendiary bombs which, we were told, had been dropped by the Italians. No wonder they did not ignite; Mussolini was not famous for his warfare. We had to laugh. Had the bombs gone off, our school might have caught on fire.

In my fourth and last term, my life changed drastically. I umpired the school's tennis matches and scored for our cricket games which we played against younger Public School boy teams. I generally had more responsibility at school, such as supervising the younger pupils. I played "Left Wing" in field hockey against other schools and was surprised to find that I was not a bad athlete. I was a fast runner, and it was a thrill for me to see that the whole team had to run along with me when I succeeded to have the ball in my possession.

Once a year, in the Spring, the school invited boys to our school dance. Naturally, it was a big event. We were all excited and looked eagerly forward to that day. At the first dance, one of the boys asked me to dance with him. He became quite smitten with me, and afterwards wrote me long letters, hoping to see me again. My schoolmates, when they saw that I was receiving letters from a boy, envied me because this rarely happened to a girl. However, this romance was overshadowed by the fact that I had fallen deeply in love with Faye Cooke. She was the Headgirl of the school, captain of the tennis team, athletic, good-looking, with intense brown eyes that looked directly into yours; a small, beautifully formed upturned nose and short cropped dark hair. Above all, she also excelled scholastically and was an accomplished speaker. The entire school looked up to her as their role model.

I figured out that the only way that I could get close to her was to help her with her German. She had once mentioned to me that she was having difficulty in that subject. We arranged to take long walks together in the woods surrounding our school; I would correct her conversational German. Once, on a rainy day, after one of those walks, I remember getting into her bed, since we were both shivering from the cold; all we did was lie next to each other for comfort. My non-sexual crush on Faye did, however, brighten and heighten my otherwise dull days in school.

One day, a few of my schoolmates and I decided to go to the woods to smoke cigarettes. Unfortunately, we were caught and confined to our school grounds for three months. It was a terrible punishment because, before that incident, I did occasionally get permission to leave school for an afternoon if a parent of one of my friends took us out for tea in town.

In our house there was an infirmary where, at all times, our health was very carefully monitored. Every time we had our period, we had to sign a book with the date. When I first came to school, I missed three months. Because it was believed that I might be pregnant, the doctor came to examine me in the dorm. Of course, it was not possible because I was a virgin, but it caused quite a stir with the other girls who somehow heard about it.

Going to church twice on Sundays proved to be a terrible bore. It was all very well for my father to give permission for me to learn all about the teachings of the Church of England, but he was not the one who had to attend church services, which were very close to Catholic teachings. I was bored by the endless hymns, even though I found the music quite beautiful. To make matters worse, once a month we had to write a book review about a religious book that we had read. By this time, I was fed up and had managed to find books with paper jackets which summarized their contents and just wrote a synopsis in my own words. Luckily, I got away with it.

I cannot say that my school days were happy ones, and therefore I counted the days when I would be able to leave school behind.

In retrospect, however, my strict upbringing at Boarding school probably contributed to make me into a stronger person, so that I was able to deal with the many struggles and difficulties which I had to endure in future years.

Chapter VI

After Boarding School/Mac

After two years of feeling protected in a secure environment, leaving Boarding School made me feel very anxious. To go out into the "real world" meant that I would have to find a place to live; that I would have to make a living in order to support myself because there was no more money for me to continue my education. As it turned out, both problems were easier solved than I had anticipated. By 1941, many men and women had been drafted into the Armed Forces or into a factory, so that I immediately found a room in a hostel right in the center of Bournemouth. Also, I was extremely lucky to share my room with a charming girl, named Esmé. She was not only beautiful, but she was also very refined as well as fun. We became good friends and shared many experiences. These were anxiety provoking times and it felt comforting having someone to share my concerns. Both of us were never sure whether we would survive the next bomb attack. On good days, we enjoyed long walks along the boardwalk in Bournemouth which was located on the south coast of England. Of course, we could never go out on the actual beach since the whole coast line was surrounded by barbed wire. On week-ends, we would go to the tea dance at the Bournemouth Pavilion. We were both pretty nice looking, and the boys in the English Air Force and, later on, the Canadians and Australians who joined them, would ask us to dance. At one of these dances, I met a very sweet, innocent English boy who was barely nineteen years old; his name was David. After seeing each other only a short time, we thought we were in love. I believe that I was just flattered to have such a good-looking boy interested in me. It has always been my downfall in life that looks were so important to me, instead of looking at the inside of a person. There really was no physical or emotional attraction between us, as I recall. Shortly after we met, David was shipped out. He wrote me many letters and sent me photographs of himself which I tacked over my bed. I never found out what happened to him. While I was not upset no longer hearing from him, I thought about him sometimes. But I had to concentrate on earning a living.

My excellent education did not help me much in my search for a good job. Because I had to earn money immediately, I took a job as a cashier in one of the largest department stores in town, called Beale's. In the basement of the store, pneumatic tubes were sent down to provide customers with change for their purchases. Mathematics had always been my weakest subject in school. Coming from Vienna, where everything was counted in decimals, it was hard for me to remember that there were twelve schillings to the English pound instead of ten. The sales girls were very amused when I sent up the wrong change and they would send back two or three tubes containing money and at the same time with a note which read: "You did it again!" Sitting in the dreary basement day after day without a ray of sunshine was no fun; the job was horribly depressing.

Fortunately for me, during that time period, I had met a man, named Mac. It is strange to think that I don't now remember any details of that first meeting, particularly since to this day, I cannot get him out of my mind. Mac was a gunner in the Australian Air Force, attached to the R.A.F. He was fourteen years older than I; a man who was sophisticated, with dark brown hair and soulful brown eyes; a man who seemed to know so much more about life and love than I did. I looked up to him because, of course, I was still a virgin. I was flattered that this man who was extremely handsome and sexy was so in love with me, that he did not mind that I was not willing to have a full-fledged affair with him. He could have had anyone he might have wanted in this crazy hyped-up war-time. Seeing him on week-ends made it possible for me to endure the boredom of my dreary job.

Shortly after meeting him, he was transferred to Yorkshire. I received many letters telling me about his flirtations with other women, but assuring me always of his love for me, and trying to figure out how we could meet again on his next leave. Because of the constant bombing which we experienced in Bournemouth, situated on the coast, and because the war had escalated, I was very concerned about his safety. I must have expressed it in one of my letters to him, because I received the following reply:

"Cherie," he wrote. (He always called me that, and I found it so charming.) "I don't want to give you a lecture because I would rather give you consolation, but you must not worry about me. I know this sort of thing is easy to say, but it won't do you any good, and it won't help me. In the first place if anything is going to happen to me, it will come, no matter how much we try to avoid it, and in second place nothing will, if I can help it. I am a great believer in self preservation and I believe in my luck, and if you can keep on thinking this too, well everything will be O.K. I have to do my 200 operational hours, and then I am given a rest before I do another 200. This war is going on for a long time yet, and lots can happen in the future, but my death is not one of them. So in the future, darling, try to look at things on the bright side where I am concerned and think of the happy times that we shall have in the future. 'Nough said, dearest. You know that I want nothing from you that you are not prepared to give without regrets. But when you change your mind, as you no doubt will, as you get wiser, I shall be around if the R.A.F. lets me."

Shortly afterwards, a second letter arrived. Things had gotten even worse. It seemed to us as if we had lost the war. It read:

"Hullo Cherie. This is just a note to let you know that I am still on deck after having taken part in the raids over Cologne and Essen. These were my first night operations and they certainly were an initiation. The first time we were shot to hell, and the second, well the good Lord must have been watching over me, we only just made it each time. For the present keep your fingers crossed for me. Love from Mac."

In another letter, he wrote: "I can't wait to see you and as soon as I get my first leave, we will be together again."

Then came a telegram: "Trying to arrange for a week's leave. Will telephone Wednesday after 9 p.m. Stand by for broadcast. Love Mac." I was elated. We arranged to meet in a London hotel, where we had two separate rooms. We would embrace and cuddle, but it never went further than that. Still we so enjoyed our time together, going to the theater, out to dinner and we both loved to dance. But mostly, it was being with each other, and talking about each other's lives. He told me all about Australia, which was a country I knew nothing about, but which I romanticized because of him. I told him about my past life in Vienna, my schools, my summers spent on a farm and about the holocaust. How many of us had escaped to Paris and how I had left for England alone without my mother. He was shocked; but as most people during that period of the war, he knew nothing of these horrors. We were two people from two very different worlds which the war had brought together. It was a fact that the war accelerated relationships. Each moment became more precious because none of us knew how long we would live. Not only could the boys in combat be killed at any moment, but we, the civilians, could die in a bombing. Because it was such a precarious time, we lived to the fullest, in a constant state of anxiety, but at the same time, it was the most exciting time of my life.

The letters from Mac kept coming. I answered all of them knowing how important mail must have been for him far away from home. I also wrote him about the other boys in my life. He did not expect me to sit home. I experienced occasional disappointments with some boys who promised to call me and never did. This, of course, being so young, I took much to heart. I tried not to write too much about my more successful flirtations. In one of his many letters, he once wrote: "Your letters, cherie, are so wonderful. You write exactly like you talk." He would console me and give me fatherly advice.

In July 1942, a letter from Mac arrived which really upset me a lot. He wrote: "This is to let you know that I am still O.K. After having crashed in Suffolk the other night, I was slightly injured which is not as bad as it sounds. The pilot made a belly landing and the plane was completely smashed up. It ripped the bottom clean out of it. No one else was injured, though we were all very slap happy after the crash, just like being drunk. I didn't know for about an hour afterwards that I was injured. We all thought we had had it and wished each other best of luck on the inter-com. My only consolation was that I was going somewhere where it was warm. Amazing what thoughts pass through your head in such few seconds. I had my neck x-rayed and of course I am grounded. All's well that ends well."

Mac had to have complete rest and was given a week's leave to recover which he spent at some distant relative's house. Luckily, he did recover and wrote me: "We must meet again." We did manage to meet again in London. During that week-end, we went to the Hammerstein Palais, a huge dance hall, where the big bands played, among them the famous Glenn Miller band.

Before I went to meet Mac this time, I happened to run into another Australian who, by chance, knew Mac. He said to me: "Do you know that Mac is married back in Australia?"

I was very shocked and upset. It was hard for me to believe because Mac had never mentioned it. I decided to confront him and waited for the right moment: we were dancing and he had his arms around me when I said: "Mac, how come you never told me that you are married?"

"Darling," he answered, "you never asked me."

I was speechless. I decided to either accept our relationship or never see him again. Because I cared for him too much, I did not have the heart to break it up.

After that incident, Mac's leave was up and I saw him off at Waterloo Station. Standing on the platform, as the train pulled out, we embraced, saying good-bye till the next time. We waved till the last moment until the train was out of sight. It seemed to me then that I was always the one who was left behind. I had the gut feeling that I would never see Mac again. I turned around and walked along with many other girls seeing their boyfriends off and took the train back to Bournemouth, thinking about our week-end, but feeling very apprehensive and sad. A few weeks later, my premonition was borne out when a letter I had written to Mac was returned to me. Shortly afterwards, I received a telegram which was marked: "On His Majesty's Service". It read: "I regret to inform you that your friend Sgt. McMichael has been reported 'Missing on operations against the enemy' on the 12th August, 1942. It is some consolation that quite a number of airmen reported missing are eventually found to be prisoners of war and we sincerely hope that it will be the case in this instance."

I was devastated, deeply moved, incredibly sad. Once again, I experienced a terrible loss. At my young age, I had lost first my country, then my mother and some other members of my family, and now Mac who had become the most important person in my present life. I guess, in retrospect, he was like a father figure because of our age difference. This meant a great deal in those days, because a girl of nineteen was usually sexually very inexperienced; a man of thirty-three, fighting in the war, grows up quickly and as a result becomes much older than his years in the process. For many days, after knowing that he had died, I would start crying whenever I thought about him and, to this day, writing this makes me teary-eyed. Mac has been a very important person in my life and I will never forget him. Did it really matter that he was married? At least he had a few happy times before he died. I have always kept a lasting memory of him— a man who cared so much for me—a man who accepted me totally for myself and asked little of me. While not becoming my lover, he still had a decisive influence on my emotional development.

One Sunday morning, shortly after Mac got shot down on a mission over Germany, fate intervened: the Germans must have thought that the department store where I worked was a factory and bombed it. That day it was completely flattened. We would all have been killed, had it been an ordinary work day. As it was, at that very moment, my friend Esmé and I happened to walk on the other side of the street when the bombing occurred and were spared.

After that incident, Esmé and I developed shingles, "a nervous disease, probably due to shock," the doctor said. As I mentioned previously, I just had a few cuts which the nearby drugstore bandaged, and I was all right.

The day after the bombing, the whole town gathered on the square to inspect the damage which had resulted from the bombing. We asked the store owners whose stores had been set on fire from the bombing whether we could help. I remember helping one clothing store, where the owner was very grateful for our help in loading clothing into a truck. At the end of the day, he insisted on paying us, even though we had not expected any reward. It was touching to see how the whole town stood together.

Very soon afterwards the townspeople began to rebuild and we, too, had to get on with our lives. The reality was that Esmé and I had to recover from our horrendous experience, having come so close to death. Once again, fate intervened.

A few days after the bombing, I received a draft notice giving me the choice of either joining the army, the A.T.S., or working in a factory which would have meant having to go up north to one of those horribly depressing industrial towns. Even though it meant signing up for three years, I told the Labor Department that I thought I wanted to join the Army. "But," I told them, "first I am taking a week's vacation to think it over." They agreed and I was to report back after my vacation.

As luck would have it, I had just received a letter from my old friend Janet from Vienna who had just finished her schooling in Leicester and who had recently moved to Cambridge to work at the Lion Hotel, one of the oldest and most famous hotels which, in the old days, used to be a coach house. One could still see where the stables were kept in the back of the hotel. She was lucky to get a job there as an Assistant Housekeeper since she had graduated in Domestic Science. "Why don't you come and visit?" her letter said. "I can manage to smuggle you into my tiny room, and it won't cost you anything." I was thrilled to finally see my old school friend again, and also to visit Cambridge, which I knew to be one of the most beautiful university towns in England, famous throughout the world.

I will never forget walking into the Lion Hotel lobby where Janet was waiting for me. I was thrilled to see her. We had not seen each other since the day I had left her at the station in Vienna almost three years before. It seemed like a century had passed because so much had happened to both of us. Since Janet was on duty that day, she had to leave me right away.

"My friend, an American Captain in the Air Corps by the name of Badger, will look after you until I get off work," she said, and quickly introduced me to him.

"Would you like a drink?" he asked me right away as we sat down in the Lounge. I think I fell in love with him right there and then. As I looked at that stunning, slim man with beautiful blue eyes and blond hair, looking so handsome in his uniform, it was love at first sight, as far as I was concerned. I looked at his delicate hands and began to think that I would love to have them touch me. (Hands always tell me a lot about a person. My mother taught me that.)

On that fated day, not only did I meet the man who was to become my first true love, but on that same evening someone at the next table called my name. It turned out to be a cousin of my father's from Vienna. "What a small world," I thought. She asked me what I was doing and when I told her that I had plans to join the A.T.S., she said, "You are crazy, you will be stuck in England for three years and it will take such a long time for you to be able to join your father in America when the war is over."

That evening completely changed my life because, by chance, Janet had a friend, Henrietta, who worked at the Cambridge Instrument Factory, a factory right in Cambridge.

"We will call her up and see whether you can't get a job there," she said. "That way you can move here and we can be together."

I was extremely lucky that it all worked out just as we had planned. I got the job at the factory. Back in Bournemouth, I presented the letter from the factory that I had been hired to the Labor Department, and was off the hook from the Army. I packed my few belongings and said good-bye to Esmé. I was very sorry to part from her, but we promised to write as we embraced and said good-bye. I moved to Cambridge, leaving behind my school years and my adolescence.

Chapter VII

Cambridge

My first week in Cambridge, I lived with Janet in the Lion Hotel, where she managed to smuggle me into her tiny room provided by the hotel, enabling her to work late hours when she was required to do so. Since it had a separate entrance, it was possible for me to go in without being seen.

On my third day in Cambridge, which I spent sightseeing, I climbed up the winding staircase leading to Janet's small room and found a Red Cross letter addressed to me under the door. It read: "We are sorry to inform you that your mother was arrested at the police station in Paris and has been sent to a concentration camp, which we believe to be in Auschwitz. We will let you know as soon as we get further information." I let the letter drop in disbelief.

During the time I was living in Bournemouth, I had received a few Red Cross letters from her in which she was only allowed to write a few lines. In those letters, she had asked me how I was, whether I had enough money, and how I was managing alone in England during the war.

But this was final. My shock and grief were so intense that to this day I avoid talking about it. Writing about it is almost unbearable and I just want to negate that it ever happened. A few minutes later, Janet found me sitting on top of the stairs, sobbing. She put her arms around me and tried to comfort me. But how could anyone comfort me when we both knew that my mother's survival was highly unlikely. From what we had heard, no one came out of Auschwitz alive. To lose one's mother is one of the worst tragedies that anyone, particularly at a young age, can ever get over. For days I walked around depressed and sad. I could not believe that I would never see my mother again. I never did: she did not survive. The reason that I seldom talk about it to my friends is, that even so many years later, it is just too painful to relive. Thinking back to the time of this painful letter, I can now see that my grief was exacerbated by my sense of guilt, since my mother had made it so difficult for me to love her during my early years.

I did not want to jeopardize Janet's job at the Lion Hotel, and I moved into a room with one of Janet's friends; her name was Henrietta and she had a room in a typical suburban house which belonged to Mrs. Howell. Our landlady was very pleasant, but she hated the "Yanks." Every morning Henrietta and I went to work at the factory. My job consisted of calibrating thermographs, which were used on naval ships for temperature regulation. First I had to dip them in hot oil, up to five hundred degrees, and then into crushed ice, mixed with salt, to below freezing. I had to be extremely careful not to drip hot oil on my legs. I saw that many of my co-workers had horrible scars. In addition, I had to stand on my feet fifty hours a week, and was required to work overtime. It was a horrible job and I came home totally exhausted. Fortunately, after a few months of working these dreadful hours, I developed a stomach ulcer; the doctor said: "The pressure and stress must have caused your symptoms." I was vomiting and felt dreadful. He wrote a note to the factory, and I was relieved from my duties there. Shortly afterwards, I was extremely lucky to get a job as a secretary for a pleasant middle-aged lady child psychologist in Cambridge's Town Hall. Mornings were spent working for her; afternoons I was required to visit children's nurseries. I was in charge of supplying them with cans of food, paper goods and whatever other supplies they needed. The nurseries were dispersed around Cambridge, but I managed to get around by bus. I was very welcomed by the nursery management and they invited me to stay for lunch on a regular basis. This was a real treat since food was strictly rationed. I always made a list of their needs which I brought back to the Town Hall. As a rule, I was through by three p.m. and could go home and relax. It was a cushy job, and I was so relieved not having to work at the factory for the rest of the war.

By this time, Janet was also drafted for war-time work. Since she was a trained dietician and had studied Home Economics at College, she got a job in a school which was considered war-time work and, reluctantly, she left her beloved Lion Hotel. Together we rented a large room in a house on King's Parade, right across from the famous King's College. The house belonged to the *Ballet Joos*; while on tour they rented it out. We shared one kitchen with various other young people living there. Since the owners were away, we were able to have friends visiting us and we had many parties and a great time. Americans we knew always brought us food; once Badger brought us a dozen frozen eggs which, when we opened them, smelled so terrible that we had to throw them all out, much to our disappointment. Another time he brought us a chicken which still had its feathers; we spent hours plucking it. It is hard to think back to those days today and to realize how excited we would get to get a chicken or eggs, which we today take totally for granted.

After work, Janet and I would take a book and sit on the banks of the River Cam, outside Kings College, listening to "even" songs in this beautiful calm setting, where the grass was so well kept that one could count the blades. We watched students and tourists punting along the River Cam, a famous pastime in Cambridge when the weather is good. It is a way of seeing the backs of all the historic famous colleges.

But once the *Ballet Joos* returned, we had to move out. We found an apartment which was our dream come true, because it was below street level. We had both read and enjoyed the book *My Sister Eileen*, where two friends watch people's legs as they pass by their apartment window. We also tried to imagine what the people actually looked like, "What a crazy idea," Janet's mother said when she visited us. "You will be sorry when you get older and suffer from arthritis from all that dampness." Of course, she was right. We had a fireplace and lit a fire every evening to keep warm. We loved having our very own apartment and, best of all, having our own entrance. Mrs. Parfait, our landlady, was still relatively young and since her husband was in the army, we saw another serviceman visiting her from time to time. Therefore, she never complained about our visitors.

Food continued to become a big problem for everyone because it was severely rationed. Janet and I were fortunate to get a free lunch, but for supper we started making a soup on Monday, add potatoes on Tuesday, and whatever we were able to find on the market the next day. We never had an orange or a lemon all throughout the war. Often Janet went to the butcher to ask for bones for our soup. "My sister is sick," she would say. A few days later, I went in with the same story. We did not fool the butchers, but they were accommodating, knowing how little food there was. On Fridays, we were able to buy fish; my boss always gave me time off to stand in line at the fish shop. Sometimes, we also bought fish and chips, wrapped in newspaper. At other times, Janet brought back a few tins from her school. She hid them in her bicycle basket, covered with a dish towel. Our American boyfriends gave us their ration cards, which helped a lot. On weekends, Badger took me out to dinner in a restaurant, and Janet, too, was taken out. We did not starve.

While I was working at the factory, life was very bleak and miserable. Badger's loving attention was the only bright spot in my life. It was not surprising then, that at last, since we had been dating all along, he and I spent a week-end together in a pub, called the *Black Rose*, where they had bedrooms upstairs. That's where I lost my virginity. Afterwards, I felt very guilty, like a "fallen" woman. From the beginning, we had a very intense sexual relationship. Badger, although twice my age, became my steady boyfriend for the remainder of the war. He did not look his age and was stunning, tall and thin in his Captain's uniform.

Despite the fact that I was in love with Badger, a love that deepened after we became lovers, I knew deep down that it was somewhat like a father-daughter relationship since he was thirty-eight and I was just nineteen. I had never had a real father, and this was a man with so much greater life experience and who seemed to truly love me. Sex was not the reason I cared for him so deeply. He could never do enough for me. It is true that he brought me gifts, not the conventional ones in return for sexual favors, but they mostly consisted of food which he could bring from the post. However, it was the little personal touches that really mattered to me. Often, when I came home from work, he would be waiting for me, having just polished my one and only pair of good leather shoes. It was touching because clothing was also severely rationed.

Since our apartment was too small for privacy, we often spent week-ends at our little pub on King's Parade, opposite the colleges and the river; a wonderful setting. The rooms were charmingly furnished in an old English style. We would register as "Mr. and Mrs." The registration clerk was used to this and he just let it go. This was wartime and no one in Cambridge was going to make trouble for a couple in love. But on other week-ends, staying in London in a fancy hotel was a very different story.

One week-end, we registered at the elegant Greene Park Hotel requesting two separate rooms in our own names. The bellhop showed us to a suite, consisting of a living room with two adjoining bedrooms. We were sitting in the living room talking when there was a knock on the door: "You are to leave the hotel immediately," the Manager said. "This is a decent hotel, and we don't allow this sort of thing to go on here."

"But," we said, "we are just having a drink together and are not doing anything else."

He was insistent and our protesting did not change his mind. We were furious. It was the one and only time that I ever got thrown out from a hotel. We checked into another, less fancy hotel, and consoled ourselves by going out to dinner and to a ballet. Even though it was wartime, it was still possible to do this.

Back in Cambridge, the officers' mess gave fantastic parties. Buses escorted us back and forth to the post, which was just outside of Cambridge. They were festive events: the bar was stocked with bottles of every conceivable drink; the buffet table was laden with food we had not seen in years. There was a huge roast beef, ham, coleslaw and potato salad, and, above all, hard boiled eggs. With our ration of one egg per month, this was the biggest treat. We always carried our one egg home from the grocery store as if it were a precious diamond. At the party, there was also real bread; the bread we could buy tasted like paper. We danced all night to a wonderful live band until they ended the evening with the "Star Spangled Banner." My friend Janet told me afterwards that I would continue dancing through this last tune without realizing that there was no more dance music.

Every so often, Badger, Janet and I would take the train to London for the week-end which was a two hour ride from Cambridge. By this time, the war had escalated. Back in Cambridge, we felt relatively safe because the Germans and the British had made a deal: "You don't bomb Heidelberg and we won't bomb Oxford and Cambridge." Miraculously, the Germans actually kept their word. In London, ducking the V.E. rockets and buzz bombs that arrived without any warning whatsoever, was really scary. But despite the fear of the bombs, it was wonderful to be able to see a play, and go to a good restaurant; we took our chances. We lived dangerously, for we were young and six years of war became a way of life.

Badger and I often talked about the fact that he was married. It was understood that once I would come to America after the war, we would get married. "I am definitely getting a divorce, darling," he told me. Deep down, however, our age difference began to worry me. When I am going to be forty and still a young woman, he will be close to sixty, I thought. I was beginning to think about it often. I already began to get the feeling that I needed to be in the company of people my own age.

One evening, Badger was not coming into town, and I had already told him in so many words, that I needed some space and, of course, he was not thrilled to hear this; still he thought it was best to let me have my way. At the "Dorothy" that night, I met Johnny. He was exactly my age, and absolutely adorable. He was a fighter pilot who flew P-38's. (I still have his photograph.) We began to have a sweet platonic friendship which both of us knew would lead nowhere, but we didn't care. His home in America was Kokomo, Indiana, a town I had never even heard of. I think he had a girl back home, but all of that was not important at the time. That first evening when I met Johnny, Janet told me: "Badger came in unexpectedly in the hope of finding you. He was extremely upset since he had heard that his eighteen-year-old daughter had fallen off her horse and is in the hospital." I felt very guilty, not having been there in his hour of need, but I still continued to see Johnny. We were kids together, enjoying ourselves, despite the constant threat of death. I worried about him every time he went on a mission, and for good reason, since so many boys were getting killed. It was always so good to see him again. We always had so much fun together. One day we decided to bake a cake; another day, we went punting on the River Cam, out to Grantchester, to have tea in the famous garden; the poet Rupert Brooke had lived in that village. We enjoyed a typical afternoon English tea hour, where tiny sandwiches, scones and strawberry jam, covered with clotted cream were served. Since Cambridge was surrounded by farms, they grew vegetables and fruits and also made their own jam.

These moments in this serene setting were unforgettable, in contrast to our days which were threatened by the war.

Somehow, I managed to see both Johnny and Badger. My feelings became ambivalent, I felt guilty not to see Badger that often. I knew that I loved him and I thought that I did want to marry him despite our age differences. On the other hand, I enjoyed being with Johnny and just having fun. I did not want to give him up.

In early 1945, the war had already gone on for six years. I got fed up with living in England, and I was just dying to leave for America to join my father. I could no longer stand the constant rain, not seeing the sun, and the endless rationing of food and clothing. I needed a way out. But how? I had heard rumors that it was possible to stow away on a naval ship headed for the U.S.A. Being young, and I must say, in retrospect, pretty gutsy, I decided to take the train to Southampton, stay in a hotel overnight, and then hang out in a pub where sailors go to drink, and try to talk one of them into helping me to stow away. It was a preposterous idea, but I was willing to give it a try. It also appealed to my adventurous and romantic spirit. It made me feel as though I was in a movie. It also convinced me that I was not a cowardly person.

All worked according to plan. I found a room in a small hotel, and, in the evening, I found "the" pub which was the sailors' favorite watering hole. I was lucky and started to talk to a sailor: "I am desperate to leave England," I told him. "I have been stuck here all through the war without my parents, and I want to join my father in America."

"I understand your dilemma," he said, "and I'll do everything I can to help you, but I can't promise that it'll work. I'll meet you tomorrow at 11 a.m., after I speak to someone in charge, and let you know whether it can be done. I take it your papers are in order?"

I assured him that this was so; or so I thought.

I was very excited when I got into bed that night, but I also told myself: "Don't be disappointed if it doesn't work. At least you tried."

The next day, my sailor arrived with many apologies: "I spoke to the person I told you about, but he was afraid to take a chance."

I had sort of expected it, thanked him profusely, said good-bye and took the train back to Cambridge, feeling sad and disappointed. Janet was not a bit surprised that it had not worked out. "But at least I tried," I told her.

Three months later, the war was finally over; it was V.E. Day (Victory in Europe), and we were ecstatic. My favorite cousin, Jules, who had been in the French resistance, came from Paris to visit me and we went to London to celebrate. Picadilly Circus had truly turned into a mass brawl that day. People were going crazy with joy that the war was over, at least in Europe, and, of course, everyone got drunk. No one could blame them. Wives couldn't wait to see their husbands returning from war, children were waiting for their fathers, and we were happy that our boyfriends were safe; that is, of course, those who had survived that horrible war. Jules and I went to a posh restaurant, ordered champagne and a fabulous dinner. When the bill arrived, it was horrendous. The maitre d' thought we were drunk and added on a few English pounds, which we indignantly refused to pay.

Victory in Japan (V.J. Day) came three months later, August 14, 1945, after America dropped the atomic bomb in Hiroshima. A catastrophe for the Japanese, as we all know today, but, at the time, we did not know what repercussions the atomic bomb would have for the rest of the world.

To celebrate the real end of the war, Badger and I went to Edinburgh for the week-end. We stayed at the Hotel Balmoral on Princess Street. It was a stylish, old-fashioned hotel somewhat reminiscent of the Plaza Hotel in New York. My only memory from that time is that we were often strolling up and down the main street with the castle high up overlooking this charming city. It is a custom of the people of Edinburgh at a certain time of the day. I also recall how terrible the food was, and that all we seemed to eat was a thick Scotch broth.

But this trip had little to do about good food. It was about feeling incredibly relieved that the war was finally over.

Shortly after our visit to Scotland, Badger left for America, supposedly to ask his wife for a divorce and straighten out the obstacles confronting our future. He was also going to see my father in New York before going home to Indiana. He did indeed do so, and I would have loved to have been there and to overhear their conversation. At last I, too, was preparing to leave for America, thanks to my father's intervention. My dream was coming true, or so I thought then.

A lot of American service men had already gone home. Cambridge began to look a little deserted. In a way, it was somewhat of a let-down. To console ourselves, Janet and I went to the tea dance at the "Dorothy." At a table, next to us, sat four English R.A.F. pilots. They were totally involved in their "pilot talk" and didn't even notice our existence. "Look how stuck up the English are, compared to the Americans," Janet said to me. All during the war, the English and the Americans were competing with each other. The British would say: "They are overpaid, oversexed and over here." They never wanted to admit that if the Americans had not joined the allies, England would surely have lost the war. We were just discussing this, when one of the pilots asked Janet to dance. On the dance floor, he told her: "I am going to India, but I will be back in two weeks and I will call you then." They seemed to get on very well. On the way home, she told me: "I am smitten." Two weeks, three weeks went by, no phone call. She certainly was very disappointed.

One evening, I felt like going dancing, but Janet did not want to go with me, because she had arranged to work on a translation with a friend. I went alone.

Suddenly, someone asked me to dance, and it turned out to be none other than the English pilot who had flirted with Janet before his short trip to India.

"Why didn't you call my girlfriend?" I asked him.

"I was embarrassed to call her," he said. "We had such a short time together, and she might not even remember my name."

"Well," I said, "why don't you walk me home after this is over? She would love to see you."

Little did I know then that my oldest friend, Janet, had met her future husband.

Arriving at our apartment, I yelled up: "Guess who I brought home." Janet was thrilled to see him again, and invited him up for coffee. Coffee was the only item not rationed, since the English preferred tea, which they drank in large quantities. Following that evening, Janet and Hugh started going out with each other, and I often joined them, since Badger had already left for home.

I was now making plans to leave for America. My father had sent me an affidavit, but no money. Since I didn't want to wait to leave by boat, I decided to try to fly on Pan Am, one of the first clippers to make this journey. It cost $379.40 one way, and I just barely managed to save $280. I desperately needed another $100. But how to get it?

One week-end, I was at the elegant Park Lane Hotel in London, sitting at the bar with some friends. I was introduced to an older English lady, and I told her my predicament: "I have this fabulous stamp collection which I've brought with me when my mother and I fled from Vienna, which I would like to sell," I told her.

"Oh," she said, "let me see it. Perhaps I'll buy it from you."

I brought it to the hotel the next day. I was very apprehensive.

"It's really fabulous," she said. "I'll give you the $100 you need to get to America."

I was sure that she did it out of the kindness of her heart. I accepted the money, thanked her profusely, and promptly went to the airline to buy my ticket. I gave notice to my employers, packed my meager belongings, kissed my dearest friend Janet good-bye and, with great trepidation, boarded my very first plane. It never occurred to me, however, that it might be dangerous to fly. I was so excited that my dream to go to America had finally come true. My only regret was leaving Janet behind.

We stopped in Shannon for refueling and I remember how green the grass was in Ireland. I suppose it's because it always rains there too. At the airport they served us a delicious Irish Coffee while we were waiting. I looked around the beautiful duty free shop. Of course, I couldn't afford to buy anything, but it was exciting to see the luxurious objects displayed. When we got back on the plane, I was counting the hours. I was looking out of the window when suddenly half way over the Atlantic, the pilot announced: "We have to turn around and go back to Ireland because of engine trouble."

Looking down at the vast ocean below, we were all very scared. Would we even be able to make it to Shannon? "Why do these things always happen to me?" I thought, and "will I ever make it to America?" At last, we landed in Shannon many hours later. We were taken by bus to Limerick where we spent the night in an incredibly dilapidated Bed and Breakfast place. I could hardly believe that on this very expensive trip, the airline would not provide us with a decent hotel. We took off again the next morning, a little apprehensive. On the plane, I did not talk to the other passengers, as far as I remember, because I was so deep in my own thoughts.

What would it be like to see my father again, now that six years had passed since he left me alone at the gate of my boarding school? What would New York be like, and for that matter, how would I find a job and a place to live; would I make new friends? What would it be like in the "New World?"

I loved flying, I realized, and I admired the pretty air hostesses. I made up my mind on that first flight that I, too, wanted to become a stewardess. In 1945, being an airline flight attendant still represented real glamour and prestige. I found out later that I was not the required height, that I was too short, and that a college education was also necessary; thus I was not a candidate.

At last we landed in Philadelphia. There was my father waiting at the airport and there we were, at last together again, six years later.

Author's first Boyfriend, Captain Badger

"Flying fortress" bomber used in Britain against the Germans

Author's young friend, Jonny who flew fighter planes (P-38), in WWII, but got killed in a test flight in America

Chapter VIII

New York

Waiting at Philadelphia's airport, I was so excited at the thought of seeing my father again after a six year absence that my heart began to beat real fast. When I saw him standing there, I was quite shocked to see how my father had aged during those years. He looked ill and much older than his fifty years. He must have seen the expression on my face, because he said: "I have just come out of hospital where I had surgery." Also from the very beginning, he made it clear to me that he would not be able to help me financially, and here I was with only five dollars to my name! I began to worry and wondered whether coming to America had been a wise decision now that my dream had finally become reality.

His early years in America had been difficult, especially since he had been a creative writer and film maker back in Vienna. In the train to New York, he told me: "For a man like me with my cultural background, with English not being my mother tongue, I could not find anything but menial work. I have had to make a living by working as a waiter at Jewish weddings just to survive. Meanwhile," he said, "I am living in a rooming house on 95th Street near Riverside Drive, where I have just one room and have to use the communal kitchen. But I have arranged for you to stay a few days with your mother's brother Salomon, who lives on the lower east side with his wife Amy and their two children; your cousin Ronny, who is seven, and his half sister, Vivian, from his former marriage, about twenty years old."

I arrived at my uncle's apartment which was on East 12th Street, next to the famous Café Royal where, at the time, the Jewish intellectuals met. I will never forget the moment I entered the apartment: my cousin Ronny was standing on the table with a toy gun yelling: "Stick 'em up." I was extremely shocked by his behavior and by my welcome, but I soon found out that such behavior was quite common during these "permissive" child-rearing practices in America. The apartment was crowded with bad reproduction furniture and many books. There were only two bedrooms, and I was to share a bedroom with my cousin Vivian. I noticed that my uncle was much older than his wife, and was always sitting in his easy chair reading books to his son, while his wife, Amy, was always in the kitchen preparing huge portions of rich, fatty food which I could not digest. After years of being deprived of such food during the war years, my stomach had shrunk so that I only weighed 110 pounds. I was 5 foot 4 inches and I wore a size seven dress. (With the years that sure changed!) At first, cousin Vivian seemed to like me and was happy to have company with someone around her age. A few days later, her boyfriend came to see her and showed great interest in me because I was the "new girl" in town and also because he was fascinated with my wartime experiences. I never understood at the time why she suddenly did not seem to like me. My aunt told me later: "She felt you came on to her boyfriend and she was extremely jealous." In reality, I had no designs whatsoever on him.

I was very excited that on my very first evening in New York, my girlfriend Janet's former boyfriend, Mel, a major in the Air Corps, came to call for me to take me out to go bowling. That very same afternoon, my aunt Amy, knowing that I had no clothes whatsoever, said: "I will take you shopping at S. Klein on Union Square and buy you a dress for the occasion." Of course, I was terribly excited and I will never forget that first dress: It was grey and had a square neckline with embroidery on it. It cost $8 and I felt that I looked stunning. Since our clothes in England were rationed, I had not had a new dress for years. I thought it was really nice of her and I thanked her profusely.

Much to my surprise, when Mel came to call for me and Amy found out that he was not Jewish, she wanted to tear the dress off my back. She was not religious in the strict sense, but a "cultural" traditionalist. This unfortunate incident caused a tremendous furor and soon afterwards when I told my father what had happened, we both decided that I had outstayed my welcome and that it would be best that I should move to my cousin Hedy's house in Garden City, on Long Island.

"She wants you to stay with her until there is a room available in my rooming house," he said.

That very first night on my first date in New York, Mel said to me: "New York is slow poison. I love it." I will always remember what he said and I have also come to feel that way over the years. Regardless, I have never left Manhattan and probably never will, despite of all the hassles, stress and dirt related to living in such a large city. It has just become my home.

I have written in an earlier chapter about my eccentric cousin Hedy—how she managed to get out of Vienna even before we were able to leave; how she had worked as a maid in England, hating the experience so much that she had smuggled herself back into Nazi occupied Vienna where, miraculously, she had also managed to avoid arrest; had married a doctor with whom she emigrated to America.

The marriage was a marriage of convenience and she did not love her husband. They went to live in Florida, where he was employed as a physician once he had received his American license. "It was a boring life," she told me. "We had no children and there was not much for me to do other than to prepare his evening meals. I felt isolated without friends and family. Every day I went alone to the beach and sat down in a café for a cup of coffee. One day, I met a man called Eric in one of these beach cafés. It was love at first sight, since by pure chance, he turned out to be also Viennese. Imagine the coincidence," she said.

After a secret rendezvous, they arranged to run off together to New York, where Eric and his brother, Otto, owned a very successful business, a leather factory, where they manufactured expensive wallets and other fine leather goods. Hers was a very strange story, but everything Hedy had done in the past had always been strange. Soon afterwards, she got a divorce from her first husband and married Eric.

Hedy and Eric bought a house in Garden City and that is where I went to stay after leaving my uncle's apartment in New York.

After not having seen each other for many years, Hedy and I fell into each others' arms; we had always felt close. Their house, in contrast to my uncle's apartment, was beautifully furnished with thick wall-to-wall carpeting which I had never seen before. Everything was elegant and modern, but what I will never forget was her clothes closet. It was filled from wall-to-wall with dresses, skirts and blouses. Because I had arrived in America with one skirt, two blouses and two dresses, Hedy's wardrobe was awe-inspiring; so was her house with the modern kitchen with every conceivable appliance.

We could not stop talking; we had so many memories to share. Of course, we also shared our sorrow about our lost family members and could barely believe that we had both managed to escape the Nazis.

The next day, we made a *Sacher Torte*, a rich Viennese chocolate cake, in memory of our days together in Vienna. Hedy's husband, Eric, left every morning to go to work, and we had time to ourselves to just hang out and enjoy each other's company.

Soon, however, I began to miss the company of boys my own age and I also became anxious to get my life together and to find a job.

I was happy when my father called me to say: "A tiny room has become vacant in my rooming house, you'd better take it right away." I said good-bye to Hedy, thanked her for her hospitality and promised that I would visit on weekends; I often did visit her whenever I felt the need to get out of the city and relax. I would meet her husband Eric after work and we would drive out together.

On my second day in New York, I had telephoned Janet's mother who, after divorcing Janet's father, had remarried a wealthy stockbroker by the name of

Ernie and had moved to New York. I think he was the same man with whom she had had an affair in Vienna, while she was still married. Ernie was a partner in a Wall Street brokerage firm and when he heard that I badly needed a job, he hinted that there might be a job opening in his office some time in the near future. "Call me when you are settled and I will arrange for you to come in for an interview," he told me. "I think I could get you some sort of clerical job filing, and your beautiful English accent would be an asset on the switchboard."

Now that I had finally moved into my tiny room in New York, I called Ernie and he set up an interview. I was very nervous when I got off the subway downtown and entered 30 Broad Street for my first interview in America. Thanks to Ernie, I was immediately hired for $25 per week. My rent was $8.00 a week. I felt so rich that I bought my father a five dollar silk tie with my first paycheck, because I felt sorry for him. I really shouldn't have done it because, as always, he already had a number of girlfriends who often cooked for him, and generally took care of him.

Once having moved into the rooming house, my father showed me his large room overlooking the Hudson River. When I walked in, I saw bundles of newspapers stacked three feet high. "What are these?" I asked him.

"Those," he answered, "are the Sunday New York Times which I try to read every week and never succeed finishing. Before I know it, it's Sunday again and so on and so on."

"But wouldn't it be time to start throwing out the old ones?"

"Yes," he said, "I must do it."

As far as I remember, he never did it.

My tiny room was on the ground floor. There was a Puerto Rican family living in one room on the other side of the kitchen which separated our two rooms. I had to walk through the kitchen to get to my room which had only a bed and a chest of drawers in it. It was horribly depressing and dark. On top of it, the Puerto Rican family made a lot of noise; there seemed to be so many of them, but they felt sorry for me and were really nice and kind people. When I returned from my first job, they were cooking in the kitchen and often invited me to share their modest meals. They owned an old jalopy and frequently after dinner, they took me along for a ride along the Hudson River. I experienced these trips as most exciting. I remember being driven along the west side highway at night with the lights of the city behind us; we would pass the George Washington Bridge all lit up, and I felt as though I was in a movie. We would then always stop somewhere on the road for a coca-cola. They were magical moments and when I had to return to my miserable room, it was a terrible let-down. I would console myself by writing in my diary about my new life.

After living in my tiny dark room for a short time, I was lucky to get a room with more light on my father's, the eighth floor. It badly needed a paint job and

I told the landlord that I would pay for it, but afterwards I found out that since the room had not been painted in many years, he would be responsible anyhow. To decorate my new clean room, I bought a Van Gogh's reproduction of a *Portrait of a Young Man*, and had it framed. At last I had my own clean room where I could almost see the Hudson River. I was able to use the communal kitchen and, if I made dinner, my father and I often ate together.

A few days after I finally settled into my new room, there was a letter waiting for me. It was from my old American boyfriend Badger, and it read:

"I'll always love you, you are the dearest person in the world to me. I will never be able to feel as close to anyone else as I feel towards you, but our priest told me that it is my duty, as a Catholic, to stay with my wife of over twenty years and with my two small boys. I cannot get myself to ask her for a divorce, but you mean more to me than anybody in this world. Of course, you can imagine how I felt when I walked out of the church. In a way, I knew that the priest was right; on the other hand, I could not, in my wildest dreams, imagine never seeing you again. I spent several sleepless nights thinking about this, darling, and I can imagine how you must feel getting this 'dear John' letter, but I decided to take a chance and ask you whether, despite that I am not getting a divorce, you would still be willing to see me. I just cannot imagine what life would be like without you. If you are willing, and I know it's asking a lot, I would try very hard to come to New York, but it will be difficult. Can you possibly come to Indiana? I would do everything for us to spend as much time together as possible."

When I finished reading the letter, I started to cry and couldn't stop. In fact, I cried myself to sleep on many nights after that. It was a terrible blow for me, especially since this was happening at a time when I was most vulnerable—when I was in a brand new country, where everything was strange—where people had no idea what it felt like to live through six years of war with the constant fear of being bombed, and where we could only live from one day to the next.

I felt that I had nothing in common with the people I met, that no one understood how I felt. Even my own father couldn't understand why I did not want to go to a Japanese restaurant with him. In England, the boys in the Army who returned from Japan told us: "In battle, we would rather face Germans because they, at least, fought face to face when they attacked us, whereas the Japanese were hiding in the trees and killing us from the back." I never forgot hearing this, and couldn't help having this feeling of animosity towards the Japanese. Thus, the timing of Badger's letter, particularly in the state I was in, was devastating. I was still young, however, and resilient, and realized that life would go on.

My job on Wall Street, although very dull, made it possible to make new friends. I made friends with an Italian girl by the name of Gallo who was about eight years older than I was. On my very first day at the office, she befriended and mothered me, knowing that I was not familiar with New York City. She invited me to have lunch with her at the coffee shop in our building. When the waitress came over to take my order, she asked me: "Do you want your egg salad sandwich on rye, whole wheat or white?" I was utterly stunned that there were so many choices and wanted to try all three that first day. I said to Gallo: "Imagine having the choice of three kinds of bread when we had hardly any bread at all in England, and when we did, it tasted like sawdust."

Every day I ate the same lunch: egg salad on rye toast, fruit cup and coffee. The bill came to 50¢. With the subway costing a nickel, I could well afford to eat lunch out and still live within my budget. Sometimes, for a change, we would go to *Chock Full o'Nuts* for a frankfurter and a lemon meringue pie; a great treat after being deprived for so long of food that I longed for.

Every day from 12 noon to 1 p.m., I was asked to relieve the girl on the switchboard. With my very British accent, I would answer the phone with: "Hullo, are you *theere*?" The stockbrokers would imitate my accent and laugh. "Is this 'are you *theere*?'" they would say.

Three months later, we had a three-day holiday: Memorial Day. We had the long week-end off and Gallo and I decided to take two extra days so that we could take a trip. I had heard so much about Cape Cod and it was my dream to be by the ocean, where I had not been since the age of three when my mother took me to Italy. During the war, although we lived in Bournemouth by the sea, the beach was surrounded by barbed wire and we could only look at the water. We were able to find a hotel outside Hyannis which was right on the beach and were lucky to have five perfect days of good weather.

I knew that a young man who had been a Major in the Air Force in England, now lived in Boston. I had written him, and he was so thrilled to hear from me, that he drove down to visit us for a couple of days. Since Gallo and I did not have a car, we were delighted when he offered to show us around. We visited quaint villages and they reminded me somewhat of England. I found this part of the country very special and promised myself to return to the Cape at the first opportunity which I managed to do later on. When Bob and I were alone together, we compared notes about our feelings of what it felt like to be back in the States. He also felt strange coming home after the war, and understood all too well, how I was feeling about being in a strange country after all those war years. I was relieved to have someone to talk to.

Back in New York, with the weather getting warmer, Gallo and I spent our lunch hours in Battery Park by the Hudson River. I became curious about the Staten Island ferry and wanted to find out what was on the other side. "Let's go for a ride on our lunch hour," I suggested one day to Gallo and another girl working in our office.

"Great idea," they said, "But are you sure it takes only one hour back and forth?"

"I have enquired at the Ferry station, and I was told that it is possible," I said.

Since we were all going to be away for one hour, one of the brokers agreed to cover the office. As it turned out, it was a lovely ride, but we noticed to our dismay that it had taken almost one hour to get to the other end and with the waiting time, we were very late. Two hours later, we ran all the way from the ferry back to the office, where there was a terrible to-do. Somehow, the office manager had guessed that I must have been the instigator. I am always the one who gets caught, always was and still am. The next day I got fired. It was another terrible blow for me. My father consoled me and said: "Sometimes, it's meant to be and you will get a better job." As it turned out, he happened to have been right.

On the corner of 95th Street and West End Avenue, there were four beautiful clay tennis courts. I loved the game, and enquired as to what it would cost to play for one hour, and was told that it was very expensive. I knew I couldn't possibly afford it, especially because I was now unemployed. However, I was told there are sixteen public city courts a few blocks away in Central Park where, for $2.50, you can get a season permit. Since I had played a lot of tennis in boarding school, I immediately went to get my permit. For a nominal fee, one could also get a locker and shower; the place seemed ideal for week-ends now that it was spring time. I soon got to know the two tennis pros, Maurice and Conrad, who fixed me up with tennis partners who played as well as I did. Conrad was particularly handsome, but I was told to be aware of him because he was a womanizer.

The most important thing at the time, however, was getting a new job—namely in advertising. I had been intrigued by advertisements in the subway, and I had made up my mind that I would love to work in some capacity in an ad agency. I had already approached several agencies, but at every interview, they asked me: "Do you have advertising experience?"

"How could I have experience if no one ever gives me a chance to work in one?" I asked them.

When I confessed to Maurice that I had recently been fired and was looking for a job in advertising, he told me: "It's a coincidence that you are asking me, because I have a pupil by the name of Bernice who works in an advertising agency and she told me the other day, that there is a vacancy." The next time I saw Maurice, he told me: "I spoke to Bernice, and she confirmed that there is an opening. Go for an interview."

The name of the office manager was Viola Rabkin; the address was 630 Fifth Avenue, facing St. Patrick's Cathedral and the elegant department store, Best & Co. The office was in a section of Rockefeller Center in one of the most luxurious parts of New York City. The offices were glamorous with thick carpeting. On the walls there were ads from prestigious accounts, such as Benrus watches and Coty cosmetics, amidst others. After announcing me, the receptionist ushered me into Viola's office; she seemed to take an immediate liking to me because of my British accent. After a while, she told me: "The only job open at the moment is for a statistical typist." I decided to accept, since it gave me a foot in the door in a major AAA agency. It was a very boring job, but it paid $30 a week, $5 more than my last job.

Just before going for my interview, I saw that the Berlitz School of Languages had offices one floor below. I went to enquire whether I could teach German. They told me that I could have a job if it was in my native language, and they would pay me $25 per week. Viola's offer of $30 was definitely the better deal.

My new job, even though it was menial work, nevertheless suited me for the time being, because I was getting the experience I needed to work in advertising and, at the same time, I was surrounded by creative people—something that always had and would be important to me in the future. I was sure of that.

Chapter IX

Aunt Minka

After I moved into my little room on 95th Street, I went to visit my Aunt Minka, my mother's younger sister, who had escaped from Germany to Paris with her husband, Peter, just before World War II. She lived in a one-bedroom apartment in a fourth floor walk-up on 104th Street and Riverside Drive. I had called her when I arrived in New York, and we arranged that I should come for dinner as soon as I would move to the neighborhood. Her apartment was very minimally furnished; beside her friend Carl's painting which she had brought over from Paris, where she had lived for a while, the outstanding piece of furniture was a loom on which she wove samples for a well-known fabric house, Strook & Co., where she worked as a designer. However, the great thing about her modest apartment was that she had a terrace with an unobstructed view of the Hudson. She had planted morning glories which climbed over wooden trellises; this not only gave her privacy, but also made the terrace look very attractive.

When I arrived at her apartment, she was happy to see me, but she seemed very depressed and even smaller than I remembered her in Paris; barely five feet tall. Her once red hair looked poorly dyed, and her face was wrinkled. She had aged a lot in the six years since I last saw her. I soon found out that the reason for her feeling so depressed was that her husband, Peter, had left her for another woman. He was quite a bit younger than she was, and had always been a womanizer. It did not surprise me at all because I remembered that when I was a young girl in Paris, I already felt that he was coming on to me. He would take me to a movie and hold my hand.

"Peter is now working as a medical photographer at Columbia Presbyterian Hospital," she told me. "And that's why we moved to 104th Street, so that he would be able to walk to work."

To make matters worse, she was not a pleasant woman. She always said exactly what she thought. She believed in being "truthful." She had no tact whatsoever. I remember one incident when her sister-in-law, my uncle's wife, came to visit her and wore a tasteless dress. "That's a horrible dress you are wearing," she said. Afterwards I told her: "I agree with you that the dress was tasteless, but couldn't you just have said nothing?" She shrugged it off, but as a result of her bluntness, she certainly did not endear herself to anyone. She only had very few friends who seemed to understand her.

I can't say that I was fond of her, but since she was my mother's sister, I felt it a duty to visit her once a week. She always made the same dinner for me: chicken livers, onions, mushrooms and rice, which was quite a good meal. I was happy that someone cooked a home-cooked meal for me. She had little sympathy for my problems. When I complained to her: "I have no money to buy clothes with my small salary," she would say: "You are so lucky you are young, everything looks good on you, no matter what you wear." She was incredibly frugal, never gave me any gifts, and spent no money on herself, either. She once told me: "I wanted to buy myself an ice cream cone, but it was too expensive." She spared no money, however, in sending food packages to her younger sister in Paris, who was the only member of the family she dearly loved.

One year, I was able to talk her into letting me have her terrace for my birthday, so that I could make a little party for my newly acquired friends from the tennis courts and from the neighborhood, including my friend, Alan. I provided all the food and drinks and I was very happy to have my first real party in such beautiful surroundings. All my friends loved the terrace with its blue flowers—blue was Minka's favorite color. We had a good time and it was exciting to watch the sun set over the Hudson River.

At age seventy, Aunt Minka suddenly started to paint. The amazing thing was her skill without having had any prior training. She received an award from the prestigious New York Academy of Design on 94th Street for one of her paintings which was selected for the exhibition. I think this event was one of her happiest moments. It certainly was quite an honor for a self-taught woman, and coming so late in her life; it makes one reflect what hidden talents may show up at a very late age of a person's life. I was very pleased to see her so happy at the opening, and was so glad for her and proud of her achievement, even though she paid no attention to me whatsoever. However, later on she let me choose a few of her best paintings as gifts which are still hanging in my apartment.

Years later, her husband became ill and she took him back. Shortly afterwards, he had a heart attack and died. She was totally destroyed after his death and, to make matters worse, she also developed Alzheimer's disease. This eventually led to her own death. I did not feel grief after she died. I felt that being my mother's sister and the only one living in New York, she could have been a little more generous with me when I first came to America with no money. Even my uncle's wife, Amy, who I had never met before, bought me a dress when she saw that I had absolutely nothing to wear, since clothes in England were also rationed.

At the end, when she was so ill, and during my frequent visits after work, she no longer knew that I was there. I had already long ago hired a companion to look after her and finally gave up visiting altogether.

It was ironic that although to all appearances, she was so hard up, and lived so frugally, that she managed to leave her sister in Paris close to a half a million dollars. I was pleased that she had recognized the fact that I came to visit her once a week and generally supervised her affairs when she was still well, and realized that it was a great burden for me to travel two hours on the A train, that she also left me a small amount of money in her will.

She was a strange woman. I regret that she did not allow me to know and understand her more fully.

Chapter X

95th Street and Environments

The boys in the neighborhood used to say that unless you lived between 86th and 96th Street near Riverside Drive, you were G.U. (geographically undesirable). Luckily I just fitted into this category.

I think that we all initially met in Central Park at the tennis courts. There I met Alan, who became my best male friend. He was a few years older than I was, and he was an intellectual and much more worldly than I was. We became very close, even though he was not my physical type; therefore it was easy to stay friends. We told everyone that he was my older brother, and people believed us. Since I never had a brother, even though I had longed for one, it made me feel very protected. Alan would give me advice, such as: "If you really like a boy and you don't want to sleep with him, but you do want to see him again, let him take you to your door when he walks you home, kiss him passionately on the lips, and then run quickly into your house. I promise you will hear from him again."

I don't remember whether I ever followed his advice, but I thought that what he said was funny and caring. I had never before teased a boy consciously, so this was a new experience for me.

Walking down Broadway to the Tip Top Inn, the "in" place in the neighborhood, I would listen to the young girls talking about the boys in terms of the size and make of their cars. "You know the one with the red convertible" was a typical statement. Overhearing them, I was quite shocked at their values. It was the *Marjorie Morningstar* era; Marjorie is the heroine of a book by Herman Wouk. For me, she represented the original JAP (Jewish American Princess) whose father adored her "little girl," even when she grew up, and on whom the sun rose and set. (Very different from my own father.) She was born of rich parents who lived on Central Park West. Her values consisted of going to the beauty parlor at least once a week to have her hair and nails done, so as to attract a wealthy husband. Money counted, and I was just a poor immigrant without a family background in this country. I knew that I was attractive, but it was not enough to give me self-confidence.

I always felt and still do that in spite of my bad luck in early life, I also have had good luck. I managed to survive the war. I was also lucky to live in a nurturing neighborhood in New York. Between 95th and 96th Street on Broadway, life was fun and inexpensive. In addition to our Chinese restaurant where we could eat for 99¢, there was also a drug store on the corner of 96th Street, where the Express 7th Avenue subway stopped; everyone had to pass by on the way home from work. The store belonged to my friend Michael's father, who was a very kind, generous man. He often dispensed medication for very little or nothing, depending on people's means. With his son, Michael, an attractive "drugstore cowboy," I had a chance to meet other young people since he knew everyone in the neighborhood. Two doors down was Bickford's Cafeteria which became a sort of living room for those of us who lived in rooming houses. Old and young hung out there since you could buy a cup of coffee for 5¢, perhaps write some letters or a book. But the real hang-out for us young people was the ice cream parlor across the street where, if you were lucky, one of your dates would take you after the movies on Saturday night and buy you a banana split. A great treat. Weighing 110 lbs., I didn't then have to worry about my weight.

When the winter came, I decided to skimp on my food and save every penny in order to go skiing. I lived for these week-ends. Meanwhile I had become friendly with Bernice, who had recommended me for a job at the ad agency and, luckily, it turned out that she, too, was an ardent skier. We prayed for snow so that on Fridays, weather permitting, we took our skis to the office and left on a 6 p.m. bus for Vermont or wherever there were good skiing conditions. We skied all day, hardly taking time out for lunch, so that in the evenings we would collapse from fatigue in front of the fireplace in our small hotels. After a delightfully refreshing shower and dinner, we socialized with the other skiers and had a good time. In those early days, there were not many women skiers; we met a lot of young men since we were often the only women on the slopes. I got acquainted with two brothers, Micki and Arthur, who lived in Brooklyn and who seemed to be comfortably off; they owned a 40-foot sailboat which they kept in a club in Sheepshead Bay in Brooklyn. When the summer came and the skiing season was over, they took me sailing on their boat and we often ended up at famous Lundy's Restaurant for a marvelous seafood dinner. People came from far away to eat there; it was an institution.

After a while, however, I got so involved with tennis that I decided to spend my summer vacation in New York, to watch the yearly U.S. Open tennis matches in Forest Hills. In those days, I always seemed to have crushes on men. I think it was for lack of having true love which I missed after having had a great love affair in England. That year, Tony Trabert, the then famous tennis player, was my idol. When he won the championship, I was overjoyed.

My life settled into a routine. It consisted of work, playing tennis in the summer; skiing in the winter. Nothing much changed. Only the rooming house where I lived was full of drama. On my floor lived a poor little Jewish lady by the name of Rosie. She lit candles on Friday nights. She worked as a seamstress in the garment center and after work, she cooked her meager meal in our community kitchen. Often, when I was home, she would offer me food which she had cooked. I knew that she could barely make ends meet and always refused politely, since she had even less money than I had. Another person who shared our community kitchen was a fellow from Malta who was always dressed in his undershorts, but every other Saturday morning, he would get dressed nicely because a rather elegant lady came over for breakfast and sex. We each had a shelf in the kitchen, where we kept our staples and cans of food. I remember an incident where I bought lemon oil to polish my furniture. My father, who shared my shelf, thought that this was a new product for a salad dressing and, since he loved lemons, he put it on his lettuce. I laughed myself silly when he told me this and I was hoping that he would not get sick. Fortunately, he must have been O.K., or I would have surely remembered it.

In the next door apartment lived a physician who was no longer practicing medicine. He became very fond of me, and whenever I was free, he would cook dinner for me. At the time I remember my father telling me: "I think So and So lost his license because he used to perform abortions in the past." This, of course, was illegal at the time. Because I did not see much of my father, who was always surrounded by lady friends, the kindness of this much older man was very touching and comforting to me. In some sense, he became my father substitute.

I always remember that on my birthday, he insisted that I take a taxi to work through Central Park at his expense. This was such a treat that I felt like "queen for a day."

In contrast to my life, it seemed to me tragic that all these much older people lived such cramped and disillusioned lives; they were not refugees and had not been displaced by the war like my father and I had. They were stuck in their miserable existence. I felt that my life had just begun in this New World.

A few days after my birthday, I knocked on the doctor's door to thank him for his present, but there was no answer. This went on for a day or two, and then he would emerge from his room, being this nice caring person again. These incidents had occurred in the past. Thinking back, I am sure that he was taking drugs during these periods. Some time later, after I had been able to move out of the rooming house, my father, who had remained there, told me: "I am sorry to tell you that your benefactor unfortunately committed suicide." I was very upset and saddened at the news and wondered whether I could have been of some help during his depressions which eventually led to his death, but that was unrealistic on my part, I realize now.

On the brighter side, my social life kept expanding greatly, thanks to meeting people while skiing all over the east coast. One time, Bernice and I had to travel as far as the Laurentians in Canada to find snow. Mount Tremblant was still very primitive and we had to take a sleigh in order to reach our hotel. Furthermore, it was so bitterly cold that we had to wear a fur coat (mine was a cheap mutton) going up in the chairlift which we then sent down. One day, the temperature dropped to way below freezing and loudspeakers warned us to get off the slopes. Unfortunately, it was too late and my face had already gotten frost bitten. I was all red when I entered the ski hut. With time, this has luckily subsided.

Back in New York, after my ski week-ends, I had many dates with various young men who I had met in the neighborhood, none of them serious. I particularly remember Eddy who wanted very badly to make love with me. He always picked me up with his car. We would go for a drive along the Hudson. Afterwards, he parked on Riverside Drive and 93rd Street. Across the river in New Jersey, there was a big neon sign which blinked on and off. It read: "SPRY FOR BAKING" and then "FRY FOR FRYING." This was what young people did in those days because everyone seemed to have a car. One evening, while Eddy and I were necking in the back of the car, we noticed a flashlight shining in. Two policemen who were voyeurs were trying to catch us having sex. I could see that they were disappointed since we were just kissing and fully dressed. "Move on," they said, not able to give us a ticket. It was a well-known fact that this was going on in the neighborhood. After one of those dates with Eddy, a friend at the tennis courts asked me: "What did you and Eddy do last night?"

My answer was: "We went to the 'Spry Club'," and everyone laughed.

My flirtation with Eddy, however, ended abruptly one day when I was sitting on his lap, steering his car. Eddy was supposed to have his foot on the brake, but neglected to do so. We crashed into the car in front of us and we had a bad accident. My hand went through the windshield and I was bleeding. The ambulance was called and they took me to the hospital where I received seven stitches in my right hand. This event put a damper on our relationship and thus ended abruptly.

After all is said and done, I had finally adjusted to my life in New York after those long war years in England. I adored the city and, at every possible moment, I went exploring. "New York is made up of so many nationalities and each part is like another small town," I wrote to Janet in England who couldn't wait to get my news. I went shopping in China Town, ate in Little Italy or in Yorkville, if I longed for German food. I went window shopping on Fifth Avenue and, of course, visited the wonderful museums and art galleries. I practically lived in the Museum of Modern Art, where I had become a member for a very nominal fee. I loved sitting in the sculpture garden and in the penthouse high up from where you could see the entire city. I had begun to accept the city and my life in it. But I always remembered my very first evening in New York when Mel said to me: "New York is slow poison." Now I could not imagine living anywhere else."

Chapter XI

My Social Life in New York/Central Park

Socially things began to look up for me thanks to joining the Central Park tennis courts. On week-ends there was always a long wait to play since we were only allowed to sign up for one hour a day. Sometimes we had to wait for as long as four hours to get a free court. Next to the arsenal building which housed our lockers, there was a big lawn facing the tennis courts. It was on that lawn that we spread our blankets, ate our sandwiches, and spent time socializing until the whistle blew for our assigned hour. Most of the young people slept late on week-ends and hardly ever arrived at the tennis courts much before noon. By the time we finished playing, it was usually quite late and time to leave the park. The long waiting hours were a lot of fun, because it allowed me to get to know a lot of young people my age with whom I could bond and who became a sort of extended family and a support system. The price of tennis permits had, of course, always increased each year. I remember a girl I knew saying: "I married my husband on a $2.50 permit."

"Boy, were you lucky," another girl answered. "It cost me four dollars."

Our waiting hours were also spent reading the Sunday New York Times which was a new experience for me.

On Saturdays, after tennis, some of us arranged to meet at the local Chinese restaurant, called "Gung-Ho" on the corner of Broadway and 95th Street. There, as I mentioned before, for 99¢ we got a complete three-course dinner. It was not exactly "gourmet," but we did not care: it was the price and the company that mattered. Our group was very much "into music," and we often hung out in a shop called "Thalia" on 95th Street, which had a good record collection and where we listened to music. On some Saturdays, Peggy Guggenheim, a patron of the arts, sponsored outdoor concerts at Lewison Stadium. We went there as a group and sat on hard benches outdoors, listening to classical music. Often, Paul Robeson sang there. The setting was magical and we could see the stars when the sky was clear. At the end of the concert, Peggy always came out on the stage and made a funny speech. We all enjoyed her and we were very grateful to her for making these free concerts possible.

During the week, after coming home from work and eating my solitary dinner, I often felt restless. I discovered a table tennis parlor on 96th Street and Broadway. Fortunately, I loved playing ping-pong. Because I played quite well, it was easy for me to get a partner. One day, Dick Miles, the National Table Tennis champion, came in and we happened to speak with each other. While Dick was very unattractive, with a huge nose and a very skinny body, he made up for his looks with his tremendous charm and charisma. I admired him greatly and liked him, and he seemed to like me as well. He invited me to watch him play an exhibition match at a larger Ping-Pong parlor on 54th Street and Broadway, where the better players practiced. I met a lot of Dick's friends and soon I began to spend time with him alone. We became great pals.

On one summer evening, to celebrate either his or my birthday, we decided to buy a bottle of champagne to take with us on the 112th Street ferry, which has long since ceased to exist. We had a great time drinking champagne out of the bottle we bought and were going back and forth on the ferry for a nickel. After the sixth trip, the ferryman discovered that we were still there and we were asked to get off. It was an evening to remember, and I was glad to have Dick's friendship.

Through Dick, I met Douglas, who was much older than Dick, but who was also a ping-pong tournament player. The two were invited to perform in various cities in the U.S., as far west as Chicago. Douglas, who had a car, asked me: "Do you want to come along?" I thought about it seriously and finally decided to take this opportunity to go and see my former boyfriend Badger in Indiana to find out what my feelings were towards him now that I knew that we would never marry.

I had called him on the phone, and he was thrilled to hear that we might see each other again. He immediately made all the arrangements to meet in South Bend on the designated day.

Douglas, Dick, and I took off, but no sooner had we left New York and crossed over into New Jersey, we were stopped by Highway Police for speeding. It was a Sunday and we had not noticed that there was a speed trap. At the nearest police station they treated us like criminals. The boys had to pay a hefty fine so as not to be thrown in jail. After that, we drove for miles and miles on dull highways, where one could not see any landscape, stopping only for gas, the bathroom, and an occasional hamburger. The trip seemed endless and lasted for three days. I was totally exhausted, and I was getting more and more apprehensive about seeing Badger again. Dick and Douglas were to compete in an exhibition table tennis tournament in Indianapolis, where we finally had a good night's sleep in a hotel. At last, they dropped me off in South Bend at the hotel where Badger had reserved a room for me with the understanding that I would meet the boys the next day for our trip back somewhere halfway between there and Chicago. It was an eerie feeling to be left alone in this strange hotel room with my thoughts and apprehensions. I was excited on the one hand, but on the other hand, worried and confused. What would we talk about? How would he look, now that he was a civilian in his own home town? How would we feel about seeing each other again? It had been more than a year. When would he arrive? Why wasn't he here? Was he really going to show up? What if he doesn't? If he does, and it was silly for me to think that he wouldn't, how are we going to be with each other? Suddenly the phone interrupted my thoughts. "There is a gentleman to see you." And there was a knock on the door and there he stood. We threw our arms around each other. The familiarity was wonderful, but the knowledge that we would never spend our lives together, and even the fact that these hours were stolen from his real life, had changed everything.

"Darling," he said, "I feel terrible, but I cannot stay with you the whole night, as much as I dreamt about this moment with you. I can't even have breakfast with you, but I'll see you for lunch." I was devastated, and the whole thing made me feel very sordid.

Imagine, having travelled 2,000 miles for three days and having so little time with each other! We did meet for lunch the next day, and he swore again how much he loved me, but for me things just could never be the same. He was no longer the stunning Captain in uniform, stationed in England, but a married man living in Indiana who was never going to get a divorce. We said good-bye with the promise that he would come to New York at the earliest possible occasion. My gut feeling told me, however, that I would never see him again.

It had, nevertheless, been a good thing that I had gone to see him once more, because it sort of closed a very important chapter in my life—my first lover—and it left me emotionally free to get on with my future.

Back at my office in New York, Len Tarcher, Vice President of the ad agency, seeing me struggling with typing columns of figures, said to me: "Why don't you learn shorthand so that you can become my secretary and I would raise your salary."

I became so excited at the idea that I immediately followed his advice. I enrolled in a speed-writing course in a school on 42nd Street, four days a week from 6-9 p.m. On the way there, I had only one hour and stopped at Chock Full O'Nuts for dinner. I could only afford to spend 50¢ for food because I had to pay for my tuition which I remember to be more than $100—a fortune for me at the time. After school at 9 p.m., totally exhausted, I would take the subway home. It all paid off in the end. My boss raised my salary immediately to $35 a week, even though I was only just learning to take a letter in shorthand. I am sure he realized my financial situation and that's why he did it. I was so touched by his kindness that I had a brief crush on him, although he was not at all my physical type. To get over my fantasy, I also told myself that he smoked horrible cigars which I could not stand. Furthermore, he was dating a girl in the agency who was much more glamorous than I was, and he was not interested in me. I didn't feel rejected, but it was a lesson in life: "Don't get involved with people at work." I more or less stuck to it all through my working years.

It was now time to further extend my social life. I joined the U.S.O. Club, where servicemen from all over the United States, some of them not yet discharged after the war, and others in the regular army, could go to meet young ladies.

It was not easy to become a member; we were carefully checked out before we were accepted as hostesses for their weekly dances. At the Club, I met a young man who invited me to his wedding reception: "Look for a strawberry blonde by the name of Mary Diepeveen who is of Dutch origin," he said. "I have a feeling that you two will have a lot in common."

This turned out to be true. To this day, she is still my best friend. I sometimes wonder how strange it is that by sheer accident, a seemingly insignificant event determines who becomes a life-long friend.

It was a beautiful sunny summer day when we were sitting in the garden of the Forest Hills Inn during the wedding reception. Mary and I arranged to meet again. A few days later, the phone rang: "Will it be all right if I come to New York and stay with you over the week-end?" she asked. I was delighted.

Back in my room, she told me: "I am living with my parents in New Jersey, and I am unhappy since they favor my two brothers and my youngest sister." In a way, she felt like a stepchild and I could relate to her so well, partially because we were both of European extraction, and also because I too felt neglected and unloved by my father. Because we got along well that week-end, we decided to spend a future week-end together on Fire Island. Eventually, the two of us moved into a studio together on 53rd Street, but I will discuss these events in a later chapter.

Chapter XII

Marriage and 53rd Street

It's funny how things happen in life: I was standing on top of the stairs at the tennis courts on a sunny Sunday afternoon watching other people playing tennis and, at the same time, eating a hard boiled egg, when a young man came over and asked me: "What is your name?"

What an unoriginal come-on, I thought. "Why?" I answered. "What's yours?"

"Leonard," he said, "and I hate it when people call me 'Lenny.'"

"I wouldn't call you that, because I don't like it either when people shorten my name," I answered, "so I sympathize."

We proceeded to talk, and he seemed quite attractive, but living in Brooklyn, East New York, a place I had never even heard of, made him G.U. (geographically unfit) for me.

"But," he said, "I am always in Manhattan because I am presently taking my M.A. in psychology at Columbia."

Just then my tennis partner interrupted us: "Our court is ready, let's play."

"What are you doing next Saturday?" Leonard asked. "I would like to see you again."

"Sorry," I said, "I am busy."

It was true because I had found out that in New York, unless you make your dates way in advance, everyone is busy and you are left alone without plans. This was very different from my days during the war when we lived from one day to the next.

"How about Friday night?" Leonard asked.

"No," I answered, "but if you really want to see me, tonight is the night. I am not trying to put you off."

"Well, it's not easy, since it's already late and I have to take the subway home which would take an hour, and another hour to come back to Manhattan, but I will do it and pick you up at 8:30 p.m.," he said.

Promptly at 8:30 p.m., I went downstairs to meet Leonard and, to my surprise, despite having had to take the subway to Brooklyn and back, he was already there waiting. "A good sign," I told myself. "He must be anxious and really interested."

"How would you like to go to a French restaurant where we could share a bottle of wine and talk?" he asked.

I was impressed and said, "I'd love it."

He knew of this restaurant on Lexington Avenue called *Henry IV*. It was intimate with candles on every table on red and white checkered tablecloths; very French. We had a heart-to-heart talk. He was bright, funny, and I enjoyed myself.

"May I call you next week?" he asked while we were saying good-bye at my doorstep. I agreed to the invitation; I really wanted to see him again. There were many more evenings to come.

On our second date he told me: "I must confess to you that I only earn $5 a week giving a single piano lesson, but I am willing to blow it all when we meet again." (This may sound ridiculous today, but in 1951, we managed to have dinner in a fairly nice, but modest restaurant.) I was always very creative and still am, when it comes to finding reasonable places. Furthermore, my advertising agency gave me free tickets for the "Show of Shows," the hottest TV show which was televised every Saturday night with a live studio audience. It starred Sid Caesar, Imogene Coca and Carl Reiner. The best writers, such as Woody Allen and Mel Brooks, contributed the funniest creative material to make the show a great success on NBC. It was an inexpensive way to spend Saturday night, and I thought at that time that this made Leonard more anxious to see me again. He did brag to his friends about his girlfriend's connections regarding the tickets. I might add that the early part of this courtship occurred while I was still living in the rooming house and that this fact greatly contributed to my social insecurity. Shortly thereafter, we started to go "steady."

Meanwhile, I was also seeing a lot of Mary and, as always, we had a great time together. I suggested to her that we spend a week-end together on Fire Island. I had heard so much about this island situated off the coast of Long Island which one could only reach by boat and where there were no cars. This intrigued me apart from the fact that I loved the sea. My childhood in Austria had only familiarized me with mountains and lakes; beautiful as they are, there was no seaside and it made me long for that experience. I vaguely remembered my mother taking me to Italy one summer and I could see from photographs that there were white beaches on the Adriatic, but I was very, very young then. Apart from my first vacation in America on Cape Cod, I had not been back to a real seaside resort. Mary readily agreed and on the next warm week-end, we took the train to Bayshore and a taxi to the boat which took us to the community of Ocean

Beach. The boat ride alone was already very relaxing and on reaching the island, we noticed that everyone got off in a hurry scrambling for a room. We ended up in Jerry's Rooming House where the landlady said: "In the only room I have left, you'll have to share a bed." For lack of anything better, we decided to take it. Soon, we changed into our bathing suits and spent a great day sunbathing and swimming in the Atlantic which happened to be calm that day. At the end of the day, after a shower, we changed and went to McGuire's restaurant, which overlooked the bay, for a lobster dinner. The evening ended with a drink at Goldie's, which seemed to be the local "hang-out." The restaurant also served dinner, but afterwards the tables were moved to give room for dancing. As tired as we were from all that fresh air, we ended up dancing long into the night to all the wonderful Frank Sinatra songs and loving every minute of it.

When we came back to town, Mary decided it was time to move out from her parents' house in New Jersey and, I too, wanted to get out of my rather miserable small room in the rooming house. We began looking for an apartment which we could share. Although we both had very little money, we figured out that we could split the expense of a studio apartment, and we proceeded to contact a real estate agent. Since we were both working on the east side in the 50's, we concentrated on finding an apartment which we could afford in that area. We were elated when Mr. Grasso, the agent, called to say that there was a brand new studio available on 53rd Street between 2nd and 3rd Avenues. It was a fourth floor walk-up, but being young this was not a problem for us. We went to see it and loved it; the place was so new that in fact the gas was not yet connected; we had to eat out the first couple of weeks. Nevertheless, we signed our lease and began to think about furnishing our beautiful new home. With small funds, once again, we had to be creative. I knew the husband of one of the couples I had met at the tennis courts who was in the furniture business. He offered us wholesale prices and we ordered two chests of drawers and one side table, which we were going to put between the two beds, thus creating a sitting area, making it look less like a bedroom. We found a carpenter who built us a table protruding from the wall and which acted like a Murphy bed; we only opened it when we wanted to eat.

But the big problem was getting two cheap beds. This brought about a funny coincidence. Mary and I had a friend whose name was Hubba. He liked us both and we considered him just a platonic friend, even though he was interested in "more," but he was a nice guy and just sort of hung around at the apartment. One Sunday, he told us that he would take us sailing at Sheepshead Bay where he had a friend with a boat. We took the subway and only found out when we got there, that his friend never showed up. We were standing on the dock, feeling sort of silly and embarrassed when, by chance, my ski buddy Micki and his brother Arthur suddenly appeared with their boat. Micki asked me: "Who is your friend?", meaning Mary. I introduced her to him and he seemed immediately attracted to her.

"Why don't you all come sailing with us?" he asked.

We were delighted to accept and had lunch on his beautiful 40-foot sailboat. After a short time, I saw that I was right: Micki and Mary were really hitting it off. It was funny because Mary was 5 ft. 8", and Micki was about 5 ft. 5"; they were a strange looking couple, particularly since in the past her main concern had been the height of a young man. Each time I tried to fix her up, she would ask me: "How tall is he?" not "Is he attractive?"

The two brothers took us out to Lundy's for dinner, and the next day Mary kept raving about Micki. Since we desperately needed beds and Arthur and Micki owned a bedding factory in New Jersey, they promised to send us two beds at absolutely no cost. We couldn't believe our luck. This was just meant to be and shortly afterwards, we moved into our very own wonderful apartment which allowed us to walk to work. Saving carfare was very important in those early days.

We soon found out that we had very interesting neighbors. On one side of our floor, there was a French girl by the name of Annette who we thought was absolutely gorgeous. We envied her marvelous figure, set off by designer clothes we could never dream to be able to afford. She was sophisticated and had a lot of boyfriends, one more good-looking than the next. We had adjoining bathrooms, and at night we could hear her making love through the bathroom wall. Just for fun, we asked her the next day: "Did you have a good time with so and so?" She just laughed and let it go. On the other side there was another Annette, who was American and also attractive, but not quite as chic. We became friendly with both Annettes and they would often come over for a cup of coffee or a drink. The fourth apartment on our floor was occupied by two young men, both called Kenny. They were obviously gay, but in those days they did not admit it yet. From time to time, they invited two girls over, just for "show," and we always knew when they were coming; that was the only time when the boys left their front door wide open. We lived very harmoniously with our neighbors and there was always a good feeling between all of us.

By this time, Mary was seeing Micki pretty regularly, and I was seeing Leonard. But we still had other friends over for dinner, and I still played tennis regularly in the summer, and Mary and I continued to go skiing in the winter.

Suddenly, the war broke out in Korea, and Leonard got drafted. It was Valentine's Day when I received a poem from him declaring his love for me, but he also asked me to wait for his return. We had a long, serious talk, and I told him: "I can't possibly promise to do so."

At this point, he asked me to marry him before he was going into the army. I was thrilled because there had been too many separations in the past. At last I was no longer going to be alone, or so I thought at the time.

Leonard received his orders and got shipped out two weeks later: It did not give us much time to get all the necessary papers in order to get married. We had to have a blood test and when we applied for a wedding license, we were informed that it would take at least two weeks. However, they told us that under the circumstances, we could receive a waiver if we got a lawyer who would issue such a paper. On our wedding day, March 8, 1951, we went downtown to the lawyer's office to pick up the waiver, only to find out that they had forgotten to prepare it. In my navy blue dress and with my hat which had a half veil down to my eyes, and was considered very fashionable in the 50's, I had to sit down to type this document which the lawyer signed. We then rushed over to City Hall where my father and Leonard's cousin Evelyn were waiting to be our two witnesses. Leonard had hoped we might be lucky to get a judge to marry us; instead it turned out that we had a justice of the peace with a round, ruddy face who had just finished his salami sandwich (that's what Leonard thought) and who was going to perform the marriage ceremony. He did smell heavily of garlic, I noticed. When the ceremony was over, we kissed and were pronounced "man and wife." As this was far from a fancy wedding, we took a bus to a cocktail lounge in the Gramercy Park Hotel at Evelyn's suggestion. On the way there, sitting in the bus, I suddenly felt very depressed instead of elated. I noticed that Leonard was happy and laughing, but I suddenly felt that I had lost my freedom, something I so treasured, even though I was anxious to be married and not be longer alone in this world. It had all happened so fast that I could hardly believe that I was actually married, and I had to pinch myself to convince myself that this was really so.

Unfortunately, Mary could not get time off from work to attend our wedding, but when we got back to the apartment, there was a beautifully wrapped present, and in it was a sexy pale yellow nightgown. Her best present, however, was that she had offered to spend the night in a hotel so we could have the apartment for ourselves.

We decided it was time for Leonard to call his parents with the news, and that's what he did. "Hi, Mom—your son, just to tell you that I have just gotten married."

Silence at the other end, and then: "I don't believe it, how could you do this to your mother?"

"If you don't believe it, Mom, I'll let you talk to my wife."

"Oh, you didn't marry that foreigner you told me about." (His mother was born on the boat coming over from Europe!) "So all right, put her on."

"Hi, it's really true, I love your son and we just got married at City Hall. I look forward to meeting you."

"So come for dinner Friday night, and then we will have to discuss when you will have a proper Jewish wedding ceremony. At least you are Jewish, I hope."

It really was not the reception that I had anticipated, but then I tried to put myself in her place, and I made peace with the situation. Still, I did not look forward to Friday night. On our wedding morning, Leonard got up and poured us a glass of champagne and orange juice, after which I went to work as usual. Someone had once told me that the person who gets up the day after the wedding is the one who will always make breakfast, but this turned out not to be true, as well as a lot of other vows that are made on wedding days.

Friday night with my new found in-laws was a scary experience. Leonard came to pick me up and together we went to face the ordeal. His parents lived in a semi-attached house at the end of a quiet street in East New York. The apartment was filled with poor reproductions of tasteless furniture; just the way I had imagined it. My mother-in-law had a very pretty face and must have been beautiful in her younger days. She had a bubbly personality, yet I felt right away that she was insincere. By contrast, my father-in-law was somber and not very welcoming. When we sat down for dinner, he offered us a shot of whiskey and proposed a toast: "Let's hope that what you did will turn out to be the right decision."

How lovely, I thought, that he already did not trust our judgment. As it turned out, later on, he was the one who became fond of me, whereas my mother-in-law never really liked me, and I felt the same way. She always held it against me that in her eyes we had "eloped." She arranged immediately to have the local rabbi perform the Jewish ceremony for us in her sister's house nearby.

"Another wedding!" my father exclaimed, who was not too happy about the prospect, but he did attend. There was a tremendous amount of food served afterwards at my in-law's house. Many aunts and uncles, cousins and their respective spouses attended, as well as Leonard's sister Ellen, who was only sixteen and who thought our "elopement" was "cool."

The next day, Leonard received orders to report to Fort Dix in Trenton, New Jersey for basic training and to await further notice whether he would be going to Korea or Germany. We prayed that he would not have to go to the war zone in Korea. It was a strange feeling, being married and still living in the same apartment with Mary, going to work every day as if this whole thing were not real. There were many phone calls from Leonard keeping me up to date with his daily activities, how many pounds he had to carry on his back in basic training, how many potatoes he had to peel while on canteen duty.

In his letters he wrote how much he loved me and missed me, and after a few weeks, he phoned: "I have a free day next Sunday, not enough time for me to come to New York, but if you can come to New Brunswick, we can at least see each other." In order to do this, I had to take the train the night before and stay in a hotel. It was late when I checked in and the lobby looked quite decent, but I was in for a surprise. I went straight to bed.

After a few minutes, I began to feel something biting me (a déjà vu feeling I had experienced in some of our furnished rooms in Vienna when I was a kid). My worst suspicions were borne out: there were bedbugs all over the bed. I fled out of the bed, took a long shower, got dressed and spent the night in the lobby, sitting in a chair. Of course, I was exhausted when Leonard came to get me the next morning to take me out to breakfast. But it was so good to see him, and we spent a lovely day just being together. Back in New York, a few days later, he telephoned me: "Guess what, I am going to be shipped to Germany, to Munich, with the Army of Occupation."

I danced with joy knowing that he would not be in a combat zone and that I could join him eventually. Korea might have spelled death. When I called his mother, she was not nearly as elated as I was. Her "little boy" was leaving the U.S., that's all she could think of, and I had to convince her how lucky we were that he would be out of danger.

Loving letters from Leonard arrived almost daily. I wrote back regularly and was busy making my own arrangements to leave. I had to give my boss notice and Mary had to find a new roommate.

Finally, the day came; this time I left with the French ship, the *Liberté*. I was given a farewell party on the boat and friends and family came to say good-bye and stood waving until I could no longer see them. I was a little sad, but this passed when I realized that Leonard and I would soon be united. From Le Havre I took the train to Paris. It was painful returning to France eleven years later with all my sad memories and the thought of losing my mother. My relatives in Paris were thrilled to see me. They were happy for me because just before leaving New York, I had become an American citizen and I was very proud returning to Europe as such and as a married woman. Leonard had written me that his friends in the army couldn't wait for me to arrive in Germany. They needed someone who could translate the menu for them, since they ended up eating the same dinner every night: a steak. I eventually turned them on to "Wiener Rostbraten" and some other wonderful German dishes, and they were all glad that Leonard's wife had arrived.

Munich is now and was then a specially beautiful city, only it was badly destroyed by the allies. It was sad to see that there were ruins of churches and other destroyed buildings all over this magnificent city. It was not easy for us to find a place to live, but we managed to find a room in a Pension, not far from the center of town. Leonard was stationed at the hospital and was working there as a psychologist.

He had signed on as a PFC (Private First Class) in order to serve only two years instead of three years as an officer. In retrospect, it was a big mistake, because we would have had a much better life had he been an officer; the army would have provided us with good housing and all sorts of other privileges.

Instead, we had to find a place to live and generally had to fend for ourselves. But, at the same time, it was worth it just to be together and we were looking forward to starting a new life in New York. Leonard had his meals at the post, where he was also able to shower. However, I had to go to the Public Baths, since the pension did not have bathrooms. Armed with my soap and towel, I went there daily. "Here comes the crazy American, she bathes every day," I heard them whispering amongst themselves, thinking that I did not understand German. I skipped Saturdays because this was the day when the Germans took their weekly baths and it was too crowded.

My aunt in Paris had suggested that I should try to track down the actor, Fritz Kortner, at the Theater on the Maximillian Strasse, in Munich. "You were very friendly with his daughter when you were a little girl," she reminded me. It was a great suggestion because I managed to track Manny down. She was around my age, and we immediately became good friends. She introduced me to the café which was near the theater on the Maximillian Strasse, where all the actors and other creative people "hung out." It was in that café where I spent most afternoons and where I always found interesting people to have a good conversation with. After work, Leonard, who knew where to find me, would join us and we had the most fascinating time comparing notes about Germany during the war years in contrast to my life during the war in England. These were all people who claimed to have been politically dead against Hitler and the Nazis but, who nevertheless did not leave Germany for one reason or another. After all, it's not easy to uproot your family, leave your profession, particularly in the theater, and your country unless you are absolutely forced to. I know this all too well.

Even though I spoke perfect German, I tried to avoid any confrontations with most Germans. There was only one exception: because Leonard and I had to move out of the pension, we had to look for another place to live. After much searching, I found a room in a good neighborhood in a very lovely apartment, beautifully furnished. We moved in rather reluctantly because it meant sharing the kitchen with a German couple. They were outraged when they saw that Leonard helped me to get a meal together in the evening. "A man does not belong in the kitchen," the landlady said.

"I don't think that's any of your business," I told her. One thing led to another, and we had a terrible fight, when apparently I lost my temper and hit her lightly. She pretended to be hurt, which was utterly ridiculous because she was twice my size and I had hardly touched her. I guess I must have let all my rage against the Germans out on her. We paid a lot for rent, and I couldn't even use her bathroom because she claimed it was too expensive to heat the water heater. Living with Germans was a very uncomfortable situation for us, but we had no choice. There was no housing to be had because so much had been bombed.

Even though it was the Germans who had started the war, I had mixed feelings about seeing so many historical buildings destroyed.

Apart from meeting in the café and sight seeing, I was busy trying to earn some money because Leonard's army pay was very meager and we wanted to travel while in Europe. We had access to the P.X. (army store) and I was able to buy coffee and cigarettes at cost. Since we didn't smoke (or rather gave it up) and since the Germans were unable to buy either, they had to buy these items on the black market. This is where I came in. I felt as if I was in a B-movie when I approached an antique dealer opposite the best hotel in town (the "Vier Jahreszeiten") casually asking for the price of an antique piece of jewelry in the window, whispering under my breath whether he was interested in the two commodities. He was very responsive and we made a deal.

Every week I delivered my goods after first making sure that no one was watching our transaction. I always pretended to buy something before we made our exchange. With my profits, we were able to travel and decided to take a trip to Italy.

Later on, when Leonard was transferred to Frankfurt, where we once again had to share an apartment with Germans, I was forced to look for a new source. How I found it, I can't remember, but it was a furrier whom I supplied with coffee and cigarettes. This time, I had to try on fur coats before selling my wares.

In the winter we went skiing in Austria with my profits. It all helped to make our stay in Germany bearable. We were also able to travel free in German trains, and from time to time we went to Paris to visit my favorite aunt, Mussia, who was so happy to see us.

Before we knew it, Leonard was prematurely sent to an army camp outside of New York as punishment, due to an argument with a supervisor. I took this opportunity to stay on a bit longer in Europe, and I returned to Vienna to recapture my childhood days.

In an earlier chapter, I described this visit to Vienna and my meeting with my childhood girlfriend, Hasi, which left me angry and disappointed. The city, even though still magical, with its parks full of flowers and lilacs in the spring, but because at the time it was occupied by three foreign powers, was not like the old Vienna I had remembered as a child. Disappointing as it had turned out to be, it was good that I did return, because the visit was a closing chapter of my childhood in Vienna. I have never since felt like returning again. But that may change in the future.

After returning from Europe, Leonard and I at first found a studio apartment on Third Avenue, then moved to a three-room apartment in a brownstone, and later, to my present four-room apartment on East 14th Street, where I still live today and probably will always remain because it has a fantastic view. I soon managed to find work in two advertising agencies, while Leonard had trouble finding work.

In the ups and downs of fourteen years of marriage, there are four events that stand out in my mind.

The major one was the birth of our son, David, named after my mother's first initial. While still working, I carried the baby until I was in my eighth month till my bosses, though very understanding, found my big belly a little embarrassing when I relieved at the reception desk where I had to greet our clients.

I don't want anyone to think that for me giving birth was not the most important event in my life. It was. It is hard to describe what it feels like for someone who has not gone through it, and therefore cannot possibly relate to it. For me it was a miracle which completely changed me from being a single human being to having another person totally dependent on me. On the one hand, it was a great responsibility; on the other hand, it was so wonderful to have a son who hopefully would always be part of me.

Leonard and I had spent a holiday in Nantucket in a Bed and Breakfast on 12 Gay Street, a cobblestone street, not far from the Main Street on this delightful island. Even though we were trying to make ends meet, we took this well-deserved holiday in this very special place. There were only a few cars and we rented bicycles to get around and to go to the beach. After a few days, I discovered that I felt nauseous in the morning. At first, I thought that it was from something I had eaten, but I soon realized that I was pregnant. My gynecologist had once told me: "I don't think that you will be able to carry a baby."

When I got back to New York, he confirmed that I was indeed pregnant. Leonard was not working and it seemed like a bad time, but being a Catholic, the doctor said: "With a baby comes money."

All seemed to go well for a while, but at a party in Westport, I had problems and I was afraid that I would lose the baby. Luckily, however, this was not the case.

At the time, Leonard was still unemployed because he had come out of the army and couldn't find a job. But I was working at Hirshon-Garfield advertising agency on 57th Street and Fifth Avenue. I took the 3rd Avenue El to work every morning from our 30th Street apartment until my eighth month, when I could no longer waddle up the stairs because my belly was too big.

It was wonderful not to be working. I was able to spend a lot of time at the Penthouse of the Museum of Modern Art, where I became a member for a nominal fee. It felt very luxurious to be a lady of leisure.

In my ninth month, when my water broke, Leonard rushed me to St. Claire's Hospital, where I was taken to the delivery room, but I was not ready to give birth. Leonard was getting very anxious. When two days later, I still hadn't given birth, he went to see many Charlie Chaplin movies. Finally, on the third day at

12 noon, after the doctors were already going to send me home, my son was born. Luckily mother and child were fine, because in a Catholic hospital, when it's a matter of saving the mother or the child, it is the child that is saved.

Leonard and I were ecstatic. I had wanted a boy and we gave him the name of David, "D" being the first initial of my mother's name. My friend Mary arrived with a dozen of the most beautiful tulips—her father, being Dutch, imported them from Holland. A few days later, a lady doctor came in to tell me: "Your son is now a man; he has been circumcised."

A week later, I left the hospital, my belly curiously just as big as before. It was difficult to climb the four flights to our charming brownstone apartment, where we even had use of the garden. It began to be a problem, however, with the carriage, the groceries, and most of all, the baby. I always had to make three trips. Leonard finally got a job as a Probation Officer, and we then decided to rent a small, modest apartment for the summer in Long Beach, where Leonard was able to commute to the city and David would be able to run around nude in the garden. It was much healthier for him. We were also lucky to have a lovely landlady who sometimes baby sat for us. In the evening, when I didn't want to cook, we were able to take David with us in the stroller and sit outside a restaurant. Sometimes we would take him for a walk along the boardwalk after our dinner. Older people often stopped us: "How can you take a baby out at this hour when he should be sleeping in his crib?" they asked. An old-fashioned idea, we thought.

I loved having a little baby boy. It reminded me of my Italian doll, Alma, with whom I played back in Vienna. I loved the way he clung to me. I loved the fact that he was so helpless and that I could cuddle him and give him my undivided love. During those first months of David's life, I had no interest in Leonard whatsoever. I felt that he was in the way of my relationship with my baby. I felt a little guilty about this, but my landlady, who was quite a bit older and who had had adolescent children, said, "Don't feel badly—it's normal." Of course, these feelings passed soon.

During the first months of David's life, while we were living in Long Beach, I used to wake him up around 10 p.m. and give him a bottle. He was such a good baby and never woke up during the night. He then let me sleep till 10 a.m. the next morning. It might have been the good clear sea air which enabled him to sleep twelve hours around the clock.

One incident I have never forgotten: one evening I was changing David's diaper at 10 p.m. in the same room where Leonard was sleeping. There we had set up the bassinet. I didn't turn on the light because I didn't want to wake him and therefore I did not see that David was lying too close to the edge of the high bassinet. I suddenly heard a thump—David had fallen to the hard floor. He screamed so loudly that it woke up the whole neighborhood. I was hysterical. I was sure that I had killed my son. We immediately called the pediatrician who said: "It's a good sign that he screamed, but bring him in tomorrow." Of course I was so worried that I didn't sleep all night. Thank goodness he was all right, the doctor said to my great relief.

When the summer was over, we realized, however, that we would have to change apartments. Leonard who, in the meantime, had landed the job as a probation officer for New York City, managed to find us a four-room apartment with an elevator.

Before we moved to Long Beach, we had hired a nurse called Louisa. She was Haitian and, when I told her that I was nervous about handling the baby, she always said: "Don't forget he is just a human being." On her first day off, my friend Mary came over to help me out. When the baby woke up and cried, we both ran to the refrigerator to get the bottle of milk to feed him. Being inexperienced, we couldn't understand why David rejected the bottle and cried. Finally, it dawned on us: we forgot to warm up the bottle! We soon learned; Mary subsequently had four boys.

I found that having a child had many great rewards: amidst them were the letters David wrote when he was old enough to go to camp. One of the funniest letters read: "Dear Mom, I need UNDERWEAR. I forgot to BRING IT. Love, David."

There were many other letters telling us how homesick he was, and there was one memorable letter he wrote us at home after Christmas, thanking us for the gifts and saying how very sorry he was that he unwrapped them the night before. "I will never do it again," he promised.

Of course, bringing up a child is not easy. Many times David would come up from the playground downstairs with a bleeding finger or, another time, with a broken arm, after playing baseball. Luckily, Dr. Schwartz was our next door neighbor, and since I could not stand seeing blood, I would ring his bell and he would bandage the wounds.

There comes the time when your child has to go to Kindergarten and he has to cross the street alone for the very first time. It is a terrible moment in a mother's life. On the one hand, I had to let him go alone, so that he would become independent; on the other hand, I was terrified that he might get run over. I did let him go alone, but ran downstairs after him and watched him cross 14th Street, making sure he did not see me.

After a couple of years, Leonard got a job as a psychologist at Long Island Jewish Hospital and things improved greatly for us financially. We were able to rent a summer place either on Cape Cod, in Wellfleet, and later on on the North Shore of Long Island, in Huntington or Centerport.

One summer, we saw an ad in the New York Times and we rented a house sight unseen on Martha's Vineyard. It sounded intriguing because the ad read:

"House situated on a half acre, walking distance from the beach." When we arrived, to our horror, the half acre was a swamp with a pond and the house was a fisherman's shack. We got used to the primitive house, but not to the fact that rats appeared in our bedroom in the middle of the night. I was so horrified that I sat up in a chair all night long (deja vu from New Brunswick, years before).

The next day, the landlord sent over an exterminator, and it seemed to do the trick. Despite these problems, we really did have a wonderful small bay beach five minutes' walking distance from our house. There, we met in no time, people from all walks of life, and soon found out that no one had a house much more elegant than ours; that's just the way it was in Menemsha, still a primitive fishing village without pretensions.

At an auction, I got to know a very interesting woman by the name of Gloria who was bidding against me every time I raised my hand. She and I became friends, and the friendship included our husbands so that we went out as couples. Gloria owned a fabulous contemporary house in a community called Gay Head built by an architect according to their specifications. It sat high up on the cliffs overlooking the ocean, with a cantilevered deck on one side, adjoining their living room on the second floor. One evening, we were invited to a cocktail party at their house, along with thirty other guests. Their children and my son, David, aged six at the time, were playing downstairs while we, the grown-ups, were enjoying ourselves upstairs in the living room. Toward evening, four elderly people went out to sit on the deck and to watch the magnificent sun setting over the ocean. We were inside when we heard the most horrendous crash. The deck had collapsed and, as much as we were worried about the people sitting on the deck, our worst fears were that our children below would have been crushed. We heard screams all around us. I ran downstairs to look for my son. I saw he had some cuts and was bleeding, but otherwise unharmed. It was an incredible relief that none of the children were hurt, but the grown-ups on the deck suffered from broken bones. However, luckily no one was fatally injured. I was in such a state that after I saw that David was alive and not seriously hurt, I went to the bathroom and vomited. About fifteen minutes later, the ambulances were screeching towards the house and that quiet island turned into a disaster area with the people on the collapsed deck being transported by ferry to hospitals on the mainland. But I am jumping ahead of myself.

When David was two years old, we decided to take the boat, the *Liberté*, to England, since we had not had a proper vacation by ourselves in years. This was made possible by the fact that my friend, Janet, offered to take David for the two weeks while we went off to Palma on the island of Mallorca in Spain. Janet, in the meantime, had married Hugh, the R.A.F. pilot, with whom she had three children, two boys and one girl. They lived outside of London, in Twickenham, where they had bought a big house with a beautiful garden. To this day, she runs a nursery school from her house. "So one more won't make any difference," she told me on the phone. "It will be wonderful seeing you again after all these years."

In 1957, we paid only fifty dollars a week in Palma for a double room with three meals. We stayed in a charming room with blue shutters and a little terrace overlooking the entire magnificent Palma harbor. Even though the room was outstanding, the meals were another story. They were not very good and consisted mostly of starch. We would say: "Steak on Monday after the bullfight on Sunday." We actually did go to the bullfight, even though we did not like the idea of killing an animal. I guess the music and the ambiance were so outstanding that we, too, experienced the excitement of the performance and we did not want to miss the long time honored Spanish tradition.

In our hotel, we met an English journalist by the name of John. He was so witty and delightful that the three of us became really good friends and palled around together. John, though gay, was quite taken with me because we had much in common, both having gone through the war in England. I noticed that Leonard became a little jealous of our friendship. One day, the three of us decided to make an excursion to Formentor, on the other end of the island. It was a resort with a luxury hotel and had lovely, sandy white beaches. John and Leonard went swimming and after a few minutes, I saw that they kept diving under the water to look for something. John came out and said: "Leonard has lost his wedding ring while swimming and is desperately looking for it. I am going back into the water to help him."

It just so happened that our rings were sort of special. They had been hand made for us in a store called Lobel's in Greenwich Village; very fashionable in the 50's. Our rings had up and down lines, meant to be symbolic of the ups and downs of marriage. "How true," I said to myself as the marriage went on. Ours were in silver; we could not afford gold. Leonard and John searched for a long time and while I was sitting on the beach, I was thinking: "Is this an omen of things to come? Maybe I will return to this place many years later. I will order a fish dinner and there in its belly will be the lost wedding ring."

While these things were going through my mind, the two came back and said: "No luck, the ring must have fallen deep into the sand."

Many, many years later, I did go back to Mallorca. I never found my ring, but I found something much more precious.

The other event which was most shocking was the suicide of my cousin Hedy. By this time, my father had remarried for the third time a woman who was not much older than I was. Evelyn was American and she was extremely jealous of me because my father did occasionally take an interest in me. Leonard and I went to their wedding which was held in Croton-on-Hudson, in an institute where my father was working as a psychologist for research advertising. Evelyn also was very resentful that I had a healthy child because she had given birth to two retarded children from a former husband who had died a few years before she married my father.

When we heard that Hedy had committed suicide, we all drove to Cape Cod to attend her funeral. I was devastated since Hedy had always been my favorite cousin. After leading a very bourgeois life and having given birth to two boys, she moved from Garden City, where I first visited her, to another suburban house in Closter, New Jersey.

One day, during this time, her husband Eric bought a dog home, a bulldog, which they and the children all adored. Eric had to train the dog and it seemed, while doing this at a kennel, he met a French lady with whom he fell in love. He would come home late with lipstick on his shirt. Hedy could not bear the humiliation any longer, and they finally divorced. She was terribly upset and depressed because in those days, divorce was still an unusual occurrence.

Through some of her friends, she met a Senator from Massachusetts who talked her into selling the house in New Jersey and moving with him to the Cape, to Brewster, where he had a beautiful, sprawling house. In her desperate state, she accepted and moved there with her two boys, Kenny, 10 years old, and Tommy, 14. Shortly after she got there, it seemed the Senator started no longer coming home after work, and she found out that he had a mistress living in the same town whom he visited frequently. Having gone through so much trauma in her childhood with an unloving mother, a divorced father, and a husband who deserted her, this was the last straw. She took an overdose of sleeping pills, leaving a note explaining what she had done. When the Senator returned, she had passed out. Instead of immediately taking her to a doctor in Brewster to get her stomach pumped out, he drove her to a hospital in Hyannis, many miles away, and by the time they reached the hospital, she had died, leaving two boys without a mother, and a father who had moved to California and was not in touch with them anymore.

On the way to the Cape, driving up in my father's car, I was very apprehensive, upset and sad about my cousin Hedy's funeral, who had been like an older sister to me.

When we finally arrived at the Senator's house, we saw a black hearse parked outside; not exactly a comforting sight. The house was very large with stuffed animal heads mounted on the walls of the enormous living room. Murray, the Senator, was sitting at a table with a woman who, we found out later, was his mistress. Various friends, as well as Hedy's brother-in-law and his wife, had also come up from New York to attend the funeral. Murray employed some lackeys who prepared dinner for all of us. The atmosphere during dinner was quiet, sinister and eerie. We, the family, were convinced, and still are to this day, that

Murray had wished her death. In a sense, it was murder, but murder which we could not prove.

The next day it was pouring with rain as we drove to the funeral parlor. After the service, everyone passed the open casket. Looking at my cousin's dead body, I broke down and cried. I had never seen a dead person before. It was the only time during my marriage that I remember my husband having real compassion for me, knowing how much I had loved Hedy; he put his arms around me to console me. Standing over the grave site at the cemetery in the rain, I couldn't help but being reminded of the movie "The Barefoot Contessa," where Ava Gardner is standing over her husband's grave in the pouring rain. The worst part was seeing those two little boys standing there who now lost their mother, having already lost their father. Miraculously, and in spite of their tragic childhood, they managed later on to become successful and well adjusted adults. Kenny went first to boarding school and on to college. Later he became a psychologist, graduating from Berkeley University. He also studied the flamenco guitar and spent time in Seville, Spain, where he played with well-known flamenco groups and was known as "El Kenny." Tommy went to UCLA and subsequently won the O. Henry Award for the best short story. He now teaches creative writing at Stanford University and has published two books; the last one is about his mother's life and eventual suicide.

As for my married life, it was going through a bad period. I became increasingly restless making three meals a day, cleaning our apartment, and taking care of David, who was growing up and was already nine years old. When I would bring up the subject of going back to work, Leonard would say: "A mother's place is at home."

When I enrolled in an adult evening course, he would come home and demand dinner, and would almost make me miss my class, on purpose. I had just gotten to know my friend Lois, and when, one night, we two wanted to go to a dance recital, he was furious that I was going out.

The turning point in my life occurred when I read *The Feminine Mystique* by Betty Friedan. I suddenly realized that I was not alone being discontent and that my feelings about my marriage were shared by many other women. I told Leonard: "I want to go back to work: I am bored staying home."

His answer was: "If you go back to work, I'll divorce you."

Nevertheless, I found a job and with my first paycheck, I bought a dishwasher which I sent home with a note: "This will replace me." Leonard did not think it was funny and must have decided to do his own thing. He would come home for dinner and afterwards pick a fight with me over nothing, storm out of the house, get in his car and drive off. I was too naive to realize that he was having an affair. Finally, one day, he confessed: "I am seeing a young nurse half my age who is crazy about me. I want a divorce." It figured: you trade in your old wife who had helped you through school and who has furnished your office, and you trade her in for a new model. Today it happens so often, but then in 1965, it was still rather unusual. People who were married for a long time just stuck together for the sake of the children. My going back to work had just been an excuse for Leonard. He was going through his mid-life crisis. After 14 years of marriage, it broke my heart. I could not see how I would be able to pick up the pieces: my temporary job was over and I had not worked at a full-time job for ten years. I was totally desperate. To top it off, it all happened in the middle of July, in a heat wave, and I was sitting all alone in my apartment without air conditioning. We had sent David to sleep-away camp for the month of July.

Leonard's friend and co-worker, a psychiatrist, came to see me to help me over my depression and prescribed tranquilizers. He was a great help. I was also lucky that my friend, Sonny, spent a lot of time with me in an effort to console me.

Leonard and I had previously made a reservation in a hotel in Spain for the month of August, and I decided to go alone and take David with me.

Leonard moved out of the apartment with his piano.

For the first time in 14 years, I was alone in my apartment with no meals to cook, no child to look after, but I could not cope with my new found freedom. I would sleep all morning and turn my days around. Often, at 10 p.m. at night, I would go to the laundromat to do my laundry. My friend, Mary, told me to come out to spend a week-end and a couple we both knew invited me to the Berkshires. They kept talking about Leonard and I soon made the decision that I could not be friendly with people who were still his friends.

"No hard feelings," I told them, "but it's either Leonard or me." I just could not be friends with people who were still on his side. Whether I was right or wrong, that's the way I felt. This only left my friends Mary and Lois.

Lois had become a very close friend. We had met in a very strange way a few years before when Leonard and I went skiing to the Hunter Mountain area in Shandaken and were staying in an Inn called *Auberge des 4 saisons* run by a French couple, Annie and Dadou. They served the best meals and we could not wait to get back from the ski slopes for their wonderful dinners. On that particular day, there was a heavy snow storm when we drove up from New York. We entered the Inn quite shaken up, as we almost skidded into another car on the way. There was a couple sitting by the fireplace. The husband said: "Hi, you look like you had a bad time driving, where did you come from?"

"New York," we said.

"Did you come from Manhattan?"

"Yes."

"From the lower east side?"

"Yes."

"Did you come from 14th Street?"

What was he getting at, we wondered.

"Do you live in Stuyvesant Town?"

"Yes," we said again.

"Hi, my name is Fred Gerard, and this is my wife Lois; we are your neighbors living in the building behind yours," he said.

We were stunned; what a small world it is, we thought. We found out that they had lived in France for many years and that we had a lot in common. That's how I became friends with Lois. We saw a lot of each other when we returned to New York, because our children were about the same age, and we would often sit in the playground with them. I was lucky to have them as a couple on my side. But at the time when Leonard left, they were in their country house in July, and it still left me alone in the hot city. I realized that I had to do something. I picked up the phone and called England.

"Hi, Janet," I said. "Can I visit with David in August, Leonard and I have just split."

"Oh, darling!" she said, "I am so sorry, of course, make your reservation and you can stay as long as you like."

When David came back from camp, we left for England. I explained to him: "Daddy can't come with us—he has to work, so we are going alone." I did not want to tell him the truth at this point; he would have been too upset and it would have spoiled his holiday. After spending a week with Janet, we left for Paris to see my aunt who was very upset about my upcoming divorce. We then took a plane to Malaga, Spain, where we arrived and, to our horror, found the airport in total darkness because it seemed that the electricity had failed. It was about midnight when we took a taxi to Marbella on the Costa Brava, to the Hotel Columbus, only to find out that they had not honored our reservation and they could only have a room for us on the next day. However, they could put us up on the fourteenth floor in a condo building next door. Here we were in the dark, David, aged 10, and I, in the middle of the night, in Spain. The porter carried our bags up the fourteen flights since the elevator was not working either; we dragged ourselves up behind him and finally fell into our beds totally exhausted. Things looked up, however, on the next day when the elevator started working again. We were able to move into the hotel next door where we had had our reservation. It was right on the beach with a lovely pool, where luckily David found other children to play with. I tried to hide my grief from him, but I spent much time on the phone with Leonard. He called frequently to see how things were going and I was secretly hoping for a reconciliation even though in my heart I knew that it really could never be. The days passed quickly, sunbathing and walking on the beach, but in the evening, while sitting in the dining room, just David and I, it dawned on me that I was going to be alone in the future and I felt very, very sad.

Upon our return to New York, Leonard took David out and said: "Mommy and I are getting divorced; it's no one's fault. You will live with your mother and I will see you on week-ends." David was devastated and was unable to accept the situation. It was very rough for him, since all his friends' parents seemed to be married, except for one boy in his class. The following year he told me: "Now half the class has divorced parents, you got divorced one year too early, Mom, or I would not have felt so badly." (I guess I was always ahead of my time.) How well I understood his feelings: I had gone through the same trauma myself as a child with divorced parents, and I could share his grief.

At age 14, David decided to move in with his father. It broke my heart, but I could not stop him. I was told that a boy is best off living with his father, and I had to let him go. During this time, he did not want to see me, but I would go to Stuyvesant High School at 3 p.m. and wait for him to come out. We then went to a coffee shop together and it made me so sad to let him go again.

Before I knew it, a couple of years later, I received a letter which read:

"I am leaving for Israel in an hour. Just wanted to say have a nice six months, and I will write, I promise. Love David."

David, who loved hamburgers, had the bad luck to go to a vegetable kibbutz, and it wasn't long before he came back to New York.

I was happy that I could see him again. That year, on Mother's Day, my bell rang. When I opened the door, there was a delivery boy with the most beautiful bouquet of flowers. The card read: "Happy Mother's Day. Don't faint. Love David." I called him back to thank him and said: "I didn't faint: I just passed out."

I was very touched and happy to have my son's love again.

Reflections Upon Marriage

On reflecting upon my marriage, I see now how easy it is when you are young and feel lonely to let yourself fall in love, even though secretly you may have doubts about the other person; this is especially true when there is peer pressure for girls to get married. I had been in love with the idea of love. How little we know about each other when first dating and not living together before marriage. Among other things, I soon discovered that my husband was a morning person, getting up early and going early to bed, whereas I loved staying up late. I could have gone out dancing when he was ready for bed.

After fourteen years of marriage, I had to confess to myself that we really had been strangers most of these years. I often felt more lonely during my marriage than after my divorce when I was free to choose my own life style again.

I can never recapture those years of my youth when I could have married someone with whom I might have been more compatible and with whom I might have had a lasting, loving marriage, giving me the companionship which would have been a comfort to me in my old age. But how lucky I was, nevertheless, I thought, to have conceived a child to care for and to be responsible for and to whom I could give my love. This gave and continues to give meaning to my life.

Author with son David about 2 years old in Long Beach

Chapter XIII

Final Divorce

The divorce was very traumatic. It had taken over two years of arguing with each other's attorneys and with each other. Since Leonard was required to pay child support and some small amount of alimony, he went as far as subpoenaing my modest pay check at my advertising agency, which was most embarrassing; I was only making $125.00 a week; not enough to pay rent and food. I finally agreed to the divorce settlement which was hardly adequate, nor did it have a cost of living increase, but I could no longer stand the constant stress and harassment. It was hard enough to work from 9-5, worry about where David would go after school and rush home to make dinner for him and take care of his clothes.

On the day when I was to sign the final divorce agreement, I entered my attorney's office to find Leonard sitting there with his attorney. They handed me the divorce papers and, to my horror, there was a paragraph which read: "In the event that I would have a man staying in my apartment, all payments from Leonard would stop." I couldn't believe what I was reading.

"Gentlemen," I said. "There is no way that I will sign this agreement. What does that mean? Does that mean that if a man sleeps over, payment stops? Or does it mean that if a man moves in with his dog and stays for a week that I lose everything? There is no way I am signing this."

The three men looked at me in astonishment. I guess they thought that I might not notice this clause. Talk about macho pigs, all three of them, including my own lawyer. There was complete silence while all of them stared at me. "Wait outside," my attorney said to me. A few minutes later, when he called me back into the office, he buzzed his secretary: "Kathy," he said, "please strike paragraph X in the agreement and retype the page." That's how I finally got my divorce.

Celebrating Divorce

That summer, while David was again in camp, I felt that after two years of intense fighting for my life and the harassment I had been put through, I deserved a special vacation. As a little girl, I had dreamt of two places where I wanted to go when I grew up: one was Hollywood, since I was then crazy about movie stars; the other was the French Riviera, where I believed only the jet set could afford to go. Since the dollar was very favorable that year compared to European currencies, I bought a ticket to Nice on Air France. It was a beautiful sunny day when I arrived at the airport. I hailed a taxi to take me to a small hotel where I had made a reservation from New York, not knowing much about the city. Luckily, my French is pretty fluent.

The cab driver looked at me and said: "Mademoiselle, you don't want to stay there, that's a hotel for old people. You are a pretty young lady, and Nice is not for you. It's much too bourgeois and you don't look like you want to get all dressed up every day. But I will pass by there so that you can see for yourself. I'll take you to *Juan les Pins*, a charming small village by the sea, and I'll help you find a little inexpensive hotel. Then after 10 days, I'll come and take you back to the Nice Airport."

He really was an unusually kind person, I thought. We did pass the hotel in Nice, and he was so right, it was not for me. His fare was reasonable and he drove me around *Juan les Pins* until we found a hotel, appropriately called: "Hotel Welcome." The owner, a nice middle aged Frenchman, was very impressed when he saw that I was alone and without a car, and I had come there specifically to visit all the museums and art galleries in the area. He put me in a little room next to the garden where I could enjoy my breakfast sitting outside.

Driving along the Mediterranean had been a wonderful experience, and passing through all the little villages where people were sitting in outdoor cafés, was just how I had imagined the Riviera: the blue sea, the blue sky and the bright sun made this drive magical for me. We drove by mansions and there were flowers blooming everywhere in all the most gorgeous colors. It was like a dream come true. The owner of the hotel and I made a plan that I should follow as much as possible to take buses in order to get around. My big excursion was to go to St. Paul de Vence to the famous *Galerie Maeght*. It meant changing buses to take me up to the village of St. Paul and from there I had to walk more than a mile through a forest to reach the museum. With the help of my French, I made my connection, but I had to have a coffee while I was waiting for the second bus. Once in Vence, I decided to have lunch before my walk to the *Gallerie Maeght*. When I finally arrived there, to my utter amazement, there was a sign that read: "Gallerie closed today due to the installation for the Miro show." This was just too much.

"I have now travelled 3,000 miles, taken two buses, walked over one mile to see this museum, and nothing is going to stop me from going inside," I said to the lady at the entrance, in French.

She looked at me and didn't have the heart to turn me away. There were two Americans standing behind me, and they were able to tag along thanks to my persuasion to let us in. In the end it was well worth it. The architecture of the building itself is quite outstanding and I was able to see the marvelous permanent collection of paintings despite not being able to see the Miros which were still being installed. On that particular day, to celebrate the opening of the Miro show, the tables were elegantly set in a garden in the center of the museum. The rich contributors and collectors were going to dine there that evening. I felt a little like an outcast, not being able to take part in the festivities; instead I had to walk back through the forest and I again had to take two buses in order to get back to my hotel. On the way out of the museum, I was, however, also able to see the magnificent sculpture garden with fine works by Henry Moore, Giacommeti and Picasso, amongst others.

The next day, the owner of my hotel hearing about my difficulties in getting around without a car, told me: "I am going to Antibes on business, and I can drop you off at the Picasso Museum." Of course, I accepted. The mansion, dating back to 1608 was so breathtaking because it was built high overlooking the Mediterranean. The entrance is filled with antique furniture and the museum is known for Picasso's ceramics, rather than his paintings. These seem to be influenced by the Greek and Cretan civilizations depicting flowers, sea urchins, birds, as well as fawns playing the flute, and other mythical creatures. I could not take my eyes off this outstanding collection with the wonderful blues of the Mediterranean strongly visible on urns, vases and plates. Picasso himself used the fourth floor of this mansion as his studio in 1946, where he lived with Françoise Gilot. This was the time when the famous photograph of Picasso was taken, when he was walking behind her on the beach, protecting Françoise from the sun with a large umbrella.

My very first day upon my arrival in Juan les Pins, I went to a café not far from the beach to have lunch, and I ordered a "Bloody Mary." The waiter, about twenty years old, at most, and very good-looking with blonde hair and blue eyes, said to me: "Mademoiselle, you are the only American in Juan les Pins this year because of the student strikes in Paris which have prevented tourists from going to France. Therefore I am not charging you for your drink."

I was speechless and thanked him. He insisted on treating me for my one lunchtime drink during the whole time I was there. Needless to say, I tipped him generously. This incident has always proved my point that if you speak or at least try to speak the language of the country where you travel, people are going to react very differently towards you than if you insist on speaking your own language.

It turned out that my hotel was very well situated, walking distance to the beach and to the railroad. On my last day, I decided to take the train to Cannes, known to be the chicest place on the Riviera, and famous for its yearly Film Festival. I was walking along the "Croisette," when someone suddenly grabbed me from behind. Shocked, I turned around to see that it was Fred, my friend Lois's husband.

"Lois is across the street, trying on a bikini," he said. "Is she going to be surprised and thrilled to see you. What a small world it is."

We both knew that we were all going to be on the Riviera, but somehow I didn't exactly know where and when I was going to be there, nor did they. Lois couldn't believe it when I walked into the store.

"We are staying at the Carlton Hotel," Fred said. "Why don't you come to dinner with us? We have a reservation in one of the three-star restaurants, a country house in the mountains."

"How could I?" I asked. "My last train leaves Cannes at 8 p.m. How can I get back, and besides, I need a shower." I felt like Cinderella.

"Don't be silly," they said, "We have a car, and of course we'll drive you home and you can take a bath in our hotel."

I suddenly felt very protected, so different from having been on my own for the last ten days. I was overwhelmed and touched to be with friends in a foreign country, so far away from home.

Entering the posh Carlton Hotel, I saw Ed Sullivan, T.V. host, at one table, Harold Robbins, the writer, at the next one, both sipping a cocktail. I couldn't believe the opulence of this hotel which, at the time, was considered to be one of the most luxurious on the Riviera. The lobby was carpeted with plush rugs and lit by huge crystal chandeliers. The busboys, dressed as though in a Hollywood movie, were pushing expensive luggage around.

Entering my friends' suite overlooking the magnificent Mediterranean, I was amazed to see that the bathroom was as big as my little room in Juan-les-Pins. I revelled in my bubble bath. But the best was still to come: Fred drove us to a restaurant, somewhere in the country behind Cannes. Unfortunately, it was already dark so that I couldn't see the wonderful landscape of Provence with its fields of lavender, the scents permeating the air. The restaurant looked like someone's private house where you enter into a salon before being ushered into the dining room. At the time it was the only three-star restaurant listed in the Michelin Guide, where I had ever eaten and yet I cannot remember the menu, but I do remember that the meal was outstanding. It gave me, however, a taste of the life that the very rich lead, but then the price was so much less then than it would have been today. After dinner, as promised, Fred drove me home.

On my last day, my faithful taxi driver arrived early; we had a last cup of coffee together in the garden and set off for the airport. On the way there, he stopped by the sea, so that I could have a last look at the blue Mediterranean. It was so unbelievably nice and sensitive of him; I considered myself lucky to have met him. My days at the Riviera totally came up to my expectations and I felt very special having been there.

Following my ten days of bliss, I had arranged to meet my friend Gloria in Dubrovnik on the Adriatic seacoast of Yugoslavia. This was *my* year and Dubrovnik, although so different from the Riviera, was a fascinating town, surrounded by a medieval wall. The city's architecture is strongly influenced by the Italian Renaissance. It was at one time, the most important trading port between Venice and the Middle East. No cars are allowed within the city's walls, creating a sense of timelessness.

We were able to stay in a luxury hotel in a room facing the aquamarine Adriatic. The lobby, beautifully furnished with antiques, has a bar from where one could see the pool and the open sea beyond. Quite a change from my Hotel "Welcome" on the Riviera. Many of the locals came to the hotel bar for a drink and that's how I met Yani, a Yugoslavian rock star. He was a singer in a group called "The Dubrovnik Troubadours," famous throughout Yugoslavia, and similar to the Beatles in England. We got acquainted and a few times he took me out to dinner in a local restaurant. On several occasions, when we walked into town, young girls would asked him for his autograph. It made me feel proud walking along the street with the local celebrity. Our relationship stopped abruptly, however, after he suggested: "Let's go to the 'Island of Love,' just across from the mainland. It's a romantic place which you must see."

Getting off the small boat, I saw an array of beautiful flowers and budding trees everywhere. There were hundreds of birds chirping away. It was obviously the place where young people went to make love. Yani started to kiss me, but it seemed to me that he hadn't bathed for at least a week and our love affair ended abruptly without being consummated. To this day, I don't quite remember how I managed to get out of this embarrassing situation. Nevertheless, before I left, he gave me one of his records and sometimes when I want to remember my days in Dubrovnik, I play it and think back to that day on the "Isle of Love," wondering whether I could have overcome my cleanliness mania. For all I know, he could have been clean, but sweaty in the hot climate.

It had been a wonderful vacation, but I had to go back to my son David, back to work and back to reality.

In New York, I was informed that the divorce papers had finally been signed after years of struggling.

Chapter XIV

A New Life

"You were reborn," the well-known painter, Milton Resnick said to me many years later. He was so right. It became a new life for me, being a woman living alone with a ten-year-old boy at a time when this was still not the norm. How well I remember going out at night by myself for the very first time. I always loved the theater and there was a play in Greenwich Village which I wanted to see. I made a reservation and went to the box office to pick up my ticket just before the beginning of this play. The agent who handed me the ticket was one of the actors in the show, and must have liked the way I looked.

"We are having a cast party after the show and would love for you to join us," he said. I felt extremely flattered and decided: "Why not, I'll go." It certainly was a good beginning for my first time out alone, and it helped my self-image tremendously. Here I had led this sheltered life for fourteen years and I soon began to see that men were attracted to me. But even more important for my ego was to find a job.

I was lucky that during my marriage I had worked for a short period for Judy Wald, who owned an employment agency serving the advertising industry. I called Judy: "Come in," she said. "I'll send you for an interview with a small ad agency who just moved from a brownstone since they were expanding to bigger offices on Third Avenue and 44th Street."

They seemed to like me, but told me: "You have to pass a typing and shorthand test." I was afraid to fail, not having worked for many years, but Judy talked them into letting me take the test at her agency, where she knew I would be much less nervous.

"You will pass," she said. They hired me on her say-so.

My new life was beginning to fall into place: every morning, I took the bus to my new job. I was hired as secretary to the Director of Research. He kept asking me what it was like to be a "gay divorcée," because I think he was playing with the idea of divorcing his wife. I did not like him and, as luck would have it, a week after I started working for him, the President of the agency fired his secretary on the spur of the moment for something she had allegedly said to a client.

He came over to me and said: "I guess you'll have to sit outside of my office for the time being, if you don't mind." I did not mind at all and even though I was very apprehensive working for the president of an advertising agency, I thought I'll give it a try. Doug Warren was very good-looking, tall and impressive, thirty-five years old. He was one of the youngest presidents in the business. I respected him enormously, but I was afraid of him, even though he was not pretentious. The job was a challenge for me. I must have been doing all right, because he kept me on as his executive secretary for five years.

My biggest problem, however, was that when David came home from school at 3 p.m., I always worried whether he was all right. Even though he had strict instructions to call me the minute he came home, he conveniently forgot to do so and, a lot of times, simply went to a friend's house. I would be desperately calling all over the place. I was frantic sitting there helplessly in my office. "Is David there?" I asked the mothers who already knew my voice. I was so relieved when I tracked him down. I did not know whether to give him hell or tell him how much I loved him. He would promise to call me the next day after school, but often neglected to do so.

Between going to work every day from 9-5, doing the marketing on the way home, and making dinner for David and myself, there was not much time left for myself. Week-ends were the exception. Since it was still fall and the weather was good, I was able to go and play tennis on the lower east side by the East River. By now our season permits had gone up to $50, but it was still a bargain, considering one could play as often as one would like.

My big problem was that I was going through a horrendous divorce with Leonard. He would call me almost every evening and taunt me about one thing or another. In our discussions, he would never bend as to his visitation rights, due to his rigid nature. If there was something special that I wanted him to help with, he absolutely refused. As it was, I had to get a baby sitter every time I wanted to go out in the evening. At the beginning, before I began to have a social life, I stayed home a lot. But then, one evening, my girlfriend Lois and I went to the famous Cedar Tavern which was frequented by a lot of painters, and shortly thereafter a few of them asked me out. There was no one in particular I was interested in, but it was a diversion from my usual routine. One day, I was coming home from work on the bus when I saw an incredibly attractive man looking at me. I was immediately drawn to this tall, dark, handsome person. I thought about him constantly and then as luck would have it, I saw him again on the bus and we both smiled. It was obvious that he was living in the neighborhood. I was just about giving up on seeing him again when, suddenly, at the tennis courts, there he was playing on the court next to me. I could not believe the coincidence. We both walked off the courts when the whistle blew and looked at each other. "I believe we have met before," I said rather nervously. It took all my courage to say this.

"Yes," he answered, "you look familiar."

"I think I saw you on the 14th Street crosstown bus," I ventured.

"Do you live around here?" he asked me.

"Yes, on 14th Street."

By this time, we had sat down on a bench, watching some of the other players.

"What do you do besides riding the bus and playing tennis?" I asked. Someone had to carry on this conversation, I told myself, or I will lose him.

"I am an actor in a soap opera," he replied.

I can't let this man escape, I told myself. What do I do next? I am new at this game.

"I am walking home," he suddenly said. "Would you like me to walk you home, or are you planning to play some more tennis?"

"No," I said, "I must go home and make lunch for my son." I thought he might as well know where I stood.

"Are you married?" he asked me.

"Not really," I said, "just separated."

We walked along the river and my heart was beating rapidly. I was very sexually attracted to him. When we reached the door of my apartment building, he asked: "When are you going to play tennis again?"

"Next Saturday," I answered.

"What time will you be there?"

"Around 11 a.m."

"Let's meet there," he said. And so we did. Gino walked me home again, and since it was the week-end when Leonard had David, I was free to invite him in. We had a drink together and I found out that he played the part of a doctor in a soap opera, one of the first of its kind. It was called "Search for Tomorrow." Of course, all the nurses on the show are in love with him, I thought, and so am I.

I soon found out that Gino was married, but it was too late and it did not stop me. For the first time in fourteen years, he made me feel wanted and it developed into a great love affair. It was a love affair right out of a movie. I was technically still married and so was he; we had a problem getting together, which made it all the more intriguing. On Saturdays, he came over with his tennis racquet and when my apartment was available, we gave up playing tennis. When David would leave the house to go to the playground, we were able to make love. Sometimes, David would hang around because he was impressed that his mother was going out with a television star; so were most of my girlfriends' mothers who watched this soap opera. Gino was also nice to David and brought him to the set one day; he took him behind the scenes to show him how a television show is produced. Afterwards he bought him lunch: a hamburger and french fries, David's favorite food. (To this day, it's David's favorite food.)

"Why don't you and Gino get married?" he would ask me.

"When you are older, I will explain it to you," was my answer.

When I did not hear from Gino, I felt very upset, even though I knew that he could not get away. Then suddenly, he would call and show up with a red rose and when I looked at him, I forgave him. One Christmas, he went to Canada and I had gone skiing at Hunter Mountain in the Catskills with my father and his wife, Evelyn. As usual, we stayed at the "Auberge des quatre saisons." David spent Christmas with Leonard. Gino and I had arranged to meet at midnight in my apartment in New York. He was flying in from Canada and I took the bus back to New York. The city was very still, since it was Christmas Eve; the streets were deserted. His plane was supposed to land at 11 p.m. I was so excited about seeing him again that I was unable to rest and was walking up and down in my apartment in anticipation. What if he doesn't show up? What if his plane crashes? All these thoughts were going through my mind when I heard the bell and there he stood. I will never forget that moment and how happy I felt. Years of deprivation of love and romance had made this meeting meaningful and special.

One of the funniest moments was that Christmas when he had pre-taped the soap. We were sitting in my bedroom where I keep my television set and watched him on the screen kissing another woman. Another time, he would rehearse his lines with me. It made me feel very privileged to be with a well-known television personality. I began to be the envy of my girlfriends who were stuck in boring marriages.

I couldn't believe my luck to have met Gino at the critical time of my life, when I most needed to be loved and to regain my self-esteem. It was a terrible blow to my ego to find out that my husband of fourteen years was cheating with a twenty-year-old nurse. Even though I tried to tell myself that he was going through his mid-life crisis, it still didn't help me to overcome my grief and feeling rejected. I felt that Gino was my salvation. In addition to being an actor on a soap, he was a Canadian actor who had trained there. His ambition was to be a classical actor, but since he had to support a family, he was grateful to have a job in television where the pay was much better. During the two years we saw each other, he did manage to have a part in a play by Molière, a classical French playwright, which was produced at Circle in the Square, in Greenwich Village. I went to see the play and felt very proud of his performance; he was a brilliant actor. He told me afterwards when I congratulated him that the pay for off-Broadway was an unbelievable sixty dollars per week. Hardly a livable wage, even in 1966.

We saw each other for two years, two years which I treasured and will always remember because we were not only lovers, but we also shared our great love for the theater with each other. We also shared our feelings, talked and laughed with each other. Gino, who was also a father of a young son, understood only too well how I felt about David. Unfortunately, this kind of euphoria cannot last.

During the time we knew each other, he had met only one of my friends, my friend Sonny, who was also an actress and who had held my hand during my very emotional separation from Leonard. At the end, when I had not heard from Gino for some time, she called me up: "If you are wondering why you haven't heard from Gino," she said, "I met him in the street in the Village buying a Christmas tree, and he told me to tell you: "He will always think of you with love, but he has decided to get his marriage back together, you must forgive him."

I told myself: I seem to be good at involving myself with married men who go back to their wives. I had better stop it or I will get hurt over and over again. I really must change my ways.

I decided to get away from the city and that summer, I rented a house on Fire Island with the divorced wife of one of Leonard's colleagues. Gloria and I had just been left by our respective husbands, both psychologists. It was a coincidence that she also wanted to have a place near the beach where we could relax after work. We both had full-time jobs; she was a buyer at Macy's. Also, since neither of us could drive, Fire Island seemed the logical place for a summer house. We took the train to Bayshore and then the ferry, and with the help of a real estate agent, we were lucky to find a small house.

Chapter XV

Fire Island/Greece

I do not want to make it sound as if the affair with Gino was just forgotten, because I was grateful that he had given me back my self-esteem and he had made me feel like a woman again. I knew that I would never have married him even if he had been free.

Actors are simply not good marriage material by and large. They are too absorbed with themselves. I was looking for a man who would be a good father to my son and for a man who could love me freely. Fire Island was certainly not the place for that. But it was a magical island and being free for the first time in my life was important to me. Just getting off the ferry and breathing in fresh air was enough to make me feel high. With no cars, there was no pollution and, with the ocean on one side, and the bay on the other, one had the feeling of being on a ship in the middle of the ocean. The island is very long, but in some communities it is no more than half a mile wide. Our house was only about three houses from the ocean. It had two small bedrooms, a living room with a potbelly stove and a small kitchen. It had a large deck with a walkway leading to the sea.

Our first week-end there, Memorial Day, it was freezing. We tried to find wood for our stove, but so did everyone else, and we ended up having to buy logs for $1.25 apiece. The locals sure took advantage of the city slickers who had no choice. We huddled around the stove to keep warm in the evening. The following week-end, we were lucky, the weather had changed drastically, the sun was shining and everything looked just wonderful. There isn't any place in the world quite like this island. I was totally happy.

Since we were in Ocean Bay Park, a community consisting of mostly houses, hardly any restaurants or shops, we had to go to Ocean Beach, the next village, if we needed supplies, or if we wanted to have some fun. I decided that I should have some transportation to make life easier. I had Macy's ship a bicycle to me via United Parcel. Sherry-Lehmann, the liquor store on Madison Avenue, shipped us a case of wine. With our little red wagons we went to the ferry to pick everything up. The wagon is parked near the ferry, so that on arrival, one can put one's luggage on it, and take it back to the house which in this case was quite a distance from the ferry landing. On Fridays, we would also bring some groceries from the city, since food on the island was very expensive. When we arrived, tired from a weeks' work and the commute we did not have to go shopping and could immediately cook our dinner. It all became a routine:

I would leave my office at five p.m. and by seven p.m. I could be standing by the ocean with a drink in my hand. After dinner, we often went into town, to Goldie's restaurant which was the "hang-out" for locals, as well as the yachting crowd and the renters. The bartender, John, became my friend and I tipped him generously at the beginning of the season in order that he would look after me. It was the local custom to do so and it paid off, since he would warn us if a male customer would try to get us drunk by ordering doubles. Approaching Goldie's, we could already hear Frank Sinatra's song "Strangers in the Night" echoing through the stillness of the evening and with the roar of the ocean in the distance, my memories of the city were left far behind.

The very first time that I went to Goldie's, I had beginner's luck. I met Robert who was a "regular" on the island. His parents had taken him there ever since he was a little boy. He loved the island more than anything else. "It's a fantasy island," he told me. "It's unreal and has nothing to do with the rest of the world."

He was so right. Those were exactly my own feelings. We became good friends and it blossomed into a summer romance which made my first time there even more "special." In fourteen years, I had never experienced such utter freedom. David was in camp, first as a camper and later on, as a counselor. He only came out once or twice during the summer.

My friend Sonny, who had been especially supportive the first month after my marriage broke up, had already bought a house just around the corner from our rental house. Her next-door neighbor, Terry, who was also divorced because she had "cheated" on her husband, always kept an "open house." Although she had three small children, and despite the fact that she was now alone, she always managed to keep her marvelous sense of humor; we would hang out at her house on rainy days. The summer when America sent its first men to the moon, it rained almost all the time and we ended up watching the event on television at her house. We could not get over the fact that science fiction had suddenly become a reality.

On sunny days, our large deck was open to visitors. We invited friends for the week-end, or we had neighbors over for a drink or for a small cocktail party. In turn, we were invited to other people's houses. At the end of our walk, lived a single man in a huge beautiful house right on the ocean; he often asked many of his neighbors over to watch the sunset from his deck.

During four years, we rented the same house and we were able to meet a great variety of people. I had my flings during those first carefree summers after years of a destructive marriage and began to feel like a whole human being again, but I finally began to outgrow Fire Island. I realized that there is a big world out there; it was time for a change. When I now think back to those days, none of the people I met were really that memorable, but at the time they were as carefree and fun-loving as I was.

Since I had also spent my two-week vacations in our house on the island, I felt the urge to travel. I had always lived for my vacations and finally my boss at the advertising agency agreed to give me three weeks off instead of the customary two. At last I could go back to Europe!

Greece

An ad in the New York Times which read: "$250 round trip to Athens, Greece" intrigued me. I had never been to Greece, a country which I was longing to visit. With only one address of a painter, named Costa, I flew to Athens by myself. Costa turned out to be as fun-loving as "Zorba the Greek." I had to remind myself of the saying: "Beware of Greeks bearing Gifts." This turned out not to be true because Costa and his friend couldn't do enough for me to make my week in Athens memorable. They had no money, but were extremely hospitable. With Costa's old jalopy they showed me the city and its surroundings. We went to the long beaches, with white sand near Athens, the fish market where we ate fabulous meals consisting of the "catch of the day," the freshest fish I have ever eaten; to Kolonaki, the fashionable part of Athens where the rich live and, of course, we had dinner in Plaka, the old town, where Greek musicians serenaded us. On days when I was alone, I would go to a museum, like the famous Archeological Museum, or sit in a café on Constitution square, watching the people go by. One day, when it was too hot to go anywhere, I took a taxi to the Hilton Hotel, since an American businessman I had met on the plane, had given me his room number and had said: "Feel free to use the pool if you want to go swimming in the event that I am not there."

Soon my marvelous week in Athens was over, I said good-bye to my new found friend Costa and flew to the island of Corfu. I stayed in a rather nice hotel, a little bit out of the center of town. It had a pool, but though it faced the port, there was no beach. Since I was longing to go swimming in the sea and since it was difficult to get to the beach, which was quite a distance away, I decided to hitchhike. I was embarrassed to be seen by the bellboys of my hotel and I stood a little past the entrance sticking out my thumb. I felt somewhat afraid doing this, but my wish to get to that beach was so strong, that I had the courage to do it. The very first time I was lucky to get a ride on the back of a motorbike with a tourist who looked respectable and who turned out to be harmless. The beach on the Northern part of the island was absolutely breathtaking, with miles of white sand, and almost deserted in those days. It did, however, have a little taverna where I was able to get a moussaka, a typically Greek lamb dish, a Greek salad and a glass of Retsina wine. I needed the wine to give me courage since I was worried about getting back. Luckily, I easily got a ride with people who were just leaving the beach at the same time as I was. I was incredibly relieved to be back in my hotel in one piece. What an adventure, I told myself, but I could not resist returning to this paradise. Two days later, I decided to give it another try. This was really not smart, since Greek men have a bad reputation with single women. I did choose my ride very carefully, however, and had learned the one Greek word which is most necessary: "Oichi," which means "no." Going there was no problem, but on the way back I was not so lucky and had to walk back the long path which led to the beach, continue along the main road for a few kilometers before someone gave me a ride. I think that this finally cured me and ended my adventures in Corfu. I was lucky to get away unharmed and I would not suggest that other tourists hitchhike, but these were different times since the Military Government was still in power and for this reason, few tourists were travelling to Greece. I spent the rest of my time at the hotel pool or took a bus into Corfu city to visit the shops and cafés, but I was not particularly impressed and I wondered why Laurence Durrell had written such a glowing description of this island, but that was in a different time.

I was glad to leave Corfu behind and flew to the island of Mykonos which was quite another adventure.

The boats from Athens can rarely land on the island because it is extremely windy, and the waters are shallow and dangerous, so that one has to take a small boat to get ashore. Balancing down the gangplank with my luggage and the wind blowing, my "at the time fashionable" Dr. Scholl's heel-less shoe fell into the sea. I screamed, but it was too late, even though other passenger tried to save my shoe as it was rolling down the gangplank. I limped off the boat, feeling rather foolish. It was the beginning of a very strange and yet wonderful week in Mykonos. The windmills above the village were perpetually turning around and this constant wind made me feel high and very energetic all the time. My hotel, the *Xania*, was right next to the windmills and in order to go down to the harbor, I had to walk through a maze of little white winding streets which made it difficult to find the way down. There was a shop which had a pretty dress hanging outside and this was always my sign to make a right turn. One night, on the way back, the shop was closed and I did not see the white dress; of course, I lost my way. The island was known to European homosexuals and jet setters; it had become a very fashionable place. There were charming little places to have a drink in the plaza and romantic restaurants for lovers. There was a whole unwritten routine involving the certain time in the evening when one should be at what place. Late at night we all ended up at the discothèque next to the harbor.

Our days were spent at two of the best beaches in Europe, with fine white sand, quite a rarity on the European continent. The nearer one is called "Paradise," the other, a nude beach, is a hang-out for the "gay" community; it is called "Super Paradise." Right on "Paradise" beach are many tavernas where we would eat our lunch. I had met some people at my hotel who often joined me. If we were a large crowd of people, the waiters would set up a table right on the beach facing the ocean. I remember one day, we were a group of ten or more international tourists consisting of a mixture of the "beautiful" people. Because I speak three languages, I was very popular and often found myself to be an interpreter. The whole scene reminded me of a Fellini movie. With the sun shining, the heat, the gorgeous setting, the sound of the ocean roaring and the many bottles of wine we drank, we all felt "no pain." After that, a siesta was strongly indicated before starting to party again in the evening. One day, sitting in the café by the harbor for breakfast, my coffee cup flew away in the wind; and it was not made of styrofoam. As I said before, I loved the wind which made me feel high, but I did not love it that much. My friend Joan had joined me that year and since she wore contact lenses which irritated her eyes, we took the next boat to the island of Ios.

Ios was yet another story: Joan and I checked into a little hotel in the village. We decided to stay there for a few days since we liked the look of the island. The first thing Joan did was to wash her hair. Suddenly I heard a scream coming from the bathroom. "My hair is full of soap and the water is cut off," she shouted. "What am I to do?"

I don't remember what we did, but we did eventually go to the square to get some breakfast. A few minutes later, we saw a procession of people all dressed in black carrying a child with an I.V. on a stretcher. Seconds later, a helicopter touched ground and the child was transported to a hospital in Athens. We were both totally taken by surprise, very shocked, but comforted by the thought that help was nearby, should we ever need it, while on this or any other island.

The following day, we walked over a small hill to the other side of the little island to the beach. We were sunning and bathing in the warm sea when we saw a group of people crouched on the sand listening to a radio. Suddenly, President Nixon's voice could be heard announcing his resignation. It was a historic moment. Being on vacation, we rarely bought a newspaper and did not know what was going on back home. Since I am an ardent Democrat and disliked Nixon, I was happy that he was leaving the White House and the presidency.

For the next four years, Joan and I went back to Greece looking for the "perfect" island. She, too, fell in love with this country, where one could have a wonderful time and meet interesting people from all over the world. We visited Kos, Skiathos, Ios, Patmos, Rhodes, Paxous and Samos.

One year we took a small boat from Samos to Turkey to visit the world-renowned archeological site, *Ephesis*, for the day. It was one of the worst sea voyages I had ever taken; the sea was so rough that I was seasick for over two hours. Arriving in Kusadasi, we did not join a tour group. Instead we decided to take a taxi by ourselves. This turned out to be a grave mistake. The taxi driver drove and drove along the sea for what seemed to be a very long time. We could not communicate with him and fantasized about being kidnapped in Turkey. We already imagined a headline in a New York paper which read: "Two American tourists disappear in Turkey on the way to archeological site in *Ephesis*." We were most relieved when we finally spotted our group at the entrance of *Ephesis*. We made up our mind then and there never to leave the group again. We had a wonderful guide who made this an outstanding experience. *Ephesis* is one of the most fascinating sites I had ever visited with ruins that go back thousands of years and that give a visitor a good understanding of how people lived in those ancient days. Unfortunately, we had to return on that awful boat, where I was even more seasick on the way back than on the way there. It became unbearable and I said to Joan: "I can't stand it anymore, please throw me overboard." She ignored me and lied to me: "We are almost home," she said. The strange thing was that the moment we arrived on solid ground, I felt fine and we immediately went into a small bodega (wine cellar) where we tasted a good Samos wine, telling the locals about our adventure.

One year, I went ahead to the island of Hydra, where Joan was supposed to join me a week later. Hydra was a special island because there were no cars and only donkeys were used for transportation on its cobblestone streets. One day when I was going down to the harbor for breakfast, I saw an incredible sight: all the Greek women, dressed in black, were standing on the dock, crying, as they saw their sons going off to war in boats. Unbeknownst to us, a war had broken out between Greece and Cyprus. There were no more waiters in the café to make our morning coffee. I remember sitting there with the well-known painter, Brice Marden and his wife, Helen, drinking beer instead. The banks were immediately closed for exchanging foreign currency and we were unable to convert our dollars into drachmas. There was no more mail and the telephones were cut off. Joan was supposed to meet me a week later and I did not know how I could reach her in New York. It was a rather desperate situation, and I was a little frightened. Luckily, I met a nice Swiss couple in my hotel and together we discussed what we should do next, since we saw that all the other tourists were desperately rushing to catch the boat back to Athens.

We felt that, if by chance, bombs were going to be dropped, surely Athens would be the target, and not this small island. We thought it was safer to stay put.

Because we became very anxious, we ended up drinking too much in order to distract ourselves and danced all night in the discothèque. A few days later, the owner of the hotel where I had stayed before, was kind enough to change my dollars into drachmas and I was able to make some phone calls. After hours and hours in a telephone booth, I finally succeeded to reach Joan in New York who told me: "I am coming to meet you, regardless of the war."

"Are you sure?" I said, "because I would understand it if you decided not to come."

But she insisted on coming and we arranged to meet in Athens at the Hotel Galaxy, where I had stayed before. The next day I took the boat and left Hydra to meet Joan.

When she arrived, she told me: "I was interviewed by reporters at Kennedy Airport. 'How come you are going to Athens, knowing that there is a war on between Greece and Cyprus?' they asked me."

"I promised my friend that we would spend our vacation together in Greece, and I am going. I am not afraid," she told them.

The next day, things seemed to have calmed down. We walked down to Constitution Square to the bank, since Joan needed to change her money. I was standing outside waiting for her to come out when she motioned to me from inside that they were closing the bank again. "This is ridiculous," I said to her. "Let's go back to the hotel and call the American Embassy to find out what we should do."

The Embassy told us: "Go to the island of Corfu which is further north from Cyprus and you should be all right." The nice receptionist at our hotel secretly changed our money when no one was in the lobby. We packed and rushed to the airport where there were hundreds of people all trying to get out. We put our names on the waiting list and were extremely lucky to get the last two seats to Corfu. Once there, things really seemed to be somewhat calmer, as if there was no war. A few days later, however, the whole mess started again. With the banks closed and the fear of being bombed, I said to Joan: "I've had it. Three weeks of uncertainty are enough; this is no way to spend a vacation. I am leaving for Nice where I can stay with my friend Jacques."

Joan, too, wanted to leave for Paris, where she had friends. We said goodbye to each other and flew our separate ways.

Just an hour later, Jacques met me at the Nice airport. There it seemed as if they had never even heard of the war; as if this experience had been a bad dream. People only a few hundred miles away, hardly knew about the war in Cyprus nor could they care less. As usual, they were sitting around in outdoor cafés, enjoying the splendid weather and the pleasures of the Riviera. This peaceful scene reminded me of the first time I had visited there, a few years back, after my divorce had finally come through.

Chapter XVI

Puerto Rico

In 1969, just before Christmas, I had a severe sinus infection. "There is really nothing that will help you relieve this in New York's damp climate," the doctor said. "If I were you, I'd go somewhere down south where it is warm and hopefully the sun will dry out your sinuses."

Since I usually get very depressed during the holidays when everyone seems to be with family and since I don't have any to speak of, I took his advice to heart. When I saw an ad in a travel agency window which read: "$99.00 round trip to San Juan, Puerto Rico," I bought a ticket.

Coincidentally, one day, sitting at a beach in the middle of a hot summer day, a friend had told me: "If you ever feel like getting away in the winter, I know a fabulous place in Puerto Rico which I know you would love. It is called 'Denise-on-the-Beach' and it is run by a French lady by the name of Denise. She is a little crazy, but she owns this wonderful inn where, when you step out of your room, you are literally on the beach. It is a short distance from town and more quiet than the busy Condado area. For some reason, the most interesting people from all over the world have found the place. The Inn is very simple, rather primitive and unpretentious, but you will never feel alone."

I remembered this conversation and called Denise from New York. "Just call me when you arrive at the airport and I'll have a room for you; then give the taxi driver my address," she said. I followed her advice and I was thrilled to see that the Inn was, in fact, on a quiet street off a main road and right on the ocean.

Denise showed me to my room which was very simply, but tastefully furnished with just a bed and a chest of drawers; on it stood a vase with hand-crafted colorful paper flowers which the natives are known for. I had no sooner taken off my warm winter wardrobe and changed into my summer clothes when I heard a knock on my door. "Be at the bar at 6 p.m.," Denise said: "I have a date for you; he is a tennis player, so he can't be all bad."

I guess she saw that I had brought my tennis racquet. It was like her to try to fix up people who she knew came down alone. I went to the outdoor patio which was covered and thus it was protected in case of rain. It also served as the dining room where breakfast was served. The bar was in one corner and when I sat down, a fairly attractive American by the name of Jim introduced himself to me. A little later when Denise came in and saw that we seemed to be getting along quite well, she asked: "Do you both like *Paella*? If you do, I will drive you to Old San Juan to a little restaurant where you can have dinner together."

Since neither of us had been to San Juan before and were eager to see the old town, where we did not know our way around, we were delighted to accept her offer. I felt wonderful being in this warm climate in the middle of winter. After dinner, we took a walk along the picturesque streets of the old town. Even though we enjoyed each other's company, there was no real "chemistry."

When we got back to the Inn, we had a cup of coffee on the patio. A pleasant Frenchman by the name of Jacques joined us. He seemed to be more interested in me than Jim was. We started talking, and since I speak French, he offered to drive me around the island the next day. Ours developed into a platonic relationship because we both enjoyed each other's company. I loved the fact that we could explore parts of the island by car, since I was unable to drive. We drove west through the rain forest and passed small villages where the locals lived in huts in extreme poverty. I noticed that the children had distended bellies, a sign of malnutrition. The contrast between the life style of the tourists and the rest of the population was very upsetting to me. On the other hand, I found the locals to be generally courteous and warm, showing no resentment towards the tourists.

I returned to New York, my health vastly improved and happy with my vacation.

From that time on, I went to Puerto Rico every year to stay with Denise. We even became good friends and she often took me aside to talk to me. One day she told me her story: "I was married to a Frenchman who was an executive with Air France. We have two children who are now grown-up. After a few years, we divorced and soon afterwards I moved to Puerto Rico with the children. There I met a Puerto Rican whom I married. Together we bought the Inn. After a few months, I noticed that he started to disappear in the evenings. One night I followed him and found him in a dark nightclub with another woman. Soon afterwards I divorced him, but kept the Inn. One day, a young girl by the name of Jane arrived at the Inn. She had come to Puerto Rico to get an abortion, but the local hospital refused to perform it. I advised her to fly to the Virgin Island, but she did not have the money for the airfare. I offered to lend it to her with the understanding that she would return and would work for me to pay off the debt.

Jane kept her promise and soon afterwards we became lovers; it was a big turning point in my life," she said.

On my first visit, Jane was still tending bar. Next year, Jane had left. But as long as I knew Denise, she was involved with various women. Unfortunately, it turned out that her lesbian relationships were no more successful than her heterosexual ones. Often, in the morning, after she had been out the night before in her apartment which she kept in Old San Juan, I would see bruises on her arms. When I confronted her, she would say: "It's still preferable than having men cheating on you when you are married to them." It was difficult for me to understand that side of her, especially since she was a good-looking, extremely intelligent and interesting woman. I guess when it comes to sex, reason has nothing to do with intelligence.

Denise and I remained friends for many years to come and at one time she even offered me a job. I was tempted, but I never was quite ready to give up my New York life and move far away from my son, David. However, I felt flattered that she liked me because she normally did not mix with her other clientele.

There were many more Christmas vacations when I returned to stay with Denise because there are not many places in the world where one can step out of one's bedroom barefoot right onto the beach. Also, because I travelled alone the place was ideal, and I never ended up alone; nor did I have to eat dinner by myself, which I so dreaded. One year I joined three French Canadian school teachers whose French I could hardly understand, but they understood me. Another year I actually went down with a French friend from France who was enchanted with the place.

A year later, I met a very interesting couple who lived in Germany and they invited me to visit them in Bavaria which I actually did the following summer. In many ways, Bavaria reminded me of my childhood because the German countryside is reminiscent of Austria's. There were fields and fields of sunflowers glittering in the sunshine. The forests with pine trees reminded me of my childhood days when I spent the summers on the mountain with my friend Hasi, roaming through the forest, gathering wild strawberries and mushrooms and hoping to see deer. My hosts showed me around and despite my ambivalent feelings towards the Germans (the husband was Jewish) I did feel somewhat at home.

One of the many times I visited Denise, I was about to go to sleep when I felt something tickling my nose. I turned on the light and to my horror, I saw a lizard perched on my pillow. I screamed and woke up my neighbors who, seeing the lizard, grabbed my showercap, threw it over the animal, so that it would not escape and then took the pillow and dumped the lizard on the street. What a relief, but I did get frightened. When I told Denise about the incident the next day, she just laughed. I guess she was used to that sort of thing living on the beach.

A few years passed and I had not been back. When I called to say that I was again planning to visit, Denise told me that she had moved from the beach into town and told me what had happened: "It was out of season with very few people around, when I suddenly felt something cold touching my neck," she said. "I turned around and saw a man standing there with a gun pointing at me, asking me for all my money. I gave it to him because I obviously had no choice. But it convinced me that I could no longer stay by myself in my isolated Inn on the beach. Times had changed. I sold the inn and bought a charming place in Condado in the middle of town. It has a lovely pool and garden and you'll love it."

When I went the following year, I saw that she was so right. Even though I missed the beach, there was a bus that did take me back to her former place, which luckily had not changed, despite the new owners. I would go there in time for lunch on the patio, and could sunbathe and swim in the lovely blue water. When I returned to the Inn in the late afternoon, there were always people from all over the world sitting around the pool. Somehow Denise kept her old clientele despite her craziness, or perhaps because of it. It was not a typical "couple" place and I met a very lovely French girl there, Estelle, who I still see every year when I am in Paris.

I continued to go there many times at Christmas. One year when I was between jobs, Denise invited me down as her guest and wined and dined me. She took me to visit her lesbian friends and showed me a different side of San Juan. We even went to a lesbian nightclub, a new experience for me to see all the women dancing with each other. I was relieved that I was not being hit on by any of them. Denise must have told them that I was just a guest in her hotel.

Denise has since sold the Inn and retired to a house nearby. But before that happened, on my last visit there, we became estranged because of a minor misunderstanding. She was angry with me and refused to hear me out because I had accidentally neglected to lock the outside gate leading to the garden of the Inn. It was a simple oversight, but she never forgave me. I always think of her fondly even though she had a very irrational side to her.

Once again, I had to find a new place for my winter vacation.

I suddenly remembered that my old friend Sary, who I had met many years ago in Florence, had just moved to Florida and had previously invited me to visit with her. Here was my answer as to where I could spend some time in the winter.

Chapter XVII

Sary/Key West

In 1952, while travelling through Italy, my husband and I had met Sary and Lou under a Bernini sculpture in Florence. We were all taking photographs when we bumped into this English speaking couple. "We are on our honeymoon," they told us right away. By some strange coincidence, I noticed that they were wearing custom-made wedding rings identical to ours—the only difference was that theirs were made out of gold, whereas ours were made of silver. "We had them made on Eighth Street in Greenwich Village," they said. It turned out that they came from the same store. I was already married for a year at the time.

We felt an instant rapport while talking to each other, and also because of their identical choice of wedding rings. Lou was an executive in New York's garment center. He was of stocky and short build, and it turned out that he was of German descent. "My father has a farm with lots of animals in New Jersey," he told us. Sary, too, was of German descent, but she was six years old when she came to this country accompanied by her mother. Being a petite brunette, she must have come from a different ethnic background. She was working as a commercial artist when she met Lou. She still spoke a little German.

We decided to meet for a meal, hoping to find pizza. Pizza, being a Southern dish, was hard to come by in Northern Italy, we discovered; we were too naive in those days to realize that. Since Sary and Lou lived in nearby New Jersey, we exchanged phone numbers.

Once we returned to New York, we phoned and went to visit them in Clifton, New Jersey We had all loved the cappuccino in Italy and decided to try to duplicate it in Sary's kitchen. Espresso machines where one could foam the milk were not yet available for home use. We decided to improvise by foaming the milk in a blender—milk splattered all over Sary's kitchen; we could hardly stop it and were laughing hysterically. It was the beginning of a long friendship.

Over the years, Sary and I had children, Sary had three boys—I had one son. We continued to see each other until Sary and Lou moved to New Orleans, where Lou was offered a great promotion, but we still stayed in touch. Then, one day, I had a shocking phone call: "Lou has had a heart attack and has died. He was only 45 years old," Sary said, sobbing. "I am left a widow with three small boys, an elderly mother and my mother-in-law. There is nothing for me to do but pick up and move to a house in Florida, where I will be able to survive financially and bring the two mothers along and find them an apartment. Florida is cheaper than New Orleans."

She bought a house with a pool and soon afterwards, she invited me to come down during my Christmas/New Year's vacation. By this time, years later, I was already divorced and it was a wonderful opportunity to get away from the often lonely holidays in cold New York. This was the beginning of my many trips to visiting her in the winter and, often, she came to visit me in New York because she loved the theater. Soon afterwards Sary, who was always very well dressed and loved clothes, started to work full time at Saks Department store in Florida in their sportswear department. But she almost always managed to take some time off when I visited her.

One very cold New York winter, while I was temporarily unemployed, and because my old friend Sary living in Florida could not make herself free, I decided to fly to Key West on my own, where I had quite an adventure.

A friend in New York had told me to stay at a place called *The Boatel*, a rather fancy hotel right on the water. When I arrived there and discovered that the room rate was more than I had been quoted, I moved to a motel nearby. Entering the place, there was a pool which was surrounded by only men. I immediately realized that they were all gay. What was I to do? I decided to stay there for at least one night and look around the next day. I changed into my bathing suit and when I came out of my room, I was happy to spot a "straight" couple. When they saw me, they said: "Come and sit with us and have a drink; we have to stick together."

They turned out to be a delightful, elegant, extremely good-looking Canadian couple with a great sense of humor. They had a lot of empathy for me, realizing that it is not easy for a woman to travel alone and be thrown into a "gay" scene. They took me under their wing and arranged for us to have dinner together after watching the sunset; a nightly ritual in Key West, where locals and tourists get together, usually carrying a drink. When the sun sets over the horizon, everyone applauds and disappears in different directions.

Key West is very *Ernest Hemingway*-oriented to this very day. There are many bars on Duval, the main street, where he was supposed to have hung out with his friends. One of Key West's tourist attractions is the house where he used to live. I too visited it. A little tram took me around the town and stopped there.

I was most interested to see how and where Hemingway worked since he has been one of my favorite writers ever since I was a young girl. Hemingway's house was, as I remember it, a simple, unpretentious place with few pieces of furniture. Somehow I was not surprised considering his sparse way of writing.

After spending a few lovely days with my new-found friends, they told me: "Unfortunately, our holiday is over, but we are worried about you. What's going to happen to you with all the gay boys?"

I assured them that I would be all right. They insisted that we all have a farewell drink at the bar at the *Boatel*. "Maybe you'll meet someone in whose care we could leave you," they said.

It was almost as if they had made it happen. They asked a very attractive young man who was sitting alone at the next table to join us. Edward told us that he was a college graduate who had taken a job as a fisherman to earn some money while on vacation. He was working on a shrimp boat, but because of the North Easterner which had hit Key West, he was unable to go out in the bad weather.

"These storms usually last three days," he said.

I was very attracted to him; he looked like an overgrown college student with a great build. The feeling must have been mutual, because he asked me whether he could pick me up the next day so that we could have dinner together. The couple's last words were, "He is perfect for you," and they told Edward: "Take care of her for us."

As it turned out, I was extremely lucky to have his company for the remainder of his free time.

The rain was relentless; we couldn't go out. Edward would arrive drenched at my motel with bags of cooked shrimp because I had told him that they were my favorite. We stuffed ourselves with them every day. We also played Monopoly; it passed the time. Those three days were a strange experience, almost unreal in my memory; with the rain beating down on the window panes, morning turning into night.

Obviously, since we were both very drawn to each other, we became close during these days. Edward was good to be with and had a great sense of humor. We laughed a lot about our strange dilemma, hoping on the one hand that the rain would stop; on the other hand, knowing that he would have to work and we would have to part.

When my vacation came to an end, it was time to say good-bye; Edward declared everlasting love to me and bought me a ring with our initials carved inside. It was touching considering we were only together for such a short time. Before I left, we had a last drink at the *Boatel*, looking at the fishing boats, rocking in the water without a crew.

I took the bus back over the Keys, reliving my adventure as I looked out of the window, seeing the now clear skies with only a few clouds remaining.

Sary was waiting for me in Miami.

Chapter XVIII

Max's Kansas City/SoHo

One year after returning from one of my summer vacations, my boss, the president of the advertising agency, presented me with the news: "I am leaving the agency, my partners bought me out; I am going to breed race horses."

I was stunned and said to him: "Why didn't you tell me this before I left for Europe? I could have stayed on there instead of rushing back."

"I didn't know it myself," he said, "but if you like, I'll pay your fare back."

"Thanks," I said, "but now I don't feel like going back."

The truth of the matter was that before this incident, I had already wanted to change jobs, and a year earlier I had begun to make inquiries on how to go about getting a job in an art gallery. My wish came though in a strange way: For the past two years, after some of the artists left the Cedar Tavern, which they frequented up to that time, the art scene shifted to a bar/restaurant, called Max's Kansas City on Park Avenue South and 17th Street. The owner of Max's, Micki Ruskin, an attorney, loved artists, but had utter disdain for the bourgeoisie. He arranged the restaurant in such away that the artists were drinking at the bar in the front. A few privileged ones were getting free drinks, or running a tab which they rarely paid. Instead, Micki let them barter drinks in exchange for their paintings. The middle room was set up with tables where people had dinner and that's where he was able to make a profit. The back room was reserved for the "way out" people. Andy Warhol and other celebrities frequented that room, usually late at night. At 11 p.m., a disco opened upstairs where everyone was carefully screened by a bouncer and where only we, the "regulars," did not have to pay to get in. In general, Micki had strict rules regarding those he admitted to his discotheque or to his bar. I was one of three women who were not artists and who were allowed to drink at the downstairs bar. A friend of mine who had gone to law school with Micki introduced me to him when he first opened the restaurant—thus I was "privileged." Sary Dienes, an artist, who was about 75 years old at the time, chose to hang out with us at the bar. She was eccentric and wore many political buttons on her clothes. Francine and Valerie were the other two non-artists who soon became my friends. Micki only admitted certain people into his restaurant. If he didn't like the way they looked (too square), he would ask them: "Do you have reservations?" If the answer was "no," he said: "Sorry, we are completely booked." It is human nature to want to be somewhere where only a few select people are admitted. I actually had friends calling me, asking whether I would meet them outside to help them to get in.

Max's became my life. It was like a drug even though I did not "do drugs." Just being in this place where all the creative people gathered and where one had the most interesting conversations late into the night was my "drug." It enabled me to completely forget my humdrum existence and my 9-5 job. However, I never neglected my "motherly" duties and only went out, when David was older and when he was safely asleep, leaving him my telephone number in case of an emergency, since I was only five blocks away. He was 12 years old then and did not require baby sitters any more.

My best friend was Louis, a French cartoonist who lived in Greenwich Village. I was too shy to walk alone into Max's; therefore we would meet outside and would walk in together. But once inside, we mingled with the most contemporary well-known artists: Chamberlain, the sculptor, Larry Poons, the painter who had had a one-man show at the Metropolitan Museum, Dan Christensen, the painter who showed at the prestigious Emmerich Gallery. Alan Shields worked as a bus boy at Max's, but soon had a show with the Paula Cooper Gallery in SoHo. Writers, photographers, fashion designers and filmmakers came in nightly. Of course, in retrospect, I realize that many of these people were smoking marijuana or were doing LSD.

The sixties were not only a creative time, but it was also a time when women were sexually liberated for the first time. It was due partially to the birth control pill, but also because the feminist movement demanded equality in business and at the same time acknowledged that women are also sexual beings with the same needs and desires as men. Both women and men felt more sexually liberated because it was pre-AIDS.

At 11 p.m., Louis and I would dance at the disco upstairs late into the night. Getting up the next day was very difficult, but around 9 a.m. the next morning, I managed to religiously sit at my desk. Today I don't know how I was able to do it.

Terry, Max's bartender and I became friends and I took him to see his very first O'Neill play; he never forgot it, he was so thrilled. However, on the whole, except for Louis, this was a very flighty crowd. While I was flattered to meet all the famous artists, I rarely got to know any of them intimately, because I found them to be totally self-involved or bragging about their success.

One night, at the bar, I was talking to Ken Showell, the painter. "Do you know?" he said, "that SoHo has become the new artistic center?"

"Yes," I said, "I have read in the Times that Paula Cooper's Gallery has moved there. I have already gone to see her and I have asked her whether I could get a job with her. She told me: "I can only pay very little, but I'll let you know what I decide.""

Ken replied, "Go see Joan at O.K. Harris Gallery, run by Ivan Karp, and maybe she can help you to get a gallery job." I followed his advice.

"Go see Max Hutchinson, the only other gallery in SoHo," Joan told me. "I think he is looking for someone."

Max repeated what Paula Cooper had told me: "I can't pay you what you want."

Still, I had to make a living. It was supposed to be an honor to work in a gallery, but I could not afford the luxury. However, Max, the Australian gallery owner, and I parted with the understanding that if the gallery would make some money in the future he would get in touch with me.

A year later, just as I had lost my job at the advertising agency, I got a phone call from Max: "Come in and have lunch with me, I'll pay you a livable salary, $150 after taxes."

At lunch, I said to Max, not wanting to take the job under false pretenses, "Do you really want me? I have no experience in running a gallery, and I am always on the side of the artist."

"I'll guarantee that you will change your mind in one month," he answered. "I want you to work for me." He was very direct and did not beat around the bush.

I was thrilled: my career in the art gallery was launched. When people asked me: "How did you get your job?" I answered: "I got my job through Max's Kansas City," because at that time the slogan read: "I got my job through the New York Times." As things turned out, this was to become the most exciting time of my working career. I was getting paid for the very thing that I loved most. I was working in the art world in an area which was to become the new art center. I was sure of that, even though there were only three galleries in SoHo at the time. Today, there must be at least two hundred. Max, my boss, taught me everything from installing a show, how to deal with artists, collectors and critics. The artists were demanding and difficult; the collectors had to be cuddled and only wanted to deal with the gallery owner. I got along best with the critics. I always knew intuitively which was the best or most accomplished painting or sculpture in our exhibitions (this drove Max crazy). The critics were the ones who were able to verbalize this; they would explain the reasons to me and I was grateful to them for their input. I never learned to do this.

Since I was a good administrator and was responsible, two months after I had started working at the gallery, Max announced: "I am off to Australia to visit my ex-wife, my kids and my other gallery."

"How am I going to manage all by myself?" I asked him.

"You will do all right, you'll have help with the painting, installation and lighting for the next show. The German we just hired will help you and I'll leave my phone number with you and you'll do just fine."

It was like Max to give his employees a lot of responsibility; they would then live up to it. I respected him for that; I really liked him a lot. We had already spent many hours together, just the two of us; it was a good working relationship and we laughed a lot. We worked very hard building up the gallery, and if necessary, I often stayed late. Then Max would take out the bottle of Scotch after we closed the gallery. Although Max was not tall, he exuded a lot of strength; women were crazy about him because of his rugged Australian charm and his cockney-like accent. I managed to survive the month alone in the gallery, and I called Australia whenever I needed help or advice. I wrote down a long list of questions before I called him.

Working in the gallery afforded me a lot of perks. We were invited to every museum and gallery opening in the city. I was able to put myself together in a chic manner without spending a lot of money, and was seen and photographed at the openings of the Guggenheim Museum, the Whitney, the Museum of Modern Art. I was in my element.

This was the time when it was popular for people to "streak." I will never forget when Max streaked at the opening of Joan Mitchell's exhibition at the Whitney Museum. He did it in her honor because he liked her paintings tremendously. He stripped with another artist and in one second, they both ran around her paintings in the nude. The guards were so stunned that they couldn't believe what they were seeing, but before they knew what was happening, the two of them were dressed again. The next day, Joan came into the gallery. "You were wonderful, Max," she said. She felt honored and was certainly not mad. Max was pleased and we laughed a lot about the incident. I wish now we would have had a video camera to document the event.

After work on Saturdays, all of us who worked in galleries, and a lot of the artists in SoHo would get together at Fanelli's Bar. It was a 100-year-old bar owned by Mike Fanelli, the owner's son, who was at least 85 and who was like a father to us. It was the place to find out where "the" party was that evening. In those days, there was only one party where everyone got together because the art world was still small. Robert Rauschenberg who had a beautiful house on Lafayette Street would say: "Pass the word, I am throwing a big party tonight." There would be champagne and lots of wonderful food for everyone who attended.

Later on, there were many parties on Saturday nights and it was never the same as it was in the beginning when we were like a small family; we almost all knew each other and said hello when we met in the street or in the SoHo post office. Joan, who worked for O.K. Harris, and I would meet for lunch at the Spring Street Restaurant, and we would be the only ones there. Later on, the restaurant became so popular that it expanded into three rooms. We would also meet at Raoul's for a $1.50 spaghetti meal, where you had to walk through the kitchen to go to the bathroom. You still have to do this today, but it has become one of the chicest French restaurants in SoHo. Not many people in Manhattan had discovered SoHo at that time, but European museum directors heard about this avant-garde art center and frequented our galleries. These were new and exciting times where creativity blossomed in New York. Only the war in Vietnam darkened this era.

For almost five years, I worked hard in the gallery and gave it my best; they were the most satisfying times in my working career. I was well-known by everyone in the SoHo community and I felt good about myself and my newly acquired skills.

In 1972, just before I was planning to go to Europe for my vacation, I suddenly felt sick. I went to the doctor who examined me. Because he could not find anything wrong, he just gave me some codeine for my pain. "It's all right for you to leave for France and Greece," he said.

The next day I woke up with 104 degrees fever. With what little strength I had, I called the doctor. "Call the ambulance immediately," he said, "and go to New York University Hospital."

Instead, I called my friend Lois who picked me up and drove me there with her car. It turned out that I had infected fibroids. I was operated on that very night and had to have a hysterectomy.

Two days later, when I finally awoke, I remember my good friend Mary sitting there next to me sleeping. She must have been there for hours. I had to stay in the hospital for two weeks because a post-operative infection had developed. At the end of my stay, Mary once again was there for me and took me back to her house in New Jersey to convalesce.

Despite my surgery, I was not going to give up my planned vacation. Four weeks later, I left for Spain. The German guy who was working for us at the gallery took me to the airport to help me carry my luggage. My girlfriend Lois had rented a cottage with her two children on the Costa Del Sol, the sunny Southern coast. The cottage was attached to a very elegant luxury hotel, called "Atalaya Park." At lunch time, a gourmet buffet was set up next to the huge pool which was surrounded by palm trees and lush tropical flowers. Those were the days when you could still get a cheap flight to Spain and if you had a place to stay with friends, you could live on next to nothing. Lois had rented a car and we drove around all the wonderful little towns along the coast. After my two weeks in the hospital, the sun and the good food began to make me feel like my old self again.

One day when, as usual, we went food shopping at a small nearby village, we witnessed a funeral procession passing by the village square. The men of the village were carrying the casket on their shoulders. At the same time the church bells were ringing, letting the villagers know that someone had died. The scene reminded me of the medieval Spanish paintings hanging in Madrid's Prado museum.

All too soon my holiday was over, and I had to return to the Gallery and to New York. But I was already looking forward to my Christmas vacation.

As described in a previous chapter, I had started to spend my winter vacation in Martinique in my wonderful small hotel owned by local people.

It was the night before Christmas Eve around 5 p.m. I was sitting in the gallery waiting to close at 6 p.m. I had my ticket for Martinique and my traveler's checks in my purse, and was all ready for my week's vacation. Max, my boss, having just returned from one of his trips, walked into the gallery to wish me Happy Christmas. In his loft upstairs, where he was living, an assistant was working on some of his artists' slides. The door opened and one of our artists said to Max: "It's good to see you again, come on, I'll buy you a drink at Fanelli's bar."

It was on the tip of my tongue to say: "Please don't go Max, it's dark in the street and I am not comfortable sitting here alone," but I just didn't say it. I did not want to sound as if I was afraid sitting there when it was dark outside, but I should have listened to my vibes. I had a strange premonition.

Two minutes later, suddenly a young boy in a ski jacket walked in. Without saying a word, he took out a metal pipe and hit me on the head with a very heavy blow. I fell to the floor and he hit me a second time. "Stop," I yelled, "take some money out of my bag which is behind the desk, and run for your life because there is someone in the basement who is going to catch you."

This reverse psychology seemed to work, because I don't think he knew what he was doing; he was probably drugged and needed the money for a "fix." He took $20 out of my wallet and ran, leaving my ticket and the $500 worth of traveller's checks in my handbag. The whole incident was over in a flash. I dragged myself to the telephone to call Nina upstairs who ran to my rescue and found me lying on the floor in a pool of blood. After quickly calling the ambulance, she ran to get Max. It must have been a scene to remember; there was blood everywhere, even on the walls when Max walked in with the famous art critic Robert Hughes. To relax me, Robert massaged the back of my legs, while we were waiting more than one and a half hours before the ambulance finally arrived from Beekman Downtown. Luckily, I did not lose consciousness up to that point, and was able to ask them to call my current boyfriend, John, a physician. More about him in the following chapter.

When the ambulance arrived, I passed out and only remember arriving in the Emergency Room where a young doctor sewed up my scalp with thirteen stitches; they must have shaved my head before that. I was happy when I saw John's cowboy boots heading in my direction to take me home in a taxi. He was more upset than I was that someone could have done such a horrible deed. He stayed with me all night and took care of me. However, the next day, he admitted me to Roosevelt Hospital where I remained for three days over Christmas.

They took many tests, including an EEG to see that I did not suffer from brain damage. I was extremely lucky that after such a blow, all tests proved to be negative. Because all my hair had been shaved off in the Emergency Room, I had to wear a turban for some time. My friends who came to visit consoled me by saying: "You look chic." Of course, I felt terrible even though I was grateful that I was all right. My telephone rang endlessly. My artist friends in SoHo had heard about the mugging and they were very upset that such a terrible thing could have happened in our little peaceful artistic community. "Are you a movie star?" the nurses asked me because of the many telephone calls, visitors and the flowers I received. They were especially nice to me because they felt sorry for me that this terrible thing had happened during Christmas time.

When my father came to see me, I expressed concern about travelling all the way to Martinique after such an injury. I was grateful when he said: "What's the difference whether you sit two or five hours in a plane, if you insist on going at all?" Of course, I wanted to go. I knew my friends Iria and Hélène were waiting for me.

Two weeks later, with a scarf around my head, I left for Martinique. On the boat on the way to the village of Anse Mitan, I ran into my friend Iria who had no idea what had happened to me. I was supposed to meet her there two weeks earlier, but I had no way of reaching her to tell her about my mugging. She was horrified when I told her what had happened but overjoyed that I was all right and that I managed to join her.

After my horrible experience, it took me weeks to recover emotionally. I had help from an artist who believed that telling the story over and over again would diminish the horror. She was not wrong. But nevertheless to this day, around Christmas time, I become nervous about staying out late when I am by myself. I am aware that many people are alone and become very desperate at that time of the year. And I too feel sad.

Chapter XIX

Dr. John

One evening, I was waiting for a friend at the bar in the Fifth Avenue Hotel; she never showed up, but I found myself sitting next to an exceptionally attractive man, about my age, wearing cowboy boots which I always find very sexy because they remind me of romantic Wild West cowboy movies. He was tall, had a tanned chiselled face, sharp features, dark hair and sensitive hands, which always tell me a lot about a person. We started talking and after a while, I asked him: "What do you do?"

"You won't believe it, but I am an unemployed doctor. Have you ever heard of such a thing?" he asked.

"No," I said, "how come?"

"Well, it's a long story; I have just come east from California in order to visit my kids who are living with my ex-wife here in New York. So far, I haven't been able to find a job because I don't want to open a private practice here. Believe it or not, it's not easy if you aren't attached to a hospital in New York. Thus, at the moment, I am living upstairs in this hotel."

He was so witty, had a wonderful sense of humor, and a boyish quality that I was immediately drawn to him. We arranged to meet again and it was the beginning of a long-standing loving relationship. Shortly afterwards, John got a job as a physician in a clinic. He hated it there, and he got very depressed treating sick and poor drug addicts. Soon I noticed that his drinking had become excessive. After a while, he stopped calling me and, swallowing my pride, I decided to call him.

"I am sick," he said.

I immediately rushed to see him at the hotel and found him completely incoherent. I could have been angry, but you can't be angry if someone is addicted, and besides, I owned John a debt.

Now it was my turn to take care of the situation. Funny how things happen in life. I would have done it anyway: I was in love with him.

"I am taking you to Roosevelt Hospital. I have already made an appointment," I said.

"I'll go," he mumbled, "but if they ask me what my profession is when I am being admitted, I am out of there."

I explained to him that the staff had promised me that they would refrain from asking him any questions. Unfortunately, there had been a change of shift and when we arrived at the hospital, the promise was not kept.

Ten minutes later, we were having a drink at the bar at O'Neil's across the street from the hospital. I felt helpless, desperate, but determined to help him. I cared too much for him. The next day, I called my doctor: "I need your help," I said and explained the difficult situation.

"Bring him to my office and we will get him over to the hospital in a wheelchair. I will make all the necessary arrangements," he said.

We took a taxi to the doctor's office and on the way John begged me to get him a drink. I was sick to my stomach, having to do it. We stopped at a liquor store, but I knew it was the only way to get him to the doctor. I was afraid he would jump out of the taxi while I was getting the vodka. I rushed out of the store and I thought, "I must get him admitted at all costs."

Finally we made it, and with my doctor's help, we succeeded to admit him to the alcoholic detoxification floor of the hospital, where they made an exception and gave him a private room. It only took a few days of librium injections to sober him up. I went to visit him almost every day after work.

"You are just in time for 'Happy Hour,'" he told me.

It was funny how the hospital handled this. They brought in a trolley with an ice bucket, various juices, lemons and limes; the only missing ingredient was the alcohol. John was always happy to see me, but I was shocked when he told me: "At the end of this little adventure, when I get discharged, my aunt is going to treat me to a week at Club Med because I will need a vacation."

"John," I said, "if you go to Club Med where wine is served with every meal, you and I are through; you either go to a rehab center, a 'funny farm' as you call it, and where the hospital wants to send you, or you go to a psychiatrist who specializes in addiction, or it will all have been for nothing."

He acted like a kid and assured me: "I won't drink, I just need to relax on the beach."

I was very upset and sad to lose him, but I knew what I had to do for my own sanity. When John got back, he called me: "Now what?" he asked, waiting for me to say: "You can move in with me."

I felt terribly conflicted, but I knew that it would never work and that he would start drinking again. Instead I said: "Now you have to move into the Chelsea Hotel."

That was the last I ever heard from John. I still think of him often, miss him and sometimes wonder whether I had been too uncompromising at the time, because I cared for him deeply.

Chapter XX

Randall

I met Randall at a 57th Street art gallery. I don't remember now how we started talking, probably looking at a painting at the same time and admiring it. We were sharing our impressions and must have been in agreement because before we left the gallery, we exchanged telephone numbers. As is rarely the case in New York, Randall actually called me. I felt very flattered since he was extremely good-looking—a strong, handsome face, and even though not tall, there was a presence about him. He was at least fifteen years younger than I was, but he seemed very mature for his age; also he treated me as though I was a part of his peer group. He had told me at the gallery: "I am a commercial artist, but I also paint when I have a chance and I love to play the piano."

As we got to know each other better, he helped me in many ways, such as rearranging my apartment when I had the painters, or going shopping with me when I was looking for a new couch. Then he would jokingly say: "Your son should be helping you, but I am happy to do it for you."

His parents, who lived in New Jersey, did not seem to appreciate him; especially his mother was most critical of his lifestyle. Maybe because he was not as successful as his rich brother who lives in California and who is married and has children. Maybe because he was gay; he certainly did not look it. He had no gay mannerisms. There was a moment in our relationship when he hinted: "I would really want to make love to you." Even then, long before AIDS, I didn't think it was a good idea.

Shortly after we met, we ran into each other at one of the Gotham Book Shop's book-signing parties, celebrating the publication of a new book. There Randall introduced me to a new-found friend, Robert. "You two will have a lot in common," he said. Robert just came back from living a year in France, you two can speak French together."

The three of us got along so well that we became good friends. For years we went to art gallery openings, had dinners at each others' house and eventually travelled together. (I have described our trips to Martinique and Mexico in other chapters.)

At the time I was working at the art gallery in SoHo and I had made friends with some of the art critics with whom I always got along very well. Randall had invited me to an exhibition of his paintings in a New Jersey library. I asked one of the current New York Times critics: "As a favor, can you review my friend's show?"

He actually did come and gave Randall a glorious review. Randall was thrilled and he xeroxed the review and distributed the xeroxes all through his parents' house on Greenwood Lake in New Jersey so that they would find it when they got home. He badly wanted their approval. However, they were not as excited as he was. His mother was really not an easy person. One day, she went skating on the pond and the ice broke. Luckily for her someone was able to rescue her.

Shortly after that incident, Randall bought a house on the same lake as his parents. Because it was only accessible by boat, his house was on the other side of the lake, it was also very isolated. When my birthday came around in August, he offered to give me a big party. "You can invite all your friends or whoever you want," he generously said. These parties became a yearly event for a few summers. They were particularly wonderful because it was August, and we were able to swim in the lake. The guests had to arrive at the Yacht Club at the other end of the lake. Then they had to call the house and Randall would fetch them by boat. We all brought a dish or wine and Randall provided the birthday cake. I remember one year when my friend Olivera, who was always on a diet, jumped into a boat and rowed out to the middle of the lake to avoid being talked into eating the cake. For me these parties were unforgettable, especially since my son David and his wife-to-be Steff also were able to come to one birthday party. It was such a good, warm feeling to see all my friends together. The house had a big deck and that's where we would lie in our bathing suits in deck chairs, jumping into the lake when it got too hot. The disco music was always playing and, if we felt like it, we got up to dance. The whole setting was magical because it was inaccessible and private. The house was primitive and we had to use an outhouse. We were all very amused by this. Sometimes Randall's parents or a neighbor would drop in to wish me a happy birthday.

As the evening approached, we were able to watch the sun set over the now still lake, the sky turning into a myriad of colors—a reminder of my days in Mexico long ago. One of the most memorable moments at one of the parties occurred at the end of a perfect day: Randall got the boat to take us back to land. It was already dark and as I was getting into the boat, my handbag slipped off my shoulder and fell into the lake. Randall, who saw what had happened and heard me give out a cry, immediately jumped into the lake and luckily was able to rescue my bag. Everyone applauded.

There came a day when Randall's life changed drastically. His long-time relationship with Robert came to an end. I believe he became a big drug user and as a result, he began to move more and more within the gay community. We drifted apart and only occasionally, when it was his birthday, he would invite me to his loft in SoHo, along with his family and his "straight" friends. I did not hold it against him, but I continued to see his friend Robert even though the two of them had long ago parted.

A few years later, two of Randall's friends who ran a SoHo art gallery and who I had previously met, told me: "We saw Randall on the street; he looks awful. He has lost weight and we presume that he is HIV positive."

I was terribly shocked and upset and decided to call him. The machine said: "I have gone to California to visit my brother; if you want to reach me, here is my telephone number." I called. He couldn't have been more pleased to hear my voice.

"I am O.K.," he said, obviously lying. "I am having a show of my paintings in SoHo in March, and I'll see you there. I'll send you an invitation. So nice of you to call. Look forward to seeing you."

Robert and I went to the opening. We went together for moral support. On the way Robert said to me: "I am so terrified to see him, so thin and ill." He didn't have to worry. Randall was not at his opening. Only his family and his paintings were there. He was in St. Luke's Hospital, we were told. A video camera was set up, and we spoke to Randall from the gallery, telling him how much we liked his paintings and wishing him well. I wonder whether he ever heard us. He died the next day.

Chapter XXI

Martinique

The first time I spent my Christmas vacation in Martinique, I fell in love with the island and its people. It is a mixture of the Caribbean and France with the gentlest people who, in addition to their "patois," also speak French. They are very handsome, rather slim, and "café au lait" in color. The very first time I had gone to Anse Mitan, a small village across from the main town, Fort de France, which can be reached by two ferries, I went with my friend Iria. We were met at the boat by a whole group of locals who immediately invited us to a party in a garden just across from the ferry; we could hear the sound of music. We were hesitating, but one of them introduced himself as the Hotel owner's son.

He said, "My parents knew you were coming from New York and are expecting you; we came to meet you to help you with the luggage."

We put our luggage down and joined the party, as tired as we were from our flight on Air France from New York. This is just the way it was in this small village where everyone knew each other.

When we finally checked into our modest hotel, the owners warned us right away: "Don't go out with anyone from the big city: Fort de France. These people could be dangerous."

My room was a small hut behind the main building of the hotel. On the way there, we passed chickens and a small vegetable garden. Laundry was hanging all over the place. It certainly was primitive, but my room had a clean bed and I even had a shower. When it was dinner time, however, it was a very different story. People came from all over the island for the marvelous gourmet food for which our hotel was well-known. It was served on the terrace facing the sea and we enjoyed every single course. That first night, we dropped into our beds totally exhausted, but happy.

The next morning, we were awakened very early by the crowing of the cock, but we managed to fall back to sleep. Breakfast was served on the terrace and it was extra ordinary. I had never seen such luscious fruit: fresh pineapple, mangoes, papayas and bananas. There was also fresh coffee and the croissants tasted just the way I remembered them in Paris. The next day, on the beach, I ran into Marco who I was introduced to the day we arrived. He was the owner's son, Ernest's best friend. He was thrilled that I spoke French. "Most Americans don't speak anything but English," he said.

As far as I remember, I had never before in my travels, had any strong inclination to start a love affair with a local person. I always felt that these affairs were too superficial and "same time next year" never appealed to me. But from the moment I met Marco, I felt that he was very special. He seemed extremely gentle and sensitive besides being good looking. He had soulful eyes, dark hair and a fine slim build which also appealed to me. We were both immediately attracted to each other. He did in no way come on strong, which I liked, but asked me hesitantly whether I would like to meet him the next evening after dinner. The very fact that he said: "I won't come into the hotel, but I'll wait for you on the beach after you have had your dinner," showed me that he did not want to be indiscreet.

The next evening, as promised, Marco waited for me in front of the hotel on the beach. We had no problem communicating with each other in French. I felt that he could teach me many things about the island and I learned more from him than from any guide book. Later on, when we went swimming at night, and there was a full moon, he warned me about sharks in the water and other dangers that could befall me. He made me feel protected and I felt very loving towards him. Not surprisingly, we became lovers fairly soon. He was just as gentle in his love making as he was in all his other actions towards me. Of course, I had no illusions about a future with him, since he was so much younger than I and since we had such different backgrounds, but I became most interested in his daily life. We exchanged many stories and became good friends, as well as lovers. He wanted to know all about New York, and I am sure that it would have been a thrill for him to visit me.

During my stay, we visited the local museum which was dedicated to Empress Josephine, Napoleon's first wife who was a native of Martinique. We read every single love letter Napoleon had written her, some of them were surprisingly candid sexually for the time in which they were written. While no one was looking in the museum, we were holding hands and felt that we, too, were lovers. On another occasion, Marco showed me the apartment, where he was living with his parents which was spotless and nicely furnished. I even met his mother, who was very charming and accepting of me. I don't remember meeting his father who was the captain of the ferry which went back and forth between Fort de France and Anse Mitan.

At one point, Marco told me that he loved me. It sounds like the typical "get the tourist to fall in love with you" story, but I felt at the time that he really meant it because it showed so clearly in his love making. His tenderness and his total giving of himself touched me in a very special way.

As I was leaving, I wondered whether Marco would again be there for me should I be lucky enough to return the following Christmas.

After my first year's vacation in Martinique, I so raved about the island to my two friends Robert and Randall, that they decided to join me the following year for the Christmas holidays. They, in turn, told me: "We have two other friends, Max and Leon, who are also interested in spending the holidays there."

It was decided that I would make the arrangements for the airline and hotel reservations for all four of them. Randall and Robert were to join us a few days later. Max and Leon were to meet me at Kennedy Airport at the gate leaving for Martinique.

I was in the waiting area before boarding my plane when two men came over to me and said: "You must be Brigitte; Randall described you with your white hair and young face." That's how Max and Leon became my friends, and we still keep in touch today, even though they have since moved to Florida. I had reserved a room for them at my simple hotel, the "Caridade." By the time we arrived there, we were tired, but hungry. The four of us had dinner together in the hotel's dining room. All I could think of was: "Will Marco be waiting for me again on the beach this year?" He told me that he hoped that I would return again. I told my companions nothing about Marco, but after I gulped my dinner down, I was so excited about my possible reunion with Marco, that I simply told them: "I have plans." They were curious: here I had just arrived, they must have thought; how could she have plans? It was not till the next evening that I had to tell them the truth because I did disappear every evening after dinner. Being broad-minded, they were most amused. They never actually were to meet Marco.

A few days later, Randall and Robert arrived while we were sitting in the dining room eating our dinner. Because I was unable to get a room for them in our hotel, I found them a nearby Bed and Breakfast with a nice local lady.

The five of us spent most of our days on the beach in front of our hotel. Every afternoon, at around five o'clock, the disco music started to play in a small café right on the beach; Randall named it "Fantasy Land." We would be sitting on the beach in our bathing suits when the music began. It gave us the signal to get a drink in the café. The locals gathered there as well and we all danced with each other. It was like being at a party. Randall, who I have described in an earlier chapter who was an artist so loved the place and he painted a big sign which he posted on the outside of the lovely café which read "Fantasy Land."

That year, we rented a jeep and drove through the rain forest to the other side of the island to the top of the mountain, to the famous ranch, called "Plantation de Leyritz," where the French Prime Minister, Giscard D'Estaing and President Ford had held an important summit meeting in 1974. We felt honored that we were able to have lunch in an historical place where two world leaders had met.

After dinner, my evenings were always reserved for Marco who I found to be as loving as ever. Nothing seemed to have changed between us. I always wondered whether we would feel the same toward each other in future years.

Sadly enough, it was soon time to return to New York and work. It was difficult to part from Marco, but I was happy that my friends too had enjoyed the island.

Martinique drew me back every year. The following year, my friend, Helène, came with me. In the evenings before dinner, we often walked along the beach to the elegant Hotel Meridian in Anse Mitan, watching the magnificent sunset on the way. The Hotel was very luxurious, especially compared to our little hotel. One evening we were walking through the lobby when I noticed a couple with their arms crossed, on the other side of the lobby, staring at me. I looked up and I could not believe what I saw: there was my favorite cousin, Jules and his wife, Jeanette, who lived in Paris. I gave out a scream and everyone in the hotel lobby looked at me. They later admitted to me that they were not as surprised as I was because they thought they had seen me before walking in the street with Marco.

"Could this possibly be my cousin?" Jules had said to Jeanette. Then they put it out of their minds. Still it was the most extraordinary coincidence to meet them so unexpectedly. I couldn't have been happier to be with them. The next evening, they invited me for dinner at their elegant Hotel, the Bacoua, beautifully furnished with antiques, where the lobby was decorated with exotic tropical flowers and plants. During dinner, a Martiniquain group performed a Folklorique ballet, dressed in their local costumes.

A few days later, my cousin and his wife went back to Paris, and I was left to reflect how strange life is and that these coincidences happen in far-away places. It reminded me of the time, years before, when I had met my friend Lois on the "croisette" in Cannes.

Again I was sad to have to leave Marco behind, for our relationship had miraculously remained the same in spite of the long time lapses. I immediately started dreaming of spending yet another Christmas on my beloved island.

I was to return to Martinique for another two years around Christmas. Without any communication during the year, except for one post-card which read: "I love you," Marco was still waiting for me on the beach at approximately the same time every year. It really was wonderful seeing each other again. The following year, because the Inn had no room for me for one night, the hotel made arrangements to put me up next door in a house with a cathedral ceiling which looked as though Charles Addams had drawn it. When Marco and I went in, we discovered something flying near the roof. It was the sound of an animal's wings flapping. I was terrified, but Marco put his arms around me to protect me and to comfort me. I now don't remember how we ever got rid of the bat. All I do know and remember is that Marco was always there for me. We still had the same strong feelings for each other. Too soon, my vacation was once again over. Marco took me to the airport in a taxi. Somehow that last year, I had a premonition that we would never see each other again, I was puzzled, but it turned out that I was almost right.

The following Christmas, the dollar was so weak that changing it into francs made Martinique too expensive for me. As much as I hated not to see Marco and my idyllic island which reminded me of France: Fort de France, with its little cafés and Parisian stores, I simply could not afford it.

I chose to return to Puerto Rico instead because it was much less expensive. But I would never forget Marco.

The currency exchange had since in those days long ago remained unfavorable versus the dollar and, therefore, Martinique was an expensive island; I unfortunately could not return to my magic island and see Marco again for years to come.

Time passed and I sometimes wondered what had become of my youthful love. Was he a happily married middle-aged man with a lot of lovely "café au lait" children? Had he ever mentioned my name to anybody? What did he remember about me?

For my part, our time together will always remain a most beautiful memory. I still have a photograph of him taken on the beach that first wonderful year.

Chapter XXII

Mexico

I have told the story countless times to friends, and it is a lesson to everyone who is in a relationship with another person.

In 1957, during my vacation on the island of Mallorca, Spain, with Leonard, my then-husband, we met an English journalist, John, with whom we became very friendly. We spent a great deal of time together, the three of us. After a while, he asked us whether we would look after his friend, Ted, who is also a journalist and who was planning to emigrate to the United States a few weeks after our return. We were happy to do this and when Ted called us, we invited him for dinner. He loved our apartment and we loved him. He was tall and good-looking, extremely polite, a typical English gentleman.

He told us: "My wife, Sheila, and our daughter, Jane, aged five, will be joining me shortly." On our return, he had found an apartment for them quite near us. I met Sheila who was petite, thin and pretty with blue eyes and mousy colored hair, a little distant, but I liked her; we became good friends because our children were about the same age. We saw each other almost every day after the kids came home from school and we would then take them to the park or to a coffee house. We also saw each other as couples. It's not always easy to find other couples with whom one is compatible, but this was exceptional; the four of us had fun together.

About two years later, Sheila called me one day in tears, "You can't believe what happened last night: Ted came home from work, as usual." (By this time he was working for the *National Enquirer* as a journalist and kept it a secret because it was not exactly prestigious.)

"'Can I have a beer, dear?' he said.

"'Here you are, dear,' I replied.

"A few moments later, without any argument whatsoever, he looked at me and said: 'I am leaving you, dear.' And that was it," Sheila said in tears. "We have never had an argument or an unpleasant discussion in our eleven years of marriage. So you can imagine, how it came out of the blue."

I tried to console Sheila: "You are young and pretty, and you will find someone else in time."

However, I was so shocked that I called Ted right away and told him: "No matter how you feel about Sheila, you must see your daughter. She is just a little girl and she is crazy about you."

We were good enough friends and I could say that to him. He agreed and he kept his promise.

The next day, it just so happened that while I was waiting to play tennis, a school teacher tried to pick me up. "I am married," I said, "but I have a friend who just separated from her husband. Why don't you give me your phone number, and if she is interested, she will call you."

I found out later that he had bought her a cup of coffee and immediately had tried to go to bed with her. Needless to say, she was then very vulnerable and felt horribly put down and insulted. In retrospect, it could have been that date which caused her to break down and it must have been the catalyst to what transpired the next day.

Sheila and I had been in the habit of calling each other almost every morning after our children went off to school. The morning after that date, I called and called her, and the phone kept ringing. Finally, Jane, Sheila's daughter's little voice said: "I can't wake my mommy."

"That's ridiculous," I said. "Keep trying."

She came back. "No," she said crying, "I can't."

"Jane," I said, "Don't go away, stay where you are. I'll be right over."

"O.K.," she said, still sobbing.

I remember that day so vividly. It was pouring rain when I took the crosstown bus to her apartment. Jane opened the door and there was Sheila, breathing heavily, a bottle of gin and an empty vial of pills next to her bed. I had seen a sign in the lobby with the name of a physician who lived one floor below Sheila's apartment. I rang his bell. I was in a panic. What if he is not home? What will I do? Would it be too premature to call an ambulance?

"Please come and see my friend upstairs," I begged, explaining the situation.

"I can't come," he said, "I have German measles."

"I don't care if you have the plague, you must look at her," I replied.

"Give me a couple of minutes and I'll get dressed," he said.

He took one look at her and said, "Call the police immediately; they will contact the ambulance."

Sheila was taken to St. Vincent's Hospital where she was admitted to intensive care. I called my husband and he called Ted. For a few days, it was not certain whether she would pull through. Meanwhile, I took Jane to my house until Ted picked her up, as promised.

When Sheila was finally discharged, I noticed that she had changed a lot. She seemed like a different person. Our relationship changed too because I think that I reminded her of the bad times she had just gone through. We saw less of each other and I decided to let some time pass by, hoping that she would contact me.

One day, she did call: "I am going to Mexico to get a divorce," she told me.

I saw her off, and she took Jane with her. When she returned, she told me: "I am moving to Mexico, I love it there."

Occasionally, I would get a card and then a wedding announcement arrived with a letter. "I married a Spanish surgeon, twenty years my senior. I live in a beautiful house in Mexico City. I am very happy."

I congratulated her, wished her all the best, and did not hear from her again until five years later.

Suddenly, one day, I got a phone call: "I am at Kennedy Airport in transit from London on the way to Mexico City," Sheila said. "Why don't you come and visit us?"

I was pretending that I did not resent the fact that she had totally disappeared for five years. "It happens that I have just lost my job at the gallery. I have decided to take a sort of Sabbatical," I said. "My friend Helène had rented an apartment in Puerto Vallarte for July and August, and I have been thinking of joining her. I have never been to Mexico, and would, of course, love to visit you during my trip."

That's how it happened that I fell in love with Mexico.

Sheila met me at the airport and chauffeured me to her house which was situated in the most elegant section of Mexico City. It was filled with antiques and had a large, beautiful garden full of exotic plants. A maid answered the door. To top it off, Sheila had a cook as well. Her husband, Pedro, was a distinguished looking tall man. I was in awe of him. As a surgeon at a big hospital, he was very busy during the day. We did not see much of him, except at dinner time. We had the days free to go sightseeing and Sheila was a great hostess.

She showed me the city in the best possible way; we visited the outstanding National Museum of Anthropology which is world famous, not only for its exhibitions, but also for its outstanding architecture. It is situated in the middle of Chapultepec Park—a wonderful setting. There we ate lunch in the outdoor restaurant adjacent to the Museum. We visited the art galleries in the Zona Rosa, where one could walk around since it is somewhat like a mall. I was happy that Sheila and I once again had become friends.

Perhaps my greatest experience was to see the large crowd of people, mostly women, walking on their knees and, at the same time, praying for the health of their loved ones outside the ancient Basilica of Guadelupe. Many brought flowers as a tribute. I had taken a bus tour and our next stop was to see the Pyramids of San Juan Teotihuacan, believed to having been built around the first century B.C. or as early as 300 B.C. abandoned in 600 A.D. These are the remains of the great Indian culture, destroyed by the Spanish invaders. I was overwhelmed by the magnitude and achievements of these early Indian natives of Mexico.

After a marvelous week, Pedro suggested that I should see Guadalajara, the second biggest city in Mexico. His daughter from a previous marriage and her husband had invited me to stay with them and met me at the airport. Much smaller than Mexico City, it is an enchanting city with beautiful architecture and, luckily, not nearly as polluted as Mexico City. It has one of the most famous and huge outdoor markets. I couldn't resist buying hand-woven blankets, all kinds of baskets and other treasures. My hosts were a charming young couple who lived in an ultra-modern spartan house; they owned avant-garde paintings which I helped to hang to their best advantage. They were most grateful for this, but in turn I was grateful that they showed me the city and its surroundings. They drove me to a lake community where the locals spend week-ends in the summer; there I got the feeling what it would be like to live in that town because I had always felt that I might be able to live in Mexico. I love its culture and its people.

I returned to Mexico City, where I had left my belongings with Sheila, before taking the bus to Taxco. I wanted to explore this small town, famous for its old churches and artifacts by myself. I was lucky to find a small room in a pension with a fantastic view of the whole town since the town is built into a hillside. It is renowned for its silver mines and I could not resist buying some presents. I stayed a few days, but unfortunately it started to rain non stop. With the water running down into its cobble stone streets, I was soaked through when getting on the bus which was to take me to Cuernavaca.

I had previously arranged to meet Sheila and Pedro in Cuernavaca, another small town near Mexico City. We were to get together in "Las Mananitas," one of the most famous restaurants in Mexico. It was curious that this restaurant thrived in what was then a very small insignificant place. After my third-class bus ride with Mexican peasants who travelled with their chickens and where the bus stopped at every village, I was soaked through and looked like a gypsy when I arrived at this posh restaurant. Furthermore, at one point our bus was waved down by the Mexican police and we had to raise our hands to be searched. They let us go, but I was getting even more soaked. Obviously, they didn't find what they were looking for and left.

I felt embarrassed when the doorman, all dressed in white—even his gloves were white—greeted me at the entrance of the restaurant. I passed him quickly and disappeared into the elegant ladies' room where I managed to change out of my wet clothes after I dried myself with the Restaurant's towels. I was hoping that none of the elegantly dressed ladies would walk in while I stuffed my wet clothes into a plastic bag. Soon I emerged into the garden, looking half-way decent, where Sheila and Pedro were waiting for me. They were sitting at a table surrounded by the most delicate flower arrangements.

There were bird cages hanging from the trees with the sound of birds chirping away. It looked like a Hollywood movie set. Suddenly when we looked around, we saw Peter O'Toole, the famous English actor, at the next table getting up to greet a beautiful young man whom he embraced heartily. The last time I had seen this charismatic actor was in the movie "Lawrence of Arabia." I will always remember his wonderful performance and thus I was excited sitting so close to such a famous and remarkable actor.

After our wonderful lunch together, Sheila and Pedro drove me back to Mexico City. As I had told Sheila on the phone, I had decided to take the summer off after working for so many years. Since Mexico was very inexpensive and I temporarily had no earnings, I was ready to take the apartment which Helène had rented for me in Puerto Vallarte.

A few days later, I flew there and Helène was waiting for me at the airport. She had rented a two-room apartment for me for $5.00 a day right on the town beach. It had a sit-in kitchen with the typical Mexican woven chairs, a guest room, a bathroom and a balcony. It was adjacent to Helène's apartment which faced the beach. Mine faced the colorful street and I was able to watch the natives going about their everyday business and enjoyed seeing a great variety of locals milling around, such as Mexican Indians in colorful costumes bringing their wares to the local beach. In addition, we were in a perfect location, walking distance to the village which was then still lovely. (Now it has become too touristy with high risers and big hotels.) I couldn't have been happier. I was most impressed by the Mexicans' artistic accomplishments for which they got a mere pittance, such as wood carvings and colorful paintings.

I spent two happy months there. Often we cooked our dinner consisting of the red snappers which we watched the fishermen catch right in front of our house early in the morning. We bought the fish for pennies. Helène and I usually cooked our meals together, read a lot and played scrabble when it rained. During the day, we went swimming and in the evening we sometimes had dinner in town.

One day I received a telegram from my father, asking me to reserve a room for him. He was staying in San Miguel de Allende, an artistic town, in-land, which I had also visited, but did not like very much, mostly because of the high altitude which made breathing difficult and also because the many American expatriates there were very cliquish. My father wrote that he missed the ocean. We were eating our dinner when suddenly my father and his wife walked in. I had reserved a room for them in a small hotel nearby and it was nice to have them around. We often went to the beach together in a nearby hotel situated right on the ocean, which in those days had not as yet been discovered by the tourists. The beach in front of our house was full of little restaurants and consequently many people hung around after their meals. There was one restaurant called "Dirty Dick's" where everyone gathered at "Happy Hour" to watch the fabulous colorful sunsets which Mexico is famous for. During the two months I was there, I only met three outstandingly interesting people, all of them from Denver, Colorado. A brilliant photographer, David, and two of his friends, who were also in the arts. One of them was David's ex-girlfriend, Debby, the other one was Katherine, David's best friend. All of them were as handsome as models out of a fashion magazine; they were wonderfully dressed in a very casual way. From the moment I saw David and our eyes met, we were incredibly attracted to each other. It was not just a physical attraction. There was an instant sense of intimacy and understanding between us which is very rare in life.

A few days later, David, who was a professional photographer, said to me: "I want to photograph you." We discovered this fabulous uninhabited villa, with palm trees and lush exotic plants in its garden, an ideal setting for David to take photographs. We spent the whole day together, David taking many photographs of me. One of the photographs was so outstanding that he enlarged it and sent it to me; it is still hanging in my bedroom. He captured a special part of my personality.

David, his female companions and I were together almost every day for about two weeks. They also met my father, who found them as charming as I did. We became like a secrete little family—the four of us. The reason I enjoyed their company so much was because, contrary to the few other tourists I had met, they were all personally involved in the arts: Katherine was a painter and Debbie was a stage designer. It was a pleasure to be with people who had a highly developed aesthetic sense.

Still, I was surprised when one day both of the girls turned to me and said: "We will soon have to part and we want you to have a present from us: we shall leave you and David alone and you two can then fulfill your great mutual attraction."

This left me speechless, but that is how David and I became lovers for one single wonderfully magical night. They left the next day.

Long after I left Puerto Vallarte, I could not get David out of my mind. The feeling must have been mutual, because he sent me two of his beautifully creative photographs of landscapes from Colorado. He also sent me an Al Jarreau record which he thought I would enjoy. I remained infatuated with him for a long time and could not get him out of mind. Somehow, for one reason or another, we never saw each other again, but even now, many years later, I sometimes think of him and wonder what would have happened if we had seen each other again under other circumstances. As it is, it has served as a reminder of how one person can make a difference.

On my way home, I stopped off in Mexico City to say good-bye to Sheila and to collect my things. When I finally landed at JFK, three months later, my friend Gaït was luckily waiting for me. I looked like a donkey with my blankets slung over my shoulder, carrying my baskets. She was laughing when she saw me and we had a lot to talk about. When I think back, that first time in Mexico had been a wonderful, memorable experience. Today it would cost a great deal to travel there for three months. I was lucky to have done it then when it was still possible to do it for little money. But I knew that I would return some day soon.

After I returned from Mexico for the very first time, I decided that I was now in a position to offer my services to a travel agency as an outside sales person.

I walked into a travel agency across the street from my house and I said to the nice Italian owner: "With my vast experience and with my many friends who like to travel, I feel that I can bring in some business."

The owner, Sal, immediately liked the idea and suggested: "I'll give you 40% of the commissions."

"No," I said, "Fifty-fifty."

He agreed reluctantly, and thus I became an outside sales representative for the next twenty years. I kept my part of the bargain and although I made little money, what really paid off was the fact that Sal was nice enough to put me on the IATA list, which enabled me to get a 75% discount on most airlines. I also got preferred treatment and discounts in many hotels around the world. This made it possible for me to travel even more widely since my air fares were ridiculously inexpensive.

Owner of "Max's Kansas City" showing money received from artists' auction to save his restaurant. (Photo courtesy Benno Friedman)

Chapter XXIII

End of My Soho Days
Tour Guide Through S. America

Meanwhile, back in New York, my evenings at Max's Kansas City continued, but they were being threatened by the fact that Micki Ruskin, the owner of the restaurant, had opened a second restaurant uptown which did not make it and he was running out of money. In order to save Max's, the artists decided to donate art works for an auction to raise the money. The auction was held at a Soho gallery. Because most of the artists were well known, it was a great success and a considerable amount of money was raised. Instead of taking the money to pay off his debts, Micki decided to throw a big party at his restaurant to thank the artists. The sign outside read: "Restaurant closed for a private party." It was like Micki to be unrealistic to do this and, of course, we all had a good time. However, it was the beginning of the end for the place and a great loss for me.

After Max's finally closed, he opened two more restaurants: the last one was called "Last Chance," and so it was—two years later Micki died. I attended his funeral; artists came from all over the country. Pathetically, his parents and children were walking behind his coffin. This event marked the end of an era. In New York, there has never been another place to replace the meeting ground for creative people.

To make matters worse, in early 1975, Max, my boss, fired all his employees, including me, when his rent doubled. Naturally, I was very upset, but miraculously, three days later, I got a phone call from Evelyn, a travel agent with whom I had had some dealings.

"Can you be ready the day after tomorrow and escort a group of twenty-four people to South America for two weeks?"

"But I don't speak Spanish or Portuguese," was my answer.

"That doesn't matter because you will be met by a local tour guide in every city," she said.

I thought about it for about five minutes. "Yes, why not," I told her on the telephone.

"You will be staying at the Sheraton Hotels in Lima, Peru, in Buenos Aires and in Rio de Janeiro," she said. "Pick up twenty-four tickets at Braniff and make sure your own passport is valid."

It all went according to plan and in Miami, where we had to change planes, I met the remaining passengers, three French Canadians who were to join our group. As promised, Pedro, the local tour guide, met us at the airport in Lima.

"Don't worry, I'll take over while you're here," he said. We had been told that there was a revolution in Lima, and the group had been notified as well before they left. But we were not told that we had an 8 o'clock curfew at the hotel nor, that there would be constant shooting in the streets because the military had taken over from the police. Nor was I informed ahead of time that the bar was closed in the hotel and that no one could have a drink. As a result, I had a revolt on my hands.

In desperation, I arranged with the Hotel Manager to make a room available for us where we could have a cocktail party. Even though I had gone out to buy liquor in order that we could have a "Happy Hour," it seemed that no one got happy for some reason, and there was a gloomy atmosphere in the room; my efforts were unrewarded.

On the other hand, I enjoyed having a curfew because it enabled me to meet a lot of interesting people who otherwise would have gone out to dinner. This way, they were forced to eat in the hotel. I was given the best room in the hotel with a balcony which had a view of the entire city. I had been introduced to two Frenchmen and I invited them to have a drink with me in my room. It turned out to be an unforgettable evening with the sound of the shooting in the streets as we stood on the balcony overlooking this beautiful city. One of the Frenchmen was a landscape architect with whom I stayed in touch. The following year, we met in Nice and drove along the French Riviera together, stopping at all the small villages—my dream come true.

Our next stop was going to be Buenos Aires, and in order to confirm our tickets, at the risk of my life, I had to go to downtown Lima where Pedro, the tour guide, met me. He took me to a restaurant in an arcade for lunch and had just left me when wild shooting started, glass shattered. I got so scared that I ran into the kitchen and, to the amazement of the kitchen help, threw myself under the table.

They were most surprised and told me: "We are so used to the constant shooting that we no longer pay attention."

Pedro, somewhat shaken, rushed back to console me, and it was so comforting to have him there, that I invited him for lunch. Somehow, I got back to the hotel. When I told the group what had happened, no one seemed to care. I think they were sorry that they had agreed to take the trip at such an unsettling time, even though the hotel was quite luxurious and had a huge swimming pool.

Buenos Aires was our second stop, and things were not much calmer there. It was a time when American businessmen were being kidnapped for ransom. At a tea dance in the Sheraton, an American businessman asked me to dance. He explained to me: "We are going through a very difficult time. We have to have a bodyguard with us at all times in order to protect us. Don't turn around now, but the man in the brown suit dancing behind us is my bodyguard. On week-ends, we are smuggled out to Paraguay, so that we can relax free from the danger of being kidnapped. Monday to Friday we come back to Buenos Aires to work."

I thought that the whole story was like out of a mystery novel or a movie. But that was the way it was in Argentina in 1975.

One day, getting off the elevator at the Sheraton Hotel, we heard shooting in the corridor. A few people in our group were terrified, but I tried to stay calm and I was able to say: "There is no extra charge for all this excitement."

The group became increasingly disenchanted, even though the local tour guide and I took them to see the most creative tango exhibition in the Italian section of Buenos Aires, where a couple danced as if they were glued together. We went to a dude ranch where we watched cowboys lassoing horses which I had never seen before.

Buenos Aires is famous for its beef; it is world renowned for its steak houses where the steaks are charcoaled as you enter. In many ways, with its wide streets and its European architecture, Buenos Aires is reminiscent of Paris. The streets have the wonderful aroma of the coffee being brewed in the many small cafés. I was sorry to have to leave this exciting and beautiful city.

Arriving in Rio, our last stop, was like arriving in another world. The sun was shining, the white beaches were glittering and the statue of Christ, high above the town on Corcovado Mountain seemed to be watching over everything. After many complaints from the group, such as "My room doesn't overlook the ocean, my bed is too soft or too hard," I was finally able to go to my room and, in order to relax, I took a long bath with lots of bubbles.

In Buenos Aires, José, our local tour guide, had told me: "By the time you arrive in Rio, with this very difficult group, you will need a drink. Order a 'cachassa,' you will thank me."

After my bath, I went downstairs and chose the bar overlooking the ocean. It was wonderful hearing the waves splashing against the rocks on the beach just outside our hotel. Next to me sat an American businessman. "What are you drinking?" he asked me. "It looks delicious."

"Would you like to taste it?" I asked.

He loved the drink and immediately ordered two more for us. They were very strong and as a result we relaxed and we quickly became good friends for the whole time I was there. I was lucky to have his friendship, because there was only one other person who I could relate to while there.

On our flight from Buenos Aires to Rio, the plane made one stop in San Paulo. By mistake, Ruth, a member of our group, got off there. It was too late for me to do anything about it when I counted the number of people in the group. The plane had already taken off. Luckily, she knew that we were staying at the Sheraton and was able to catch a later flight to Rio.

She felt extremely guilty having caused me concern, and invited me to the finest restaurant on the Ipamena beach. In the restaurant, we were the next people to be seated, when a man and a woman arrived together. The Maitre D' took them ahead of us. I was furious. In French, since I don't speak Portuguese, I said: "We were here first, you showed preference to them because they are a couple and we are two unescorted women. This couldn't happen in America." (This was not altogether true of America either at the time.)

He got so flushed and embarrassed that he brought out a table and chairs which he immediately set up for us. He gave the waiters orders that we should get the best service and I felt vindicated and proud that I had asserted myself. Ruth was a middle-aged woman who had not lost her joy of life and loved to travel. She had a fabulous sense of humor. We laughed at what had happened and consequently had an enjoyable evening together.

I was very lucky to have James, the businessman, as my companion most of the five days in Rio. I took him along when we went to a cock fight which is an event I never want to see again. It was a cruel experience because, unbeknownst to us, it is always a fight unto death. We also went to Ipamena beach where, unfortunately, one could not leave one's towel when going into the water, it would have disappeared. The ocean outside our hotel was too rough for swimming, and Ipamena is the beach where it is possible to swim. Most of the free time, however, was spent at the gorgeous pool of our hotel where we met for breakfast.

My trip was a very interesting experience which I would not have missed for anything, but I was more than relieved when our plane finally landed safely in New York. When I think back, I realize that I really exposed myself to the danger of getting killed in either Lima or Buenos Aires. I was lucky to have escaped, once again.

Chapter XXIV

Gaït

I had mentioned in an earlier chapter that my friend Gaït came to pick me up at the airport in New York when I returned from my first two-month trip to Mexico.

I had met Gaït at a Greenwich Village Christmas party a few years before. By chance, I had run into Ann, an acquaintance, in the street who said: "I am having a little party on Christmas Eve; if you can manage to climb up five flights, I would love to see you there. Make sure you get to talk to a charming French woman, Gaït, who has just arrived from Paris. She will be there with her husband, Jerry, who she had met on a previous visit to New York; they fell in love and got married. She just packed up and moved from Paris to New York."

At the party, I made it a point to sit next to Gaït. It did not take much coaxing to get her to talk: "After my father died," she told me, "he left me some money with the understanding that I should not squander it and that I should do something constructive with it. Being an avid reader, opening a book store appealed to me. It just so happened that the English bookstore on the Left Bank was for sale and I was able to buy it."

When I asked her where she was from in France, she continued: "I was brought up in Brittany; I was the youngest of four sisters and lived there with my parents. As an adolescent, they sent me to England to learn the language; soon afterwards I moved to Paris where I worked in an office where I could use my English. This was during World War II. After the war, I decided to buy the book shop because it suited my personality; it was a great place to meet English-speaking writers and artists. Occasionally I exhibited a few drawings and paintings. Many Americans loved to visit my shop, and it became a hang-out for American expatriates."

From the first moment I met her, I was extremely taken with her. Gaït was then a middle-aged woman with beautiful blue-grey eyes, strong-boned, handsome features, and short cropped blonde hair. I was struck by her warm smile. During the evening, she introduced me to her American husband, Jerry. It had been a late marriage and, at her time of life, I imagine that she was looking for companionship and security for her later years, because Paris was no longer the same exciting artistic place after World War II; many of her clients and friends had moved back to New York, which had meanwhile become the art center of the world. We both immediately liked each other and exchanged phone numbers, but as is often the case in a big city, we did not call each other again.

Two months later, I attended an art opening at the famous Marlboro Gallery on 57th Street, where the well-known painter Larry Rivers was exhibiting his paintings. Gaït and I spotted each other and were delighted to see each other again. When we both went over to congratulate Larry Rivers, he invited us to a party given in his honor after the opening, at around 10 p.m.

"Well," Gaït said, "since the party is on Central Park West, not far from where I live, why don't you come over to my house for dinner and then we can go together?"

I accepted gladly. Her one-bedroom apartment was located on the ground floor of a small building on the upper west side. The place was very crowded, but tastefully furnished with French antiques. She offered me a drink, then went into the kitchen and in twenty minutes she whipped up a *Boeuf Bourguignon* which would have taken me two hours to prepare. I was impressed. Jerry did not want to come with us to the party because there was a program on television he preferred to watch. We went by ourselves and enjoyed watching the many people from the art world: collectors and artists mingling in this elegant Central Park West apartment.

After that evening, Gaït and I saw each other constantly and spoke almost daily on the phone; it turned out to be the beginning of a very important friendship in my life. At the time, I was working in Soho at the Max Hutchinson Gallery. Gaït would often drop in with friends, or we would go out to lunch, or meet for a drink after work. Frequently, she would also invite me home for dinner, where she served great French specialties.

About a year after we met, it became increasingly apparent that her husband, Jerry, was not well. He withdrew more and more and drank heavily after work. When I questioned Gaït, she told me: "Jerry has been diagnosed with colon cancer." He died shortly afterwards. His death caused her terrible guilt and suffering. I tried my best to console her, but was not very successful. She felt that she had not been a good wife to him because she met her friends for drinks after work instead of going straight home to make dinner for him, and she often left him alone on week-ends.

When the summer came, I got a phone call from Gaït: "My friend, Peggy, who has a house on Fire Island, is not using it this week-end and has invited me. I can bring a friend; how would you like to come out? We'll have fun."

Peggy had bought a small cottage long before Fire Island gained the reputation as a "gay" community. Whenever Peggy and her husband did not use the house, she offered it to Gaït who, in turn, invited me. I was thrilled to get out of the city and to be with Gaït and her small dog Sasha whom we took along. She was an Abso Lasso with long, silken hair which hung over her little squashed face; typical of the Asiatic breed. I adored her.

With Gaït's old Volkswagen, we drove to Bay Shore and took the ferry over to the Pines. Unlocking the wagon left at the ferry landing, we piled our luggage and groceries on it.

"Now let's quickly go to the liquor store," she would say. "Most important. Tomorrow is Sunday, and we are stuck."

She absolutely adored red wine. The owner of the liquor store knew her well because she was a good customer, and had been coming out to visit Peggy for years. With everything piled on the wagon, we hiked a mile to the house, dragging the wagon along the twisting boardwalk. It was wonderful to catch occasional glimpses of the ocean.

Since Gaït's asthma made it difficult for her to breathe, I did most of the work. The cottage was at the very end of the community, built on stilts with a magnificent view of the sea. On the large deck we immediately put out a table, chairs and an umbrella. Gaït quickly went into the kitchen to make a *croque monsieur*; it was her specialty.

After lunch, we would read and sunbathe in the fresh air; such a change from New York City's pollution. Later on we would take a walk on the beach with Sasha, where we could not see a soul for miles. At all times we liked doing the same things together at the same time. There was never a conflict.

One of the differences between us, however, was that she did not believe in introducing her friends to each other; everyone knew that she kept them all very separate. I think deep down she was not as sure of herself as she liked to project. I can understand that now. There was an incident when I introduced Gaït to one of my friends. She became friendly with him and left me out of a social occasion. I did not hold this against her; still my feelings were hurt. Aside from this eccentricity, I felt very lucky to have found someone I was so compatible with.

Next to our house on Fire Island, was a group house, and we became acquainted with our neighbors; sometimes we invited them over for drinks; at other times they would invite us over. Occasionally, some of Peggy's friends who had previously met Gaït, invited us to a party.

After dinner, when we were alone, we often confided in each other about our past. That's when she told me: "I did not want to get married when I was young; I was having too much fun." She would tell me about the good times she had in Paris when she was younger. After an unhappy marriage, I too wanted to have fun and wanted to be free. On Sunday nights, we tried to stay on the island as long as possible before catching the last ferry back to New York and "reality."

One Easter, we flew to Los Angeles, my first trip to the West Coast. There we rented a car and drove to San Francisco, along U.S. 1, the breathtaking drive along the Pacific. On the way, we stopped at Hurst Castle, where the "stars" used to hang out in the thirties; where Gary Cooper at one time played tennis with Carol Lombard and afterwards went swimming in the gold-lined pool. The tour guide told us all about those wonderful old times.

As the years passed, Gaït's asthma got worse. There were times when I could see that she could not catch her breath; I began to get worried. She tried everything to cure her asthma, but the doctors, at that time, could not really help.

Peggy was selling her Fire Island house and it was supposed to be our last week-end there. I will never forget it. We went through our usual routine, but Gaït who always had a wonderful sense of humor and kept us laughing late into the night, went to bed early, saying that she was tired. I did not think that anything was especially wrong, except that we both felt depressed about losing the use of the house which we both loved so much.

Two days later, in the middle of the night, a phone call awakened me out of a deep sleep. Gaït's friend, Susan, who had been staying with her, said: "I have terrible news for you. Gaït has had a severe asthma attack; we called the ambulance, but it was too late. She died in the ambulance on the way to the hospital."

Once again, I suffered a terrible loss. I did not want to stay home alone that morning and went to my office, staring into space. I just could not believe that my friend had died so suddenly. The office manager, with whom I could never get along, even offered to let me go home, but I couldn't bear to be alone and just stayed till it was time to leave.

To this day, so much in my own kitchen reminds me of Gaït. Over the years, for Christmas or for my birthday, she had always given me kitchen gadgets. Now when I use my salad spinner, my oven timer, or my food chopper, I see her before me and think of the many happy meals we prepared and shared together.

We were like sisters and losing Gaït was like losing a dear family member. We had known each other for many years, starting with my SoHo days through my job at the College of Medicine and long beyond.

I still miss her very much.

French friend Gait with dog Sascha
Photo taken by author.

Chapter XXV

Corsica/Avignon

I have mentioned in a previous chapter, that when I was a tour escort travelling in Peru, I met a French landscape architect by the name of Thierry. He had suggested that he and I travel together along the French Riviera at some future date. I had told him that I intended to come to France the following summer to visit my French relatives. I was thrilled at his suggestion because it had always been my dream—to travel along the *Côte d'Azure* and the small villages in Provence. I jumped at the opportunity because I was not able to drive and therefore could never have done this alone. But I was not quite sure that he really meant to keep his promise. It was only after I actually received a letter from him, in which he wrote that he could meet me in Nice that summer that I got all excited about the prospect.

In 1975, because I had two months vacation, I decided to join my father and his third wife, Evelyn, in Calvi, Corsica, for the month of July. I like travelling alone, but it was comforting for me to know that they were in the same place, even though we stayed in separate hotels; I always wanted to be independent.

The reason that I chose Corsica was that on my first visit to Nice, I had seen a boat standing in the harbor in the old part of that city. I had asked where the ferry was heading and was told that it was going to the island of Corsica.

I never forgot my strong desire to get on that boat. Corsica intrigued me because Napoleon was born there. He had always been a sort of hero to me. I admired his great skill in battle and was intrigued with his love marriage to Josephine. Much later, when he was exiled to the island of Elbe, he was known to have said: "No matter when or where I'll always recognize the scents of my beloved Corsica." I wanted to find out for myself whether this was true. Thus I decided to spend one vacation there and my father, too, wanted to visit the island. Of course, by now, it was quicker to fly from Nice than to take the boat and that's what I finally did.

My father, who had gone ahead, had already reserved a room for me in a small hotel in the center of Calvi. It was nice and clean, but unfortunately terribly noisy since my room faced the main street. At night, the motor bikes whisking by at a tremendous speed, would virtually shake my bed, but not wanting to move, I survived with ear plugs.

Calvi, despite being a major port, also has many sandy beaches, some within walking distance; the more beautiful and deserted ones are easily reached with a little train which makes various stops along the coast. The train is so small that it looks like a toy train. The conductor collects the fares and puts the money into a big, black purse which he wears around his waist. The last stop on the train is another village, called Ille Rouse, which is not quite as quaint as Calvi, but it has several big hotels and an exceptionally beautiful white, sandy beach. My days were mostly spent alone exploring the island, but I always knew that at five o'clock, I would meet my father and Evelyn for a drink at the port in Calvi. Sometimes, I would then join them for dinner at their hotel which was a short walk beyond the port. Mostly, however, I ate in a local fish restaurant near the water where they served a delicious bouillabaisse, piled high with freshly caught fish; a meal by itself. When I did not have other plans, we sometimes met again in the café for dessert. People from all over the world were always passing by, and they were fun to watch.

While travelling, I always found it easy to meet people, and Corsica was no exception. In the beach café in Ille Rouse, I met a German actor with whom I became very friendly. Because he spoke neither French nor English, he was happy to find someone to talk to. He got very attached to me, and we often met for dinner or lunch at the beach. Long after that summer, he kept writing to me and we finally arranged to meet again one year on the Island of Ibiza, off the coast of Spain. There he proposed marriage to me, but it was a pity that I was not sexually attracted to him because he was a very nice, gentle man. Besides, I don't think I could ever have been comfortable living in Germany. As it turned out, a few years later, I sent him a Christmas card which was returned to me with a letter from one of his friends telling me that my friend had died of a heart attack. I was sad to hear that.

On another occasion, I met a young Corsican whose mother owned a restaurant/bar in Calvi. He had a motorbike and he showed me the beautiful countryside outside of Calvi. Napoleon was right, I thought, because the herbs growing on the foothills of the mountains permeated the air. From there at night, the lights of the port with its many yachts from all over Europe, illuminated the breathtaking view.

Before I visited Corsica, I had always been told that Corsicians are gruff and beware. In my three weeks there, I did not find them so, but thought they were rather distantly polite.

On my last day, before leaving for Nice, I left my luggage in the small café of my hotel, after having settled my bill.

"Madame," the landlady said, "I must apologize for having ignored you, but this is our busy tourist season. Please feel free to have a meal at our snack bar before you leave. You've been a great guest and we hope to see you again another year."

I was happy to have been appreciated; then, before taking the ferry back to Nice, I went to my usual fish restaurant for my last delicious bouillabaisse where up to now I thought that no one had even acknowledged my existence. When they saw that I had put down my luggage and I was about to pay my bill, the manager said: "This meal is on us. You have been a steady customer, and we wish you 'Bon Voyage.'"

My last stop was to say good-bye to my Corsican with the motorbike. I went to his mother's café. She greeted me saying: "I am sorry that my son had to go on an errand in another town, but he told me to give you this bottle of our local liqueur which you liked so much, just in case he would miss you."

I thanked her profusely and told her: "Give my very best to your son."

I was extremely touched by the hospitality which was extended to me in Corsica despite its bad reputation. I vowed to return some day, which I did several years later and found the island and its people just as delightful.

The boat trip back to Nice was exceptionally smooth. Lying on the deck in the sunshine, with the gentle sea breezes and the water rocking the boat, I soon fell asleep. I was looking forward to meeting Thierry again. He had called me several times in Calvi just to confirm our meeting in a Hotel in Nice. He was driving there from his home in Beziers, a town in France, not far from the Spanish border.

Just before leaving Corsica, I met a group of Germans who were sailing to Nice in their luxurious sailboat which slept six. It just so happened that they were leaving Corsica the same day as I was. They had asked me: "Why don't you come along?"

Because I had already bought my ticket for the boat ride and also because they were total strangers, I felt much safer taking the ferry. However, I told them: "I would love to join you for a drink at the yacht club in Villefranche, near Nice before meeting my friend."

Arriving at the club, I saw literally hundreds of boats anchored in this famous yacht club. Because I knew the name of their boat, I asked the harbor master to direct me to their boat. Sitting on their deck in the harbor of this beautiful club on the Riviera, made me feel as if I were part of the jet set.

I reflected that my experience in Corsica had been truly memorable, and I was touched by everyone's kindness. Furthermore, I had an attractive Frenchman waiting for me in Nice who was going to drive me along the Riviera in his B.M.W.

My friends in New York envied my good luck and since Thierry had called me several times in Corsica, I thought he was seriously smitten and would surely turn up.

We did meet at the arranged time and it did not, at first, seem as if our feelings toward each other had changed. I was flattered by his attention and devotion and was looking forward to drive along the Riviera—my dream come true.

We started our trip by driving into the mountains behind Nice, the part which is called *derrière pays* and where it is so cold that people are able to ski way into Spring. After the warm sun in the South, because of the change in weather, I caught an awful cold which was only cured when we returned to the Riviera and back to the sunshine. Our aim was to meet my father in Avignon after visiting the small villages along the way. On our way there, whenever we were hungry, we stopped and picnicked in the fields. With a fresh melon bought on the road from a farmer, the sweetest I had ever tasted, a French baguette bought in one of the village bakeries and some sausage, we had the best imaginable meal. We drove through the village of St. Paul de Vence and stayed overnight in little inns whenever we found an empty room; this is not always easy in the height of the season. We spent one hour in fashionable St. Tropez in a café where even in those days a cup of coffee cost a fortune. A few years ago, I was told that one night with dinner at the Hotel Biblious cost $1,000. We quickly escaped from the crowded, touristy coast and drove inland to the charming village of Mougins where the rich French live in the most beautiful, luxurious villas.

What I found surprising was that little villages in Provence close down early. "You must be in by 11 p.m.," our landlord told us in Manosque, where we spent the night. "There is nothing to do after that hour in Manosque," he said. I was shocked to hear that. It was true: only one café was still open at that time. We drove through the breathtaking gorges of *Les Beaux*, high over bridges with the river and waterfalls below until we reached Avignon, where the art festival was in progress.

As arranged, we met my father and Evelyn for dinner at their exquisite hotel. It looked like a place where I had imagined only movie stars would be staying. They invited us for dinner in the garden which was surrounded by the kind of colorful flowers one only sees on the Riviera where the sun shines all the time. They were the centerpiece on the elegantly set table. Of course, the meal was superb with delicacies which I had never eaten before, like frogs' legs and escargots.

During the evening, I had a strange premonition that my relationship with Thierry was not going well. Being together with my father gave me some sort of perspective. I began to feel that we had little in common. I realized because he came from a French bourgeois conservative family, our physical attraction was not enough to sustain a long-time relationship. I began to feel that it was getting more difficult to communicate with him. It was different than in Peru, where the revolution had thrown us together. I was therefore not too surprised that he, too, must have felt a problem because the following day he announced that he was going home to see his parents in Beziers and would be back the same evening. I began to feel a little suspicious, and with good reason, because he called me in the evening.

"It turns out that my family needs me at home," he said. "But I will be back in two days to see you. However, my obligations at home prevent me from continuing our trip together."

We had planned to spend the next two weeks together driving through Spain, and this left me quite desperate, not knowing what to do. The festival, which I much enjoyed, was over, my father had gone home, the town was deserted, and there I was, stranded alone in the middle of August in Europe.

I had read and knew that Salvadore Dali, the famous painter, lived in Cadaquès, Spain. He and his wife, Gala, many years his senior, had a beautiful house there. It was rumored that the fountain in his garden was filled with Coca-cola instead of water; it was also rumored that he was bisexual and that he paid a procurer to sit in the Café Maritime to watch people getting off the bus, as it pulled into the village. If a good-looking young man happened to get off, Dali's assistant would approach him and ask: "Would you like to visit Dali in his fabulous villa?" If the boy agreed, the assistant fixed up the rendezvous. Some people told me later that the visitors would be offered the opportunity to make love to Gala. Since Gala was far from young, the young men would often decline. I could never attest to these rumors since I was never invited.

Because I had heard so many stories about Cadaquès and because I knew that it was a very specially artistic place, I was most anxious to visit. But there was a snag: I was told at the train station in Avignon that it would take all day to reach my destination because of the bad train and bus connections. I also knew that with my luggage, I would not be able to manage by myself. I was deeply depressed, felt totally abandoned, and decided to have a drink in a café next to the river to try to cheer myself up and to think. The song that I had learned as a child in my French class: "*Sur le pont d'Avignon, on y danse, on y danse, tout en ronde,*"[3] went through my head. Little did I know then that I would end up sitting all alone next to that bridge. I ordered a *pastis* and was trying to figure out what to do next. One drink did not make me feel any better.

"Monsieur," I said to the waiter, "I'll have one more." At the next table sat a young French girl who also seemed to be alone and who had also just ordered a second drink. Somehow we started talking, and she moved over to my table. To my utter amazement, she told me: "I went to Germany as a camp counselor with

---

[3] On the bridge at Avignon, one dances, one dances, all around.

my boyfriend. We were both students at the University of Rennes. There," Claudette continued, "he went off with a younger, pretty German blonde girl. I was jilted and decided to hitchhike to Avignon to attend the festival. With my backpack I am camping alongside the river."

It is strange how things sometimes happen in life. By chance, she had also wanted to go to Cadaqués because she too was interested in art, being an art major in college. We arranged to meet the next day and take a picnic with us to Villeneuve, a village across the bridge from Avignon. There we would plan our visit to Cadaqués.

"I'll help you with your luggage," she said. "Let's go to the train station, find out the exact schedule and buy our tickets. Then we'll go to your hotel and see whether there is any word from Thierry."

Sure enough, there was a message which said: "I'll come and take you out to dinner tonight if you are free."

I decided to swallow my pride, even though I had been dumped. Claudette had suggested: "Let's use him to take your luggage to the station tonight, put it in a locker, and in that way, we can walk there in there morning and save the taxi fare." She was practical and I was happy that she had taken over.

Thierry kept his promise and we had dinner alone together. The conversation was strained and consisted mainly of small talk. I felt very aloof, knowing that I was leaving and had decided against recriminations. I told him: "I have made my plans and am leaving Avignon tomorrow." Thierry, of course, was happy to bring my luggage to the station. It must have somehow alleviated his guilt. I have totally blocked out our parting words. I do remember, however, that I received a Christmas card from him that year. I never responded.

Chapter XXVI

Cadaquès

Leaving Avignon, at 8 a.m. and three trains later, we arrived in Figueras, only to find out that the one bus a day to Cadaquès had left at 8 a.m. However, there was a bus to Rosas, from there we might possibly get a boat to Cadquès. In Rosas, we found out that the only boat ran on Tuesdays and Fridays. What a disaster for us! This was Saturday; we decided to try to hitchhike. We stood on the road in the heat, totally exhausted; no one wanted to pick us up because of the size of my luggage; so we decided to hide it under a tree.

Finally, we got a ride halfway on a road which was narrow and twisting and was bordered by olive trees. Again we found ourselves standing on the road waiting, thirsty and desperate to reach our destination. We wanted to cry, but started to laugh instead about our dilemma. At last a second car with young students picked us up. We arrived in Cadaquès, feeling dirty and terribly dehydrated.

We had been told before we left Avignon that it was impossible to find a room in high season in Cadaquès. Claudette had said: "If worse comes to worst, we'll camp out." The students who had given us our last ride thought there might be a room in their house, but when we finally arrived there, the landlady had gone out.

"It's Saturday, and she is at the beauty parlor," we were told.

The students sat us down at a café by the sea and said: "We'll try to track down the landlady; you just stay there and relax."

In every beauty parlor, they looked under the hood of the dryers in an effort to find her. It wasn't easy to identify her, but they finally succeeded. "It's all right," she told them, "but there is only room for one night."

We bought the boys drinks as a reward for getting us the room with the understanding that they could shower first, since there was only one bathroom available. The room shortage was due to the fact that the village had no hotels.

Later, we found out that even though this was during Franco's regime, Dali, being a famous painter, had made a deal with Franco to preserve the village so that it would never change its original character and stay uncommercial.

Since Cadaquès is an easy commute from Barcelona, rich Spaniards have their summer houses there. The village is beautiful, with its ancient cathedral looming above on a hill, where Saturday night concerts take place. Famous musicians from all over the world play classical chamber music and piano concertos indoors or, when the weather is favorable, outdoors.

Cadaquès has no real beach to speak of, but everyone swims off the rocks, diving into the sea, some in the nude. During Franco's days, the Federalès would spot them and make them put their clothes on.

The morning after we arrived, Claudette and I went to the liquor store to find out about a room. "They usually know everything," I told her. By chance, through the owner of the store, we found a lovely room with a local lady. She was warm and hospitable, so much so that after Claudette left a week later, and I stayed behind, she said to me: *"Mi casa es su casa."* Everyone I met in the village was extremely friendly. One day passing through the Saturday antique market in the village square, I met John, an English expatriate. John had left London and his former profession as a hairdresser; he had established himself in Cadaquès as an antique dealer.

"Saturday is my birthday," I mentioned after a short conversation with him.

"We'll give a birthday party for you in our tiny modest house. I live there with a native girlfriend—we'll all chip in for drinks and everyone will bring food," he said. I was touched and flattered by this invitation. Twenty people showed up for my birthday. The party consisted mostly of younger people and I was pleased that my age did not seem to make any difference. We all had a very good time together, eating a *paella* and drinking local wines.

I came to love Cadaquès so much so that I spent at least four more summers there. I told myself that bad things in life sometimes turn out to be the best. If Thierry had not deserted me in Avignon, I might never have discovered this magical place.

And magical it was. During the end of my stay in Cadaquès, I had an experience which I will never forget. Up to that time, I had never taken dangerous substances. I had lived through the Sixties without taking drugs. My two experiences smoking marijuana had left me with severe migraine headaches. At the same time, however, I noticed that some young people whom I had met, and had discussions with at Max's Kansas City who had tried drugs, were more introspective and had more insight than most of their peers. I was able to relate to them more intimately than with most other young people I had met before. Still I lacked the courage to try it.

Prior to going to Cadaquès, and while we were at the festival in Avignon, my father and I visited Arles and the hospital where the painter, Van Gogh, had often been admitted for alcohol abuse. (There is a famous painting from that courtyard.) The caretaker told us: "It was the powerful hallucinogenic drink *absinthe* which drove Van Gogh crazy in the end." I was intrigued.

In Spain this drink was prohibited, but in Cadaquès one could not only buy a bottle in the liquor store, but one café served it by the glass, just like any other drink. My friend, John, had told me about it and one night I plucked up my courage to try it at the café.

"If you promise to stay with me," I told him, "let's do it."

"I promise," he said.

Little did I know just how potent one glass of *absinthe* could be. John, after drinking two glasses to my one, disappeared immediately. I found myself sitting alone in the café, feeling stranger and stranger by the minute. The drink was creeping up on me and I felt that I was losing control over my perceptions. It was a terribly helpless feeling. I could not trust myself any more. I did not know where I was or who I was.

Luckily, Ulli, a Swiss painter I knew, came over to my table. "What are you doing tonight?" he asked, not having any idea what I was drinking.

"Ulli," I whispered, "I've done this terrible thing and feel completely out of it. I just drank a glass of *absinthe* and John left me here."

"Don't worry," he said, "I'll take care of you. We'll go have something to eat and then go pub crawling."

I must have been really out of it, because pub crawling was the last thing I needed.

There is very little that I remember about that evening, including how I lost Ulli; I only remember that passing the sea alone in the dark, it looked so ominous that it gave me the creeps, and I had an eerie feeling. I staggered over a cobblestone street to my pension and somehow managed to get into my bed. Looking at my watch, I saw it was 4 a.m. I woke up at 4 p.m. the next day.

"I am terribly sorry, Signora," I heard my landlady say, "but these arrogant Germans were slamming the doors again. I hope they did not wake you." I refrained from telling her that for the past twelve hours, I had heard nothing. She would have been shocked to hear what I had done, being a typical nice bourgeois lady.

"It's quite all right," I told her, "I was very tired last night."

I never repeated that one-time experience, and I felt lucky that I had not fallen into the sea or had a terrible accident. To this day, I remember how scared and vulnerable I felt when I suddenly noticed that I had somehow lost Ulli and was weaving home alone.

The next day John told me apologetically, "I slept on the side of the road all night and did not know where I was."

A year later, when I met Mont in Barcelona and found out that her brother owned an apartment in, of all places, Cadaquès, we spent our vacation there together. We had become very close friends in a very short time, but more about Mont in another chapter.

I was happy to return to one of my favorite places, but I never repeated my "*absinthe*" trip. I had learned my lesson.

Chapter XXVII

Deya, Mallorca, Spain, Jean-Claude

In the summer of 1977, I decided to spend my vacation on the island of Mallorca, in a small village, called Puerto Soller. My friend, Gaït, had told me that her friend Charlotte was staying nearby in a tiny village called Deya and that she had given her the name of my hotel so that Charlotte could visit me.

On arrival in Puerto Soller, I knew right away that I hated the place. The sea was dirty and the place touristy. When Charlotte came to visit me the next day, she said: "You can't stay here. You have to come to Deya. I'll reserve a room for you in a small pension. I know they'll have a room for you. Take the 12 o'clock bus tomorrow. Why stay here? You'll love Deya. It's full of interesting people. There is only one café where everyone meets and that's where I'll be waiting for you, and tell you where you're staying."

I decided that she was right. Why should I spoil my vacation and stay somewhere where I was unhappy? Deya is situated in a valley between two large mountains. The road sign reads: "You are entering Deya" as the bus approaches on an extremely narrow, winding road. A few yards later, it reads: "You are leaving Deya." Hardly a metropolis. As arranged, Charlotte was waiting for me on the terrace of the café, crowded with chic, apparently artistic people drinking and talking. We ordered coffee and she introduced me to a number of her friends, including a couple who were curators of the little local museum. A Russian friend arrived with a young Frenchman, Jean-Claude, and they both sat down at our table.

After a while, the young Frenchman, Jean-Claude, tall and slim, just my physical type, with dark brown eyes that seemed to look into your soul, invited me to his birthday party. It was to take place on the beach the next day.

"I'd love to be there," I said, "but how do I get there?"

"It's easy," he said, "You walk through the fields surrounded by olive trees just below your pension."

Deya has a small cove, which is easily reached by car, but it is a long walk to get there. It's not bad going down, but going back in the heat is tough.

I checked into my modest pension, where I had a tiny room with a single bed; the bathroom was down the hall, but the pension had a lovely garden with a terrace, where breakfast was served. As simple as this place was, I much preferred it to my previously upscale room in Puerto Soller.

The next day, I ventured down to the beach. There, a long table was set for about twenty people in front of a small café right by the water. Charlotte was already there and so was Jean-Claude. I wished him a happy birthday, and he introduced me to his beautiful sister. She said that she had been to New York and they both told me how much they wanted to visit America. Gradually, more guests arrived who seemed to have known Jean-Claude for years. Many bottles of champagne were brought out and we toasted Jean-Claude's birthday. Then a huge paella, consisting of lobster and other delicious seafood, was served. This was accompanied by large jugs of sangria. Being a newcomer, I was thrilled to be included into what was obviously an insiders' party.

Two days later, on a Saturday night, our pension gave a party with a live band. A pleasant couple I had met there suggested: "Why don't we reserve a table on the terrace for the evening and you join us for dinner? Most of the locals will come here to dance and in this way we will already be here."

I accepted with pleasure, since I never like eating dinner alone.

We had just about finished our dinner and we were enjoying a brandy when I suddenly saw Jean-Claude walking in with that same Russian lady I had met on my first day in the café. We invited them over to our table; his companion excused herself, telling us that she was meeting some friends, but Jean-Claude joined us. Soon afterwards the band began to play and Jean-Claude asked me to dance. When we came back to the table, the couple had left and Jean-Claude and I had a chance to talk for a long time; it was our first opportunity to really get to know each other.

It was one of those magical evenings. We sat outside in the open under the starry night. Then came a moment I will never forget: Jean-Claude took my hand softly into his. I felt a very strong attraction between us and something well beyond it as well. I knew then and there that this was going to be the great love of my life despite the many years difference in our ages. I also experienced a premonition that the two of us would definitely become lovers and remain in each others' lives for a long time to come.

Many years ago, when I had just married, while in Mallorca, my ex-husband had lost his wedding ring there in the sea, and I had somehow felt that I would find that wedding ring, the symbol of our lost marriage. I would jokingly say that someday I would be eating a fish and bite into the wedding ring; or that I would one day experience another emotional attachment on that island.

I was therefore not surprised about my feelings towards Jean-Claude. Even though he was thirty years younger, it didn't seem to matter. Much to everyone else's dismay, surprise and disapproval, we spent the next two weeks together, and were inseparable.

For some reason which I now don't fully understand, I decided to fly to the island of Ibiza for a week. Jean-Claude tried to talk me out of it, but I went regardless. I realize now that I was terribly scared that our relationship might end, and that I wanted to test Jean-Claude's feelings. As it turned out, I was disappointed in Ibiza, it was too crowded, too touristy. I spent the next three days at the airport hoping to get a flight back to Mallorca and to Jean-Claude; all planes were filled. On the third day, I met three other people who shared my feelings about the island and were also desperately trying to get back to Mallorca. We finally managed to get stand-by tickets to Palma, where we arrived too late and we had to spend the night in a hotel. The next day we rented a car and drove back to Deya.

It was a wonderful feeling being back in Deya again, like coming home. After the Ibiza fiasco, my new-found friends and I were so relieved that we drove to our favorite little hotel a little bit out of Deya, where we dove into the pool because it was incredibly hot. We then enjoyed a wonderful lunch on the terrace overlooking the breathtaking view of the mountains surrounding this village.

In the afternoon, back at the café, Jean-Claude's sister came up to me: "Where have you been? Jean-Claude is crazy looking for you all over. He missed you so much," she said.

I felt excited and reassured. I had missed him too. We eventually found each other and we had a wonderful reunion; we spent every moment with each other for the next two weeks.

Our relationship lasted for many years, and eventually turned into a lasting friendship. I don't remember ever being that happy before, except during World War II, while I was experiencing my first love affair. When it was time for me to go home, Jean-Claude stayed behind, but we swore everlasting love to each other, knowing full well that Paris and New York were not exactly next door.

Chapter XXVIIA

Jean-Claude Epilogue

Regardless of the fact that summer romances rarely continue after one has returned to one's own surroundings, I had a feeling that this was different, that my romance with Jean-Claude would sustain the separation and that we would see each other again. We wrote to each other very often after that summer in Deya, keeping up with each other's lives.

About a year passed. I was sitting in my office, in the Public Relations department of the College, when the phone rang. I picked it up, answering in a very business-like manner, when this very familiar, lovely French voice said: "I am downstairs."

"Don't go away, stay where you are, I'll be right down," I said. Nothing could have stopped me from running downstairs. And there he stood, like a little boy rather triumphantly that he had made it. I couldn't believe my eyes.

Jean-Claude moved in with me for the next three months. At times, it was a little stormy between us, because I had to get up to go to work every day and Jean-Claude stayed in bed, and I felt somewhat resentful, but on the whole it was a wonderful, loving time. His parents came to visit us from Paris, and we pretended that we slept in separate rooms. I am sure they knew the truth, but being French, they accepted the situation very gracefully. It was their first visit to the States and we showed them around the city. I did everything to make their stay as memorable as possible. The day before they left, I invited them for lunch. I was very nervous wanting to make a good meal. I made an omelette and baked Idaho potatoes in the oven. They so loved the potatoes that I gave them a pound to take back with them to Paris.

Meanwhile, Jean-Claude had found some part-time work, ushering in a movie house, and teaching a Japanese lady French. It was best that he had his own money and was not dependent on me. Many years later, he thanked me for helping him to make him self-reliant while in America.

During his stay in New York, Jean-Claude decided to go out West to see some other parts of America. While hitchhiking one day, the driver asked him to go out to buy a pack of cigarettes. He naively had left his bags, money and passport in the car. When he came back, the car and driver were gone and with it all of Jean-Claude's belongings. It was Christmas, and there he stood in some God forsaken town in Oklahoma without a cent, passport or papers. He went to the police and explained his predicament. They were most sympathetic, particularly because it was Christmas. They immediately called a childless couple who were happy to take him in for Christmas.

"It was funny," he said, "they called me 'Johnny,' but even though they were so good to me, I couldn't wait to come back to New York and to you."

I don't remember what arrangements were made for him to return.

All good things come to an end, and we both knew that Jean-Claude had to make a life for himself in Paris. Our age difference was too vast. It was very difficult for me to let him go, but I knew it was the right thing to do for his sake.

The following summer, I wrote Jean-Claude that I was going to Spain, to a place which is called "Mojacar." It was not very accessible, and situated in a desert where, for years, Hollywood directors had shot their Westerns since production costs were much cheaper there than in Hollywood. I called Jean-Claude from there and, once again, even though it took him two days to get there, he came to see me. It had taken him a whole night in the train, a bus ride to the nearest town where he had slept in a field outside overnight because he was too exhausted and, he also realized it was too early in the morning to arrive in my hotel. I threw him in the bathtub at once since he was totally dirty and bedraggled—I was ecstatic.

Then came the summer when I went back to Mallorca, this time to Puerto Andraitx. Jean-Claude was also in Mallorca, in another village, where he stayed with his sister. He borrowed his father's car, an old Peugeot and drove to the other coast of the island to see me. We had lunch in a little restaurant overlooking the port and were holding hands while just listening to the gentle lapping of the water in the port. I couldn't have been happier. It was so peaceful because most people were either working or on the beach. We asked the waiter for directions to the beach and he drew us a little plan. We just started down a winding road when a huge water truck crashed into our car. It ripped off our fender. We were thrown around and the car was totalled. Jean-Claude's first words to me were, "Are *you* all right?"

I was bleeding slightly from the sudden crash, but otherwise we were luckily both not hurt. We were able to telephone for help from a nearby hotel. Shockingly, the driver of the truck, who was not hurt, simply drove away.

A tow truck came to take the car away and drove us back to my hotel. It was a narrow escape. Right after the accident, Jean-Claude, who was not religious, nevertheless got down on his knees on the road and prayed. I took a photograph of him at this moment which, to this day, is standing on his parents' mantlepiece over their fireplace in Paris.

Yet another year, when I was spending my vacation in Cadaqués in Spain, Jean-Claude also came to visit and we spent a loving week together in my friend Mont's apartment.

As the years went on, we almost always managed to see each other every summer, regardless of Jean-Claude's lifestyle, either in Spain or in Paris. It's been twenty-eight years since we met, and our deepest feelings have not changed; our love affair has developed into a profound friendship; it never seems to change. Jean-Claude has been my friend who has accompanied me to my two cousins' weddings in Paris and who has, in a way, become a part of my family, too. They have totally accepted him even though they cannot quite understand our age difference; my cousin once said to me: "Why him?"

"I guess that's the mystery of life," I told him.

Jean-Claude now has two little girls with a woman he never married. I sometimes wonder why.

The last time I was in Paris, his mother invited me to a family lunch which included Jean-Claude's sister and his two little girls, but not their mother. My friend Janet was also present and commented later: "It's absolutely amazing, the whole scene reminds me of a Pinter play."

Mont, Catalan actress who lives in Barcelona

Chapter XXVIII

Montserrat/Mont

The summer after returning from Deya, I had to stop over in Barcelona for two days before my flight back to New York. There I checked into a small, depressing hotel in the *Bario Gothica* recommended by Arthur Frommer's well-known travel book. After depositing my luggage, I quickly walked down the street to the Ramblas, Barcelona's main street in the old quarter, where people hang out in the many cafés surrounded by beautiful flower stalls. Opposite the famous opera house, in the Café de L'Opera, drinking my pastis, I was deep in thought about Jean-Claude and the two unforgettable weeks we had spent together, when a young man approached me from the next table, speaking Spanish. I couldn't understand him. A kind female voice next to me said in English: "Can I help you?"

"Oh," I said, "yes please, I do need help."

"I believe he is trying to pick you up," she said.

"Tell him that I am not interested," I replied.

My new-found friend had no trouble communicating this to him and he gave up. Left to ourselves, I told her: "I am so hungry and I don't know where to eat in Barcelona."

"What do you feel like eating?" she asked me. "Would you like me to show you a little place nearby where we can get a tapa and have a glass of wine?"

So it happened that night that I met Montserrat, a charming young woman from Cataluna, with a very "sympathico" manner. She was an aspiring actress who was working in a bank for the time being.

"Where are you staying?" she asked me after our pleasant little supper.

"In the suicide hotel," I told her.

She laughed. But I explained to her that it was true, because my room was so miserable, overlooking a dreary courtyard that I could imagine that one would feel suicidal if one had to live there for any length of time. Luckily, it was the last time I had to stay there, because Montserrat and I became such good friends that she invited me to stay in her apartment the following year, and I have done so ever since for the past sixteen years. After our meal, she asked me: "What are you doing tomorrow, your last day here?"

"I plan to take the train and see the castle and church of Montserrat where the famous sculpture of the 'Black Virgin' is on view," I said.

"That's funny," she said, "my name is Montserrat, and I have been meaning to go there for some time. I haven't been there since I was a kid. Why don't you meet me in the café tomorrow at 3 p.m. when I leave the bank, and we'll go together?" she suggested.

I was happy to have a companion for the day, little did I know that this was going to develop into a lasting friendship. I guess 1977 was my lucky year.

The next day, as arranged, we took the train to the village from where the funicular goes up to the church of Montserrat. Because it is situated on a high cliff with a spectacular view of the surroundings, hikers often climb up these cliffs. Inside the church, we joined the line of tourists gaping across a heavy rope separating the visitors from a statuette of a black virgin. It was small and therefore could easily have been stolen without extra protection. This was the only black virgin I had ever seen, and it was a very special experience which I will always savor, but I have been unsuccessful in finding out as yet where the few others are located now.

That same evening, we had a farewell dinner, during which Montserrat told me: "My brother has a house in Cadaqués and maybe you can join me there next year."

This I did the following year, as mentioned in a previous chapter. It was another coincidence having been in Cadaqués prior to our meeting. In our two days together, we discovered that we had much in common. We both enjoyed museums, art galleries, theater and movies; we also seemed to have the same sense of humor and always laughed when we were together. Even though she was much younger than I, and from a totally different background (she came from a small village near Barcelona), it did not seem to matter.

She told me: "Ever since I was a little girl, I studied singing with the hope of going on the stage." Now she was hoping to use her trained voice to eventually become a performer.

Subsequently, after two visits to Barcelona and Cadaqués, Montserrat was able to visit me in New York. She was all excited since it was her very first time in the U.S. After a few days of showing her the city, we went to Asti's Restaurant known for the fact that the waiters, bartender, and clientele all participate impromptu in singing well-known opera arias. While there, I tried to talk Montserrat into singing.

"How can I get up and sing in New York?" she asked me.

"I know you can do it, I heard you in Barcelona when you took me to your singing teacher; you have a trained voice."

She finally consented to sing an excerpt from "La Traviata" and to my joy, she got tremendous applause. It was a great moment for her since she felt a little out of place wearing black pants and black boots, amidst an audience dressed in fancy evening clothes. It was a moment she will always remember to receive such acclaim in New York of all places.

Montserrat was supposed to report for work in Barcelona on a Monday and was ready to leave New York on Sunday. I tried to talk her into staying an extra day, because I was giving an engagement party for my son David on that Sunday; I wanted her to meet what little family I had invited for that very important occasion. I also wanted my friends to meet her, especially my father and Evelyn; I had told them so much about my friend. She agreed to stay an extra day, and reluctantly called her boss, who was very upset with her. The party was a great success and I was happy that she was part of an occasion which was so important to me.

A week later, I received a phone call from her, telling me that she had been fired. Her boss was furious with her. I felt extremely guilty, but such things sometimes have a way of turning out for the best. Shortly thereafter, she managed to get a job singing in a theatrical company called "La Cubana." The company started out as a form of "street theatre," but was to become very well known with bookings all over Spain and a subsequent tour of London. She stayed with the company as a singer and comedian for ten years, and at that point she changed her name to *Mont*. On one of my visits, I saw her perform in Barcelona's outdoor "Grek" theatre on opening night during festival week. It was situated on a mountain overlooking the entire city. Mont turned out to be a marvelous comedian and received very good reviews in the local papers. After opening night, champagne was served to the huge audience who had attended.

Later on she joined an even more well known company and also became involved in television sitcoms. The last time I was in Barcelona, she took me to a studio during one of her rehearsals; I was intrigued to see how complex and difficult it is to shoot just one scene. Nowadays, when we walk down the street together, people recognize her and ask her for her autograph.

In the many years that we've known each other, we've lived through a lot together. One day, while vacationing in Cadaqués, two young friends we knew, invited us to go for a boat ride in their fiberglass boat to a far away beach. We started out on a beautiful sunny day, and we were joined by a French girl. The words "small craft warnings" don't exist in Spain. Halfway to our destination, clouds suddenly darkened the horizon, and a few moments later we were in one of those Mediterranean storms, called *traumatana*. Our boat began to rock wildly and, in what seemed seconds, we were swallowing water. At the same time we were freezing, and I thought: this is what drowning is like. It was a horrible experience I will never forget. I was sure I was going to die.

For some reason or other, I have been very close to death a number of times in my life, but I have been lucky to escape every time. Despite the heavy winds, our friends managed to maneuver the boat into a cove where the rocks could easily have split the boat in half had they not been so skillful. We were actually able to climb out among the rocks and, at the same time, rescue the boat. Shivering from the cold, we climbed up on those rocks with our last reserve of energy. Our friends gathered wood and made a huge fire. We were happy to finally be on solid ground and we got completely undressed. Afraid to catch a cold, we spread out our wet clothes to dry. The guys felt obliged to bring the boat back to the harbor and to safety. But Montserrat, the French girl, and I decided to walk, even though the village was miles away. To make matters worse, the French girl didn't have any shoes, and walked back barefoot, crying out in pain whenever she stepped on thistles. It was beginning to get dark and we were utterly exhausted. We lost our bearings a few times, but finally after two hours, we reached an unpaved road, which led to the village. Here we saw a car and asked for a ride. This turned out to make matters even worse, since the driver was speeding madly on a winding road. We were sure that he had been drinking.

It was completely dark when we arrived at the Café Maritime, where our boating friends were sitting around, happily in conversation, drinking coffee and cognac, as if nothing had happened. We were wondering how quickly they seemed to have forgotten the fact that we had almost drowned. "The trip back was much easier," they told us, "because the storm had nearly subsided."

The *traumatana* is very often of short duration. They did not seem at all worried about us, and we did not feel that we could tell them about our awful experiences on our walk back. We had to keep our story to ourselves. Mont and I, however, often reminisce and remind ourselves of how close we came to drowning on what started out to be such a beautiful sunny day in Cadaqués.

Chapter XXIX

More Cadaquès/Barcelona

On my second visit to Cadaquès, I stayed in my Spanish friend Mont's brother's summer apartment, a high climb up behind the village. It was extremely primitive, but it did have a bathroom, which even sometimes had hot water so that we could take a shower. Not having to stay in a room with a landlady considerably changed my life. Mont and I were happy to have a place of our own, even though we spent little time there. When we were not swimming off the rocks, we hung out at the Café Maritime right by the sea, with the many friends we had acquired very quickly. It's easy to do when you are relatively young and everyone is open to new friendships. It was an international crowd, and with my ability to speak three languages, it made it all the easier to communicate. Often I became the translator. At times we were invited to friends' houses for a barbecue where, since no one had much money, we all chipped in. Failing that, we went to an open air restaurant, facing the sea, but we always ended up at the Café Maritime where we sat under the starry night sky till late into the night, drinking coffee ignited with cognac, which is the specialty of the house.

Sometimes, on Saturdays, we would go to a gallery opening where, surprisingly, we could see famous painters' works, and often, the artists attended. It was Dali's presence that brought artists and musicians to this small village. I remember seeing John Cage, the composer, at one of these openings, amidst others.

One time during our stay, we got up early and caught the bus to Figueras, situated in-land, where Dali has his famous museum, which is a big tourist attraction. But we were always happy to return to our village and to get back to where the sea cooled off the hot summer nights.

My vacation was ending and I had to return to New York. I told Mont: "There is no reason for you to go back to Barcelona. Why don't you stay here?"

"Are you sure?" she asked. "Will you manage by yourself in my apartment in Barcelona?"

I assured her that it would be all right and she handed me her keys. "Just make sure that you don't lose them," she said. "My sister Maria is on holiday and she is the only one who has my keys, since she lives in the same house."

I had left my luggage and return ticket in Mont's apartment and had already spent a few days in Barcelona before we left for Cadaquès together. I was not too worried that I could not manage by myself, even though my Spanish was pretty poor.

Everything went along as planned; I took the bus and train back to Barcelona, spent the night at Mont's apartment. The next morning I decided to go out for breakfast and then go downtown to spend the last of my pesetas before returning to the U.S. It was Saturday, and the shops were open. Normally, in the past, I had always divided my money, keeping it on my person before I went out. I had once been told by a German girl who I met in Lisbon: "Divide, divide, in case you get robbed." I had never forgotten that, and had put some money in my wallet, some in my pockets, and some pinned in my underwear. But because it was my last day, I combined everything in my wallet.

I was happily strolling along the Ramblas, Barcelona's tree-lined street, where there is one café next to the other and where everyone promenades up and down all day and all night. I was looking for last minute gifts in all the shops. I stopped at a leather shop to buy a belt for one of my friends' son when, looking for my money in order to pay, I realized with horror that my wallet had disappeared. I was in a panic. It was 12:55 p.m. and it dawned on me that my only chance to get Spanish money was to run into the bank, which closed at 1 p.m., with my travelers checks and my passport which I luckily had with me. The doors of the bank were just about to close for the whole week-end, but someone let me in, seeing that I was so desperate. I stood in line and told a woman in front of me what had happened.

"We are now closed," I heard the teller say.

"Please," I begged, "you must help me."

The woman explained my tragic story to the teller, who felt sorry for me and was nice enough to change my money.

Exhausted, I ran out of the bank, when it suddenly occurred to me that Mont's keys were also in the wallet. I tried to call the American Consulate, but they too were closed for the week-end. It was August, and no one works in Spain on week-ends. The town was deserted. In desperation, crying, I sat down in the Café de l'Opera on the Ramblas, where someone recognized me from Cadaquès.

"I have lost my keys to the apartment and have to leave for New York tomorrow," I told him. Together, we tried to figure out what to do.

"There is a locksmith in your part of town who might be able to open the door for you," he said, "but I don't have the exact address. Try either this street or the other one," he said.

"Too far fetched," I told myself, but I did head in the direction of the apartment and, as expected, I could not find anything open.

Whenever I am in trouble, I find that a bartender almost always is the best person to turn to; they seem to have a lot of information. So that's what I did. I walked into the first decent looking bar and, as luck would have it, there was a couple standing at the bar who overheard my sad tale.

"Do you speak French?" the woman asked. "There are two things you can do. You can either go to the police, but I am sure you are not crazy about that idea, or I'll go with you to the concierge of your friend's building to see whether perhaps she has a key."

I was thrilled to accept her offer and off we went to Mont's house. "I don't have Mont's keys" the concierge said, "but I do have her sister Maria's keys."

There we found a bunch of ten keys and we went upstairs to try to open the door. As is always the way in my life, nothing comes easy: only the tenth and last key fit. I cried for joy as the door opened. I threw my arms around both of them and invited my kind new-found friend and her husband for a drink to celebrate.

It was strange that just before this incident, I had seriously considered moving to Barcelona. I loved this city with its unusual, beautiful architecture constructed by the world-famous architect, Gaudi, the extraordinary Park Gruell with his sculptures spread throughout the garden, the seafood restaurants overlooking the Mediterranean, the Barrio Gothica with its Cathedral and old historical buildings and the Plaza Real, where one could just sit in one of the many cafés and meditate. Not to mention the many tapas bars with delicate appetizers, the fresh seafood and the good Spanish wines. At night, one could visit the elegant champagne bars, which are open all night packed with the "beautiful" people. But I decided that this theft was an omen telling me that, as I jokingly said when I got back to New York: "If I am to get mugged, it might as well be home in New York."

Chapter XXX

PR Department in a NY University

After a six months well-deserved "sabbatical," which included two months of travel in Mexico, I started to feel that it was time for me to return home and look for a job. For some reason, at that particular time, 1976, this was not easy and jobs were hard to find. After going through the usual search, answering ads, sending out resumés and going to employment agencies without success, I was getting discouraged. My situation seemed desperate and I needed to make a living. Then I spotted an ad in the New York Times for someone to work in the Public Relations office of a university attached to a medical school located in Greenwich Village, with a promise of long vacations. I applied and was glad to get the job, but disappointed with the very low salary. The office was on lower Fifth Avenue, walking distance from my house, and I figured that I would stay there until I found something better. As it turned out, I remained there almost six years, mostly because of the lure of the four weeks vacation which made it possible for me to go to Europe every summer to see what was still left of my mother's family: two aunts and two cousins. In the office there was a constant atmosphere of hysteria, tension, and altercation due to the pressure exerted on my co-workers and my bosses to write fundraising speeches. There were constant deadlines and my boss was a little Napoleonic man who had an obsessive compulsive personality. I was always very busy sending out press releases, taking care of our photo library, etc., but at lunchtime I still managed to do my grocery shopping at Jefferson Market nearby which made my life easier.

Also I knew that at the end of the day, I would meet my friends at the bar at the Fifth Avenue Hotel or at Number One Fifth Avenue, just down the street from the office.

One day, in the middle of a severe snowstorm, my son called me at work: "Mom," he said, "I have just seen an ad for an apartment across the street from New York University."

This was a perfect location for him since he was enrolled as a student at the university. We braved the snowstorm and staggered through four feet of snow, getting there before anyone else. The storm sure gave us a lucky break, because the rent was very reasonable. David moved in and was happy in his studio apartment. Two years later, I went to his graduation where he received a Master's degree in Business Administration from NYU.

After David graduated, he happened to run into a girl he remembered from summer camp years earlier. He told me: "I am in love with her." She returned his feelings. He soon moved in with her and when he got his first important job in Philadelphia, she joined him and gave up her excellent job as a nurse at the New York University Medical Center. I was very sad when David left New York. David and Steff lived in an area called Society Hill in a beautiful old brownstone. I had never been to Philadelphia before, and enjoyed that city tremendously with its historical buildings and its outstanding museum next to the river and its gorgeous surroundings. We also went to see the famous private Barnes collection, situated outside of the city, where one could only visit by prior appointment.

While working at the University, I wanted to keep in touch with some of the artists and people I knew from my gallery days. Living in Manhattan offered me the opportunity not only to visit special museum exhibitions but also to visit galleries in SoHo which, by this time, had expanded to such a degree that from three galleries in 1970, while I was running the Max Hutchinson gallery, there were now at least seventy-five in 1977, and two hundred in 1999.

At that time, going to art openings became my only way to meet people who shared my interests. At my job at the college I did not have much in common with my co-workers, but it was just a way of making a living.

Even though my salary was low, my priority in life had always been to be able to return to Europe once a year and to take a few long week-ends off to get out of town.

The job provided me with all this. In addition, it offered me great security because I was a member of the hospital union 1199. I became active in the meetings and was even asked to take a greater role in the union which I did not do for some reason or another. But I did enjoy having the opportunity for once in my life to be able to speak up. I always felt, and still feel, that employees, for the most part, are not being treated fairly by their employers, with very few exceptions.

The only person with whom I could communicate in this competitive, crazy office was one of the senior writers, Irving, who took a liking to me. I confided in him and he was always supportive; we ended up laughing about the neurotic people in our office.

One day, Irving said: "Would you like to join a sculptor friend and myself for drinks at his loft?"

"I made plans to go to an art opening," I told him, "but I'd love to join you later." Irving gave me the address of a friend's loft and when I arrived there, he introduced me to the sculptor, Fred, and to Olivera, a very attractive painter who was a neighbor. They had had a chance meeting on the adjoining roof of their respective lofts the day before. Olivera and I had an immediate rapport, both being Europeans and both having gone through World War II in Europe. She was of Yugoslavian background, but was brought up in Finland and Sweden during part of the war. The four of us went out to dinner.

After that evening, Olivera and I became good friends, and started seeing each other frequently. I admired her intelligence and found out very soon that she was a loyal friend. She often invited me to what she called her "Enchanted Evenings" at her loft and we met each others' friends over the years. It has become a tradition to spend New Year's Eve at her place and we all breathe a sigh of relief knowing that we have a lovely, comforting place to go to on, what can be a very lonely evening. When Olivera exhibited some of her beautiful drawings, shortly after I met her, Irving and I arranged to have a party for her at his loft, where she gave me a drawing which still hangs over my dining room table. To this day, we are the best of friends.

Chapter XXXI

My Hospital Jobs

I ended up spending six years in the Public Relations Department of the University, until I was told that we were relocating to the Bronx. I knew that there was no way that I was going to move with them. I wanted a job near where I lived and, also, I had to begin thinking seriously about my future. I sent out three resumés to nearby hospitals and was amazed when I received a telegram from the Director of Clinical Pathology at one of the hospitals, asking me to contact Personnel since he was looking for an Executive Secretary.

I was extremely nervous before the interview and decided to dye my hair, which had been prematurely white since the age of thirty. With a young face, it looked good, and despite several efforts later on to have my hair dyed, not one of the top beauty parlors in the city wanted to do it. They all insisted, "We love your hair color; you look great." But now it was a different story. I had to get a job and I became ash blonde overnight.

I was so nervous getting dressed the morning before the interview that in my excitement, I forgot to button the top button of my blouse, somewhat exposing my bra. I never noticed it, but my interviewer did, and she wrote it up in my personnel file. Nevertheless, I was sent to Dr. D. for my second interview.

"Can you make good coffee?" was his first question, "because I buy the best at Balducci's, and I want to make sure that we start the day that way. Which are your favorite restaurants and do you go to the theatre?" he continued, "because I am a renaissance man and since your office is right next to mine, we have to be able to live with each other."

I knew then and there that this was a man to whom I could relate, and though I can't remember exactly what I replied, I must have given him the appropriate answers, because he hired me on the spot.

Sure enough, I was to occupy the large office next to his, on the 11th floor, with a beautiful view of the park. On my first day, I told my employer: "I am very nervous."

To my surprise, he answered, "So am I."

It occurred to me that he too was hoping he had made the right decision in hiring me. I was lucky to be able to work for Dr. D. for two years. We got along splendidly and I found him to be a wonderful boss. It was a pleasure to work for him. He gave me a great deal of responsibility in dealing with our residents who reported to me in his absence.

Six months later, he told me one day: "When I hired you, I knew about your blouse being unbuttoned, but I felt that the interviewer was uptight and thus paid no attention." We had a good laugh about the incident.

Two years later, unfortunately for me, Dr. D. got a top position in a New Jersey hospital. I gave a farewell party for him which the hospital catered and I collected money for a gift. He had told me that he had seen a drawing in a gallery in SoHo which he loved. He described it to me and I was lucky to be able to locate it and found out that it was still available. After he unwrapped it, the staff presented it to him as a farewell gift at the party. I had managed to buy flowers for each table at our local Green Market; thus the entire affair was a huge success. But I missed Dr. D. a lot when he was gone.

Soon afterwards, I lost my job in the department of Pathology at the hospital for political reasons and, against everyone's advice, transferred to the Director of Infectious Diseases. She turned out to be a terror.

It was the beginning of the AIDS crisis, and my phone was the hot line for the entire country. It became a nightmare trying to calm down people who had just found out that they were HIV positive. No one at that time, at the beginning of the AIDS crisis, knew enough about the disease. I was delighted when I got fired three months later, since my boss was impossible and had had at least eight secretaries that year. Later, she herself had a nervous breakdown—no wonder.

Again, I needed work. When my friends, Max and Leon, offered me a part-time job in the Public Relations department of their music business, I accepted even though it paid very little and it gave me no health benefits or any vacation. I figured it was all right for the time being to be working while at the same time looking for a permanent job.

The office was very glamorous; a penthouse apartment on Park Avenue, right next to Regine's elegant restaurant/nightclub. But it was not the answer for a "real" job, even though I was invited to concerts since my employers had previously worked for Hurok, one of the most prestigious impressarios in the music world who handled Leonard Bernstein, amongst others.

One day, a friend who worked at my former hospital called me to say, "I have heard through the grapevine that they are looking for an Executive Secretary for the Director of Pathology at another New York hospital. Why don't you apply—it's the same job that you had before," she said.

I did just that, met my boss, who was Australian and who had a reputation for being extremely difficult. When he interviewed me and when I told him that I had an English Boarding School education, he hired me on the spot. My background must have appealed to his snobbishness.

Between my job with Max and Leon and my new situation, I was able to take off for a week's vacation. I went to Puerto Rico as my friend Denise's guest. It was a different experience from previous visits since it was out of season and Denise invited me to meet her friends, lesbian and straight. We had a nice time with each other because she was not burdened by guests staying at her Inn and we were free to roam.

My seven years working for Dr. H. were the most depressing ones of my entire career. He was a sadistic man who would yell at me if I left out a comma in a 50-page medical manuscript. Medical terminology is certainly not easy to spell. He would get red in the face while he was scolding me. After a while, I didn't put up with it anymore. I would grab the manuscript, leave his office, and say to him, before slamming the door: "While you are yelling at me, I would have had plenty of time to type in a comma."

He didn't like it, but he put up with me, knowing that he couldn't find anyone else who would put up with him or could improve on my skills.

To make matters worse, the office manager hated me from day one for reasons I was never sure of. She had been working there for thirty years and perhaps felt threatened that I would take her job away. She treated me like a prisoner, following me to the bathroom or to the file room to make sure that I didn't take extra time for myself. It was horrible, and we had many confrontations.

I complained to my boss, who had warned me about her when he hired me, but who, for some reason, had done nothing about the situation. I always wondered why, but hospital politics are very strange and no different from any other politics. I stuck it out because I wanted to get my small pension and increase my Social Security. On the positive side, however, my boss did let me have three weeks vacation and I was able to go to Europe in the summer.

In 1991, the hospital retired him and also wanted to retire me, but because of their fear of being accused of age discrimination, they did not know how to go about it. I played right into their hands by asking for my usual three weeks vacation, which I had accumulated by that time; it was denied: "The needs of the department cannot spare you," the memo stated. I was only granted two weeks.

As fate would have it, I got sick in Europe, and sent a telegram to that effect. When I was able to return, I was summoned to a meeting in which I was told that I was immediately fired. No probation, nothing, despite having worked there for seven years, and despite the doctor's certificate from Europe. It was a terrible shock, particularly knowing that the firing had been initiated by my vicious office manager.

In retrospect and in spite of the many future problems the firing created for me, it was the best thing that could have happened, because I had been eager to leave but I did not have the courage to do so. Thus, the decision had been made for me.

Chapter XXXII

Retirement

I had to fight hard in order to get my unemployment insurance to which I was entitled, as well as for my very small pension. In the end, I succeeded, but it took two years of my life fighting for what was rightfully mine. Twice I had to go to court. The first time I lost even though I had a lawyer who was assigned to me from the Unemployment Office; I then appealed and, miraculously, won my case. The second time I tried to get my pension retroactively and lost my case, but I no longer had the strength to fight for what was a relatively small amount of money. A Washington, D.C. pension officer had to force my employers to give me my pension, or I would never have received it at all.

Nevertheless, it was a tremendous relief to stop working in such an unpleasant atmosphere and for such nasty people.

On the other hand, having worked for thirty-seven years from 9-5, I felt ambivalent about retiring. I still wanted to work, at least part-time. I was terrified not knowing what to do with my new-found free time. What will happen to me on Monday morning? I asked myself. I might get terribly depressed, and I had heard that many people who retire go through this painful period of dreading what to do with their remaining years. As things turned out, I didn't have to worry.

The first thing I did was to go for counseling to help me put my life into the right perspective. I also continued looking for another job, but without much success. The other thing I did was to enroll in a computer school because I realized that not being computer literate presented a big problem; after completing the course, I was able to practice for a year afterwards. At first, I didn't find it easy, but it did give me some knowledge which came in handy later on.

Next, I looked for the right volunteer job. I didn't want to be a hospital volunteer. Nine years of hospital work were enough for me. Again I was lucky: it was the 1992 Presidential campaign, and I immediately applied to work as a volunteer; it was the most exciting campaign I had ever worked on. Years before I had volunteered when Mayor Lindsay was running for Mayor of New York City. Working on the Clinton campaign, gave me great satisfaction. I donated all my free time during the day, working at the headquarters. As the campaign came close to election day, we were all very eager for our Democratic candidate to win; we followed the results of the polls with great anxiety because it was a close election and could have gone either way.

My perks consisted of being invited to work at fundraising events; I was able to attend a $1000 a plate dinner where both Bill and Hillary Clinton spoke. Another time, at DeNiro's restaurant in Tribeca, we were invited to watch a closed circuit video in which most of the Hollywood stars participated and where Barbra Streisand announced: "The last time I sang was for a catastrophe, namely the horrible accident at Chernobyl. This time, it is to avoid another catastrophe: four more years of Bush."

It was an exciting time and, of course, when Election day finally came, we were all awaiting the results with bated breath. We finally found out that Clinton was elected, not because we saw it on television, but at the party in the Ballroom of the Sheraton Hotel, some volunteers from the rear of the ballroom stormed in, carrying the *New York Times* with the headline: "Clinton elected as 38th President of the United States." I was so moved that it brought tears to my eyes.

My friend Joyce and I went across the street to Hurley's Bar to celebrate. It was an unforgettable evening, but especially because I felt that in some small way, I had contributed to help rescue the Democratic party from total disaster.

It was the beginning of my new career, volunteering for national and local political campaigns. I found the experience very rewarding and exhilarating because, in addition to working for the politician in whom I believed, I also met people with whom I shared the same goal.

Later on, I also volunteered one day a week at the United Nations in the Housing Department. It was an interesting job because it familiarized me somewhat with the workings of a Real Estate office. I still continue to give one day a week to the United Nation.

Chapter XXXIII

Zi/Escondido

During my working years, I always tried to take a Christmas vacation in order to get away during the holidays.

One year, my friends Max and Leon suggested that I join them in Zihuatenejo and, contrary to my promise to myself never to return to Mexico because of reoccurring stomach problems, they managed to talk me into joining them because they raved about the place.

Zihuatenejo is situated in a beautiful cove on the sea. We stayed in cottages on "La Ropa" beach; "*Ropa*" means clothes in Spanish. It got its name because in prior years, the local women went there with their washboards to do their laundry.

One of my favorite friends, Randall, and I shared one of the cottages in this beautiful corner of the world, which was ideal in every way. We established our own routine: a swim in the ocean before eating breakfast on our terrace; then we would sun ourselves on the pure white sandy beach just in front of our cottages. Next door was the local restaurant, called "La Perla" where our lunch consisted of a freshly caught grilled red snapper. The service was so slow that we always jokingly said: "We have to go there a half hour before we are hungry." In front of the restaurant were hammocks set up on the beach; there we took our siesta under the palm trees. The hammocks made it easy to take a wonderful nap under the blue sky because the lapping of the water soothed one to sleep.

The actress Lauren Hutton and the well-known avant-garde painter, Larry Rivers, who lived nearby also loved the place. They came back every year and we were introduced to them and we found them both pleasant and unassuming. I really don't know what sort of roles Lauren had played in movies, but I did know that she was a famous fashion model and she still is in commercials up to the present time. Larry and I did not talk about the art world; we all wanted to get away from our city life. Our conversations were friendly, but as is usual on holidays, revolved around local gossip, where to eat in town, how many pesos to the dollar and most of all to warn each other about eating unpeeled fruit and the local drinking water.

Twice a week, we went to the village to shop for our groceries, visiting the local market for our produce and to change money in the bank. This was always exhausting, because it was so hot in town that we could not wait to return to our cottages.

From our beach, we could watch the exquisite Mexican sunset with its unusual color combinations seen nowhere else that I know of. We would then shower and get ready for our dinner in the village, which is about three miles away but reachable by taxi, or sometimes we had to hitchhike.

When we first spent our holidays there, the place had not been built up yet with its present pretentious luxury hotels nearby in Ixtapa, and there were relatively few tourists. There was one restaurant in the village, called "Las Coconuts" which was run by a SoHo gallery owner and his wife. It was the "in" place then because the food was excellent. In addition, the restaurant was beautifully decorated with many local exotic plants and flowers. We would either eat there or in other local places where the kitchens were carefully checked out for cleanliness. For five years I spent my winter vacation there and survived without getting sick, except for one year when I bought a can of tuna fish from a food stand on the beach (great mistake) and almost died of ptomaine poisoning. But after a time this lovely simple resort started filling up with tourists from the nearby luxury hotels and clubs and we felt it was time for us to find another untouristy resort.

Oaxaca

During my gallery days, one of our artists had told me: "I spend my winters in Oaxaca, Mexico, a beautiful Colonial village where I rent a house with a maid and a car for $500 a month." I never forgot it, especially since she raved about Oaxaca, describing its many museums, art galleries and the famous church of Santa Domingo, with its pure golden altar. It sounded intriguing and a few years later, my friend Lois and I left New York behind in the cold winter and flew there. We stayed in a hotel right on the *socolo* (village square), which is sheltered by an arcade, so that rain or shine, everyone gathers at all hours of the day or night in the many cafés, to read the paper, write or study their homework for the Spanish lessons which are taught in two local schools. We visited the museums, art galleries and churches. We also went to the famous archeological sites, Mont Alban and Mitla, where we hired a tour guide to lecture us on the life of the Aztec Indians who inhabited that part of the world.

At night, the Mariachi bands playing in the street next to the cafés in the square could be heard miles away. We, too, fell in love with the place and spent a whole week there until we started to yearn for a beach and a swim in the sea.

We had been told about Puerto Escondido (the hidden port) and we left on a seven hour bus trip on a curvy dangerous road over the mountains. I was scared to drive so close to the edge of the mountains, but it was all worth it when we arrived at this heavenly place which we soon called "paradise." Not only is the weather always perfect, but it is one of those places where one can meet more people from all walks of life, and from all over the world, than anywhere else I had ever been to. Every evening at 6 o'clock, we would meet on the terrace of the Hotel *Las Palmas* for "Happy Hour," which overlooked the sea; this is where everyone got together. Where else could one meet a chimney sweeper from Toledo, Ohio, a lumberjack from Canada, a farmer from Alaska or a sculptor from New York City? There were no cliques and everyone was accepted. While there, I never had to sit alone or eat dinner by myself.

I found out that there was an English lending library in my modest hotel and people could borrow books and exchange them. Carmen's Bakery also let people borrow English books. Carmen, who is Mexican, owned the bakery, and married a Canadian; together they run the business which flourishes because Carmen bakes the most delicious bread, scones and croissants. We often had our breakfast there, sharing tables and meeting new people.

But in life there is no such thing as "paradise." One day I suddenly felt very ill and nauseous. I went back to my simple room with only a bed and a makeshift wardrobe which I had, however, decorated with gorgeous tropical flowers bought on the local market. It also had a terrace overlooking the ocean from where I could watch the surfers riding the waves. The surf often was so violent that the pounding of the waves would wake me at night.

I felt so sick that I could not even swallow a glass of water, nor could I possibly conceive eating anything at all. Fortunately, a Canadian, by the name of Edouardo, whom I had befriended at *Las Palmas*, got worried when he did not see me at "Happy Hour" and came to see me.

"I feel that I am dying, I have fever," I told him.

"You must eat something," he said, "I will come and get you for breakfast tomorrow; you must try to have tea and toast. This can't go on, but meanwhile I am getting you the name of a good doctor because I think you need one."

As promised, Edouardo showed up for breakfast on the terrace of my hotel. I tried to drink the tea and eat the toast, but couldn't keep anything in my stomach. We called the doctor who, miraculously, showed up a half hour later in my room. He took one look at me and said: "We must take drastic measures. I don't want to send you to the hospital which is one hour away from here, but I am going to get the appropriate vaccine and give you an injection. Tonight you have to come to my office for a second one; you need four in all. I think you have salmonella."

"It always seems to happen to me that I get sick on week-ends," I said.

"I won't be at the office tomorrow, Sunday," he added, but I will take you to the drug store across the street which will be open tomorrow and tell them what to do. You have to go there twice, eight hours apart; there will be a girl who will give you the injections."

The next day I took a taxi and when I arrived at the drug store, there was no girl to be seen; instead a seventeen year old boy was waiting on me; he spoke no English, but was ready to give me my injection. I was really scared to think that this young boy would give me an injection in my behind in the back of the drug store behind a curtain. There was no water, and I insisted that he clean his hands before he unwrapped a needle from a sterile plastic casing. He took some cotton and alcohol and handed it to me to clean my hands (I don't know why) and then, luckily, he cleaned his hands the same way. I tried to point to my arm, but he shook his head and had me lie down on my side in order that he could inject my buttock. Miraculously, this young boy actually did it better than the doctor. I was less scared on my return trip eight hours later, but it was already dark outside and this local neighborhood was pretty deserted, no tourists to be seen. I was a little apprehensive to say the least.

After this procedure, I was still very weak, and the doctor prescribed sulpha pills for four more days. Thoughts of dying in "paradise" crossed my mind during these lonely days. I was unable to read and tried to write a little bit, but it was a great effort. Only Edouardo came to see me, usually late at night. Since I was burning up with fever, he would put cold compresses on my forehead. It was touching since we had only recently met on the terrace of the Hotel *Las Palmas* at "Happy Hour" on my first day in Escondido. I was looking for the bathroom and asked Francesco, the bartender, for the key. "Do you know where it is?" asked a male voice.

"No," I said.

"I'll show you," he answered.

Together we walked up a few stairs past the palm trees to what looked like a pretty awful toilet without a light. "I'll stand guard," he said, "so just go ahead."

When we got back to the terrace, I saw that he was a little drunk, but that he had kind brown eyes. I returned the key to Francesco. "What will you have?" Edouardo asked me.

"A marguarita *sin sel* on the rocks," I answered.

He pulled up a chair enabling us to look out towards the sea, and we started to talk. I guessed that he was about 58 years old, had a moustache and a handsome chiselled face which was wrinkled from exposure to too much sun. He had a good thin, almost too thin body, and was immaculately dressed in shorts and a shirt that looked like it had just been ironed.

"I live in British Columbia in a house miles from town with a bear and a horse in my back yard," he told me. "There is a lot of foreplay between them before they make love," he said and smiled. "What about you?" he asked.

"I'm from New York, and this is my first time in Puerto Escondido and I love it here," was my answer. "I have travelled all over Mexico, but this is the best place I've been to. It's just the right size, there are miles of empty beach with white sand and the water temperature is just right for swimming."

We went our separate ways that evening, but I saw him again walking along the beach a few days later. He didn't recognize me and I just let him pass.

The next day I almost bumped into him and said "hullo." He had totally forgotten our encounter and I reminded him. "Oh, you're Ms. New York. Now I remember you from *Las Palmas*; it's dark on the terrace and here in the sunlight people look different."

The next time we met at *Las Palmas*, he said to me: "I want to take you to the most beautiful beach you have ever seen."

We arranged to meet at Carasallilo. He was right. This magnificent cove is situated around the bend beyond the light house, reachable either by walking down a very steep incline or taking a boat from the port. Hidden in the woods behind the beach are small stands with palapas right on the sand, where the locals sell cold drinks. At the very end of this small cove, Maria has a stand with a stove which has two burners where she managed to cook the most delicious meals. We had fresh lobster and shrimps "a la plancha," the best I ever ate. Maria bought the fish first thing in the morning in the market and kept it in a cooler with ice. Nobody knew how she managed to carry everything down the steep hill. Before lunch, after struggling down this dangerous walk, we took a dip in the ocean for a delicious swim in the crystal clear blue water to build up an appetite for Maria's feast. After lunch, we had our siesta in a hammock between two palm trees, falling asleep reading a book. At the end of a perfect day Edouardo ordered the boat to take us back to the port. Since it was a windy day, it was not easy getting back to the port—the surf kept pulling the boat back in.

Edouardo who knew all the boat people, motioned to them to move faster. He enjoyed the challenge of the wild surf. I was terrified and made signs to them that they should slow down. It was lucky that I was still in my bathing suit because when we finally managed to get off the boat, we were forced to wade through the water to the beach because of the strong surf.

"Now," said Edouardo, "I'll take you to the terrace of the elegant Hotel Santa Fe for a treat: to watch the magnificent sunset."

"We'll have two fresh strawberry daiquiris," Edouardo told the waiter. It was the end of a perfect day.

Puerto Escondido, like most places in Mexico, has the most glorious sunsets. Often even the local taxi drivers stop to look at the sky turning slightly green shortly after the sun disappears beyond the horizon.

Well, here it was four days later and I felt as if I had awakened from the dead. I wanted to see Edouardo again after my horrible ordeal. On the fifth day, though still very weak, I managed to go to the "Happy Hour." Edouardo was delighted to see me. When I told him that I had not eaten for five days, he said: "I know what you need now. I am going to take you out for chicken soup for Valentine's Day."

We went to a restaurant facing the sea. The gentle lapping of the water made it very romantic, especially when he held my hand and said: "I am so happy that you are well again, but I am only sorry that you are leaving tomorrow." He couldn't stand good-byes and he would always walk away abruptly whenever we were to part. I too felt very sad having to leave him. I had grown very fond of him and thought of him constantly when I was back in New York. He had remained a charming romantic memory for me. We were not lovers because I knew that Edouardo had a woman friend back in Canada. Also I was terribly sick most of our time together and Edouardo's role in my life was a cherishing and nurturing one.

I spent the following winter vacation in Florida with my friend Sary, but two years later, I returned to Escondido. There I met Edouardo again and that's when I found out the reason he hated good-byes. "I was a little boy," he said, "when my father developed cancer. One day, he took his gun and told me that he was going hunting. He never came back."

Maybe this may account for the fact that this very kind, sensitive person is an alcoholic today, and that's why when we saw each other again two years later, I didn't wish to spend much time with him. I did watch him, however, at "Happy Hour," when the little Mexican children were selling their wares: bracelets, earrings and necklaces, and how he interacted with them. He would bargain for the entire lot so that they could go home and didn't have to stay out at night to peddle. On Valentine's Day, he got up early in the morning to go to the market and bought masses of flowers, which he gave to the help in his modest little hotel where he always stayed. The girls were ecstatic and overjoyed.

Another day, he took a group of children to a restaurant for lunch and bought them all their favorite foods, including ice cream. The local Mexicans adored him and called him "Lala." He took the trouble to learn Spanish and spoke it fairly well. He was like the pied piper and always had a group of children following him in the street. Of course, it was due to his generosity. He, himself, stayed in this really cheap hotel and could well have afforded a better place, but he preferred to spend his money on others.

At 1 a.m. a few days after I was back home, a kind voice at the other end of the phone said: "How the hell are you? I'll never forget you. I'll see you next year."

I felt touched when I hung up the phone. He had called from Canada. He had not forgotten me.

Chapter XXXIV

Billy

After my health problems in Puerto Escondido, I knew that I must never return to Mexico, and luckily fate intervened and I found Billy.

I met Billy when he was on the rebound in an elegant restaurant with a bar, called Convent Garden, in Greenwich Village.

He smiled at me as I was ordering my drink from Kina, the Swedish bartender. I knew her from a SoHo bar while I was still working at the Max Hutchinson gallery. In the early days of SoHo, everyone knew each other because SoHo was still small and had just been discovered.

Billy obviously needed to talk. "My girlfriend just died of cancer," he said. "She was forty years old. I loved her so much and I am heartbroken."

What could I say? I tried to be sympathetic and to console him as best I could. After his fourth martini, he was even more talkative.

"I am a nice guy," he said to me.

It was a strange thing to say about oneself, but I liked his openness. I decided to continue going to Convent Garden from time to time. It was comfortable to know the bartender and the place had a friendly crowd, where I often ran into people I knew from the art world. Sure enough, the next time I went to the bar, there was Billy again, having his four nightly martinis. This time, he told me more about himself.

"I am an executive in a commercial real estate agency. I had been a vice president, but as I was getting close to retirement, they had reduced my job responsibilities. I will bring you my credentials," he said unexpectedly, "when I see you again."

The next time I saw him, he showed me the company's Year End Report, which included his photograph with his title. I looked at him more closely, and here was a man in his early sixties with thinning hair, but a good lean body with regular features, though in no way memorable. What distinguished him, however, was that he always wore dark suits with a white shirt, as if he were going to a funeral. After running into Billy a few times at the bar, over a period of time, he asked me out to dinner. Of course, I realized that he was an alcoholic, but a functioning one who went to work every day of his life, and he continued to work for the same company for the past forty years. That's more than one can say for a lot of people who are not alcoholic. I felt safe in accepting his invitation. On most work days, after he had his four martinis, he would go home and be in bed by 9:30 p.m. in order to be at work on time.

We did go out to dinner, and I found myself enjoying his company. He had a great sense of humor and he made me laugh. In addition, he managed to be the perfect gentleman and escort. I decided to reciprocate and invited him to dinner at my house. He seemed not to be comfortable because I had invited my friend Bob, who was gay, or for some other reason which I could not quite understand. "In the future," he said, "I'll take you out to dinner alone."

When the summer was approaching, I told him that I was planning to go to Mallorca. "It's always been my dream to go to that island," he said. "I have never been to Europe and I had read that Mallorca is a romantic place because Georges Sand and Chopin chose to live there periodically."

"Why don't you come along?" I asked Billy.

"I'll let you know next week, and then you can book my ticket and make all the arrangements," he replied to my great surprise.

As things turned out, this was to be one of the many trips he and I took together. Even though we were not lovers, he was a perfect travelling companion in every way. His luggage consisted of his briefcase into which he stuffed some underwear, an extra shirt, a T-shirt plus a pair of white pants, and, of course, his toothbrush. He wore blue jeans and brought a sweater and a raincoat. This suited me fine, because I also travel light, since I don't want to check my luggage. Waiting at airports always makes me paranoid, afraid that my luggage might get lost. This once had happened to me on the way to the island of Ibiza. Here, I was in a heat wave, sitting at the pool of my hotel, fully dressed. It was Sunday and all the stores were closed and I could not even buy a bathing suit. I decided then and there never to check my luggage again. I just make do and always seem to have enough to wear.

Billy was a perfect travel companion in other ways, too, I reflected. He did not impose himself on me, but was always there at the appointed dinner hour, since I hate eating alone, especially in a foreign resort. How lucky I was, I thought, that we were not attached to each other, and yet how comforting to have him as a travel companion. At my time of life, I was grateful. I had found it difficult to find the right woman travel companion.

Our hotel in Puerto Andraitx, a small port resort, was modest, to say the least. Billy splurged and paid for a double room with a bathroom, whereas my single room had the bathroom down the hall. I was always frugal and still resilient enough, so that it did not bother me. The hotel had a pool, but we had to cross a busy road to get there. When it was built, there was no road there. Times had certainly changed.

Billy never complained. He would get up early, walk down to the port, where he would sit in a café and order his first glass of wine. After eating my breakfast on the terrace of our hotel, which had a wonderful view of the entire port, I would walk down to meet him; we then took a taxi to the inlet which was a few miles away. There Billy would once again seat himself down in the beach café while I went swimming. There was no sandy beach, and I had to climb down a steep ladder to get into the blue, clear water.

We spent three summer vacations together in the same hotel in Puerto Andraitx because the place was very special; not too touristy, very romantic with the sun setting over the port with its many big yachts from all over Europe, and then disappearing over the mountain surrounding Puerto Andraitx.

One of the rare days when it was so hot that Billy went to cool off in the sometimes turbulent sea, he lost his glasses. He couldn't see a thing without them and, of course, he did not bring a second pair. They were immediately washed away. I searched and searched, but to no avail. I asked everyone I saw, in three different languages, to see whether they could help me find them.

When I returned empty-handed, Billy said: "Forget it, why are you knocking yourself out for nothing, give up, they are gone." He was almost annoyed with me (or perhaps with himself).

The next day, when I went swimming, a lady said to me: "Were you the American who lost your friend's glasses?"

"Yes," I said, "Why?"

"Because I found them and handed them to the bartender in the small café with the red awning."

I retrieved them and ran up to Billy, blind-folded him, and put the glasses on his head. He just couldn't believe the whole story.

"You have to have faith," I told him.

He had resigned himself to being practically blind for the rest of our vacation. That evening, he gave me a beautiful mother-of-pearl cameo. I was touched by his generosity.

On one of our other trips, in the winter, we went to Zihuatenejo, Mexico, where I had been before on another Christmas/New Year's holiday. This was before I got sick in Mexico. There, one night, I almost lost Billy in a bar when he had too many tequilas. It was one of my worst moments, and one which I will never forget. He began to sing at the piano bar.

I was terribly embarrassed and warned him: "Come back with me, Billy, or I'll go without you."

"Go ahead," he said. "I am not coming."

He sounded like a naughty little boy. I left, took a taxi and when I got back, I began to realize that I had made a terrible mistake leaving him there. Billy spoke no Spanish. He was not even sure of the address of our beach bungalows. I was frantic. I was tempted to go back to town, but I was afraid that I might miss him while he was taking a taxi to the beach.

I paced up and down on the beach outside my bungalow and had visions of Billy getting arrested by the Mexican police. It had once happened on my first trip to Mexico that gay friends of ours were thrown into jail because they had gone swimming in the nude. The police arrested them, robbed them, and they told us that they had been raped by the guards and that they had all their expensive jewelry stolen. It was a horrendous experience. In the end they had to pay $150 in order to get released.

I remembered that and felt terrible what I had done to Billy. What would become of him? How would I explain this to his two daughters who live in Florida? I waited one hour. It seemed endless and then suddenly there he was, walking along the beach as if nothing had happened. The taxi driver had helped him find his way home. I threw my arms around him and kissed him; I promised myself that I would never again leave him alone, no matter what happened.

The following year, we decided to go away over New Year's. I had heard that the Dominican Republic was warm in the winter and inexpensive. I managed to find a hotel on the beach where I made a reservation. I was able to get very cheap tickets on Dominican Airlines and off we went on New Year's Day.

Our plane must have been fifty years old; everything was broken. I got a little worried, especially when we saw both flight attendants sleeping in the first row. Since it was New Year's Day, they had probably celebrated the night before. We asked them for a drink, but they just pointed to the galley and told us to help ourselves. The plane was almost empty, since most people must have returned home the day before, on New Year's Eve.

We were relieved and ecstatic when the plane touched ground. Our hotel was a very unassuming, but a pleasant place, where mostly local people stayed. We were given preferential treatment because I had been working as a part-time travel agent and the owner gave us his best rooms directly facing the sea. Billy found the bar as usual. I checked out the adjoining beach.

For two days, all was well. Billy drank at the bar and I went swimming. As usual, we dined together in the evening. The third day it began to rain, and it never stopped for the next four days. Since our rooms faced the sea and a terrible wind developed, we were scared stiff that the water would flood our room.

The locals told us: "This is a very rare seaquake." The sea was so turbulent that it made a huge hole in the earth outside our hotel rooms. In no time at all, this quiet bay had turned into a wild ocean and the local kids were able to go surfing—a rare treat for them. After the worst of the storm subsided, Billy's white pants became black from the mud, while we were struggling to reach a local restaurant and Billy simply had to buy new white pants.

Soon afterwards, we were invited to the other end of the village by a couple we had met by chance and who I knew because Marie had been the owner of a small art gallery near SoHo, where my friend Olivera used to exhibit her art.

When we arrived at their apartment, we couldn't find them and we were walking around in the rain in order to get to a restaurant to dry off and get a bite to eat. Finally, we took a taxi "collective" back.

This turned out to be quite an experience: local people got on at various stops, just as soaked as we were, all yelling in Spanish, drinking rum in the back in order to keep warm. Billy was a good sport throughout this ordeal; he never complained.

We took a few more holidays together after that. But one day he called: "I have been partially retired from my job and I am only here on a part time basis. I will work six months and spend the other six months in Florida where my older daughter has rented an apartment for me; you must come down for New Year's," he said. I accepted with pleasure.

Although Billy no longer owned a car and seldom drove, he had rented one to pick me up at the Orlando Airport. In his modest apartment, he gave me his bedroom and slept on the living room couch; he really was a "nice guy." He had always told me: "I like you very much, but I don't love you." Since I felt the same way, there was no conflict and it was an ideal arrangement.

Billy was particularly friendly with his former mother-in-law who came to visit while I was there. When she heard that I had never been to Disney World, she insisted that we go together to MGM's movie set. Billy didn't want to join us, but he was happy to get rid of us as he would then have the opportunity to spend the afternoon at the hotel bar across the street, where he spent most of his time. He gave her money and said: "Take Brigitte out for a nice lunch."

While driving to Disneyland, Billy's ex-mother-in-law gave me some insight into Billy's character: "When he divorced my daughter," she said, "he moved to New York, but continued to see his daughters every month. Then it became every two months, and gradually it was every six months, but he always sent child support money. Soon he used to visit once a year, and then he stopped coming down altogether, but he has always taken care of his financial obligations," she said.

I remembered having met his oldest daughter in New York while she was visiting Billy. He actually brought her to his bar and introduced her to all his buddies. She was a typical, pretty seventeen-year-old, very outgoing. "What's with you two guys?" she asked when he introduced me to her.

"We are just friends," I told her. I think she was relieved that her father was not going to remarry.

Eventually Billy moved down to Florida for good, and even though I did visit him twice over New Year's, I was not a bit surprised when I got a call one day saying: "I have met this rich widow who has a house on the lake near Winter Park, and I am moving in with her. Do come and visit; you can still use my apartment if you want to come down."

Of course, that was the end of Billy as far as I was concerned. I felt very sorry to lose him, but, I thought, it fitted in with his mother-in-law's description of his behavior vis-à-vis his children.

I somehow expected it to happen. When I once mentioned the possibility to him that he would meet a rich widow, he just laughed.

I never heard from Billy again, but as he had said: "I am a nice guy," and he was that while he was around.

Chapter XXXV

Spain/Morocco

During the summers I frequently visited Paris as well as Spain. In Paris, I was lucky to have my cousins' children as well as my favorite cousin's first wife, Nina, who was one of the chicest women I have ever known. She worked as a designer for Pierre Cardin. The first time I met her was just after I had left Vienna as a young girl. Over the years, we became good friends, not only because we were related through her marriage to my cousin; we simply liked each other. Our friendship continued even though she and my cousin, Jules, subsequently divorced. One of the reasons for this was the fact that they could not have children. Poor Nina had one miscarriage after another. My cousin, Jules, remarried Jeanette, another chic woman of Russian background, and she gave birth seven moths later to premature, but healthy twin boys. Michel and Pierre grew up to become two very charming and likeable young men who I see almost every year when I am in Paris.

Meanwhile, Nina, no longer young when she got divorced, found herself to be alone after many years of a bourgeois marriage. Despite the fact that she spoke five languages and was extremely attractive, it was not easy for her to find someone else. This always seems to be true for women; men seem to have no difficulty getting remarried.

One day, friends introduced her to Eugène, a Spaniard, fifteen years younger, who was working in a factory installing heating units. They were hardly from the same milieu, but they fell in love with each other; the age difference did not seem to affect their relationship. The rest of the family always wondered what these two people could possibly have in common. At family gatherings, whenever I came to Paris, it was always difficult to have a conversation with him. Usually, when I visited Paris and stayed with my cousins, Jules and Jeanette, we would discuss their relationship. Jeanette would say: "You see, I understand why they are together: Nina never could have children; by being with Eugène, she can look after someone who really deeply cares for her and depends on her, because she is so much smarter."

Nina's former mother-in-law bought her a small apartment in Paris and she and Eugène moved in together and eventually married. Despite their different backgrounds, they seemed very happy together. She was smart enough to give him a lot of freedom.

Eugène came from a small village in the southwest of Spain, called Sotogrande, not far from Gibraltar. His family still lived in the same village. Every summer Nina and Eugène spent their vacation there. Finally, they decided to build a house for their retirement in the same community. Eugène's entire family helped to build this magnificent place. They all gave their time to help with the construction of the house and for the landscaping of a beautiful lush garden with all kinds of exotic flowers, as well as a vegetable garden.

Eugène and Nina invited me several times to visit and I finally did go in the late eighties. On the way there, I decided to visit my friend, Mont, in Barcelona and to spend a week in a nearby village, called Sitges, which is about a half hour away by train. It is one of the few seaside towns that is not yet spoiled with fast food restaurants. But it won't be long. Being so close to Barcelona, it is bound to happen sooner or later. For the time being, though, although very crowded in the summer, it is still a picturesque village with small quaint winding streets. Overlooking the village, high up, stands a church and a museum displaying photographs of the history of this seaside resort. Sandy beaches stretch for miles along the south coast and Sitges is surrounded by these which certainly accounts for its popularity.

I stayed in a hotel which was a converted convent. The bar, which is also the lounge, is beautifully furnished with antiques. Small tables surround the bar, and this is where everyone hangs out. You can hear many different languages spoken. As far as I could see, I was the only straight person in the place, because gays from all over the world were spending their vacation there. It did not bother me, because the place was unusually comfortable and after Mont came to visit, the other guests must have thought that we were lesbians and they became much more friendly towards me. Breakfast was served in the garden, buffet style, and I observed the couples interacting with each other in the morning.

One evening in the village I happened to find an Irish pub, and there I got to know two charming people, both from Ireland, as well as a group of Italians. Often, we all ended up going out to dinner in one of the many quaint restaurants in town.

When the week was over, I had prearranged to visit Nina, my cousin, to finally see her beautiful house. It was not easy to get there. I had to fly from Barcelona to Malaga, where I had to catch a bus along the south coast until I reached their village. Unfortunately, since that road leads to Gibraltar, there was a lot of drug smuggling going on. The trip took forever because the police was continually stopping the cars in front of our bus, searching for drugs.

I finally arrived two hours late and found that my cousin was not waiting at the restaurant as planned. I felt totally exhausted from the long journey and the heat, and I had a drink at the restaurant. The bartender must have recognized me and said: "Eugène left word to call him as soon as you get here."

Unfortunately, Eugène was quite angry with me having had to wait so long.

"Not my fault," I told him, but I was upset.

The house was indeed idyllic. The typical Spanish architecture of white stucco-painted brick, with red bougainvillea climbing the walls, made the color contrast most dramatic. The house had two decks, so that there was always shade on one side to escape the summer heat. The interior was furnished with Nina's exquisite antique French furniture, which she had inherited from her mother. I had my own wing, a bedroom with a private bathroom, and it felt most luxurious.

Unfortunately, Nina, who I remembered being extremely intelligent, talented, and supportive, was suffering from the beginnings of Alzheimer's disease. She experienced serious memory loss and occasional confusion. Eugène told me: "Don't leave her out of your sight; she may wander off and not know how to get back to the house." It was hard for me to accept. On the surface she still seemed all right and was as well dressed and slim as I always remembered her. She remained attractive with her big blue eyes and blonde hair.

The next morning, the maid who came to do the cleaning was left in charge of Nina. Thus, Eugène was able to drive me around to see the countryside. I had told him: "I'd love to see your village where you were born and its surroundings." I was very happy to see this part of the country, which I had never visited. The landscape is surprisingly lush for Spain, where it rarely rains. We drove into the mountains, crossing bridges over the river, Guadalquivir, one of the largest and most famous ones in Spain. That first day, Eugène and Nina showed me the nearest beach, within walking distance from their house. From that day on, I was on my own. I spent the mornings reading in the garden and talking to Nina. After lunch, when it got cooler, I went to the beach, only returning in time for dinner. Luckily, sitting in the beach café, I met a few expatriate Brits with whom I struck up a conversation in English and was saved from boredom during the afternoons. With Nina and Eugène, I had to speak only French. Eugène did not speak English.

One day, they decided to show me Gibraltar, which I was eager to visit. It is the strangest experience to enter this port and to find the place totally British in feeling. The whole atmosphere reminded me of a Humphrey Bogart movie. It's a very busy place, and most of the cars seem to be jeeps. Since it is a free port, people come here from everywhere to shop in the large supermarkets and to buy inexpensive liquor and cigarettes not available in Spain. Even Britain's Marks & Spencer department store has a branch here. We stopped for lunch and after three weeks of Spanish food, I actually enjoyed eating English fare. Unfortunately, I never got to the "Rock of Gibraltar" which I would have liked to have seen. We had run out of time after stocking up on groceries.

Back in Sotogrande, I saw a poster advertising that it was possible to visit Morocco for the day; since it had been my dream to see that country, this was my opportunity. I went to a travel agent where they sold me a day's excursion ticket. Still, I was terrified to go by myself and also I was afraid that it would be difficult to find bathroom facilities.

The tour bus was to pick me up at a nearby hotel at 8 a.m. It arrived an hour late and I had almost given up. When it finally came, I was happy that the Spanish tour guide spoke English and German while he explained the procedure. We were driven to Algeciras, from where the hydrofoil boat leaves for Tangier. As I expected, the bathroom on the boat did not work, but jokingly I assured everyone: "We are visiting the Malcolm Forbes Museum in Tangier, and since Forbes is American, we'll not only find a bathroom, but also toilet paper." I was right.

Travelling abroad does at times present this to be a big problem. The trip across was uneventful, but before we were getting off the boat, we were told: "Everyone must give up their passports." At first, we were shocked, but then we understood that this was for our own protection. The tour guide explained to us that passports are a valuable commodity in Morocco, and are often stolen for that reason.

On arrival in Tangier, a very handsome Moroccan guide, wearing a beautifully embroidered caftan, met us at the boat and warned us: "You must stick together the whole time. Never leave the group, no matter what happens." We took him at his word. I attached myself to two very nice English ladies with whom I had been speaking on the boat.

A bus drove us at first through the European-looking part of the city with clean white buildings, trees, and gardens; only an occasional Mosque here and there was a reminder that we were in Morocco. We drove through the country side to the ocean to a point where the Atlantic meets the Mediterranean; it was very windy there and this explains why it is not as hot in Morocco as in Spain. We stopped at the Malcolm Forbes Museum which is situated in a beautiful setting with gardens overlooking the sea. This world-famous collection consists of exquisitely painted lead miniature soldiers depicting various battle scenes from many former wars. We were then taken to lunch in a typical tourist trap, where we were served the traditional couscous, but with the most delicious bread I have ever eaten. There was a belly dancer performing, supposedly to entertain us. She gave a ludicrously bad performance, totally inappropriate at that time of the day.

After lunch, the tour guide showed us the vegetable and flower market which was surprisingly clean with its colorful, fresh looking fruit and the most beautiful exotic flowers. The market was packed with lots of local people bargaining in a loud voice.

Later, we did all the expected tourist things in the old and dangerous part of town: the famous Casbah. At the entrance we were greeted by a traditional snake charmer. The snakes were rather large and revoltingly oily looking, twisting around his neck and arms. Most of us could not stand to watch, and we were glad to leave him behind.

It was a sad experience for me to walk through the Casbah and to see how miserably these poor people live in their tiny grey hovels. I had always heard stories about the Casbah, but when I saw a shoemaker working in such primitive surroundings, without electricity, or an old seamstress sewing by hand, again barely able to see, the romance of the Casbah no longer existed for me. We were quickly ushered past exciting looking native handicraft, but were not allowed to stop because the guide was afraid that we might wander away from the group and get lost.

On the way out, we were finally taken to a big house, a sort of department store with four floors; here we were allowed to shop for carpets and souvenirs. Obviously, our tour guide got a kickback there because he kept saying: "You can bargain here." Nevertheless, the prices were very high and I bought nothing.

When we left this shop, on the way back to the hydrofoil that was to take us back to Spain, we were no longer herded as before and were accosted by many vendors who followed us despite our constant refusal to buy anything. They were like leeches, and it was a very scary experience because we were running in order to be in time for the boat.

When we reached the harbor, the guide said: "This last part of the trip was for you to experience the 'real' Morocco, and therefore I did not protect you from the onslaught."

We said good-bye to our guide, thanked him, and were relieved when, upon getting on the boat, we got our passports back and we were even happier when we stepped on Spanish soil. After all, we were back in Europe, even though not in our own countries.

A few days later, I left Sotogrande and Nina's house. My departure was rather sad. She had promised me the night before to wake up to say good-bye. But when I left, she was still asleep, and Eugène never came down to say good-bye either. I had ordered a taxi to take me to the bus station and felt forlorn and sad, knowing intuitively that I would never see Nina again. She died two years later.

Chapter XXXVI

Prague

Even though now that I am retired and have free time, I do not like to travel alone; I manage to visit my friend Janet in England every year, and we travel together while I am there.

In this sense I am lucky. Most of my contemporaries have had to join groups; the thought of having to do this as an alternative disturbs me greatly. I think I would be forced to give up travelling. I never liked group travel and remember how terrible it was when I was a tour guide travelling through South America even though I was in charge.

Janet and I plan our trip early in the year for the month of August when she has time off from the nursery school which she runs from her house and she is not free until school breaks up.

One summer, we decided to visit Prague since Janet had been there before and loved the city. Also she was eager to find out when and where her grandparents had been deported since her mother's parents were Czech citizens. The last time she visited, she could not find their names in the synagogue amidst the other people who were deported and killed.

We had the good luck to stay at the Hilton Hotel, since I was able, as a travel agent, to get us a break in the room rate. (Hotels in Prague are exorbitantly expensive.)

On our first day, we immediately headed for the Jewish section which now only consists of a cemetery and several synagogues. We entered the first synagogue which was awe-inspiring and deeply disturbing. The Nazis had kept precise records of the Jews who were exterminated in concentration camps. I shuddered as I read the names of the thousands of people, young and old, who died in this horrendous way. We went through the lists alphabetically until we actually found the names of her grandparents with the dates when they were arrested, sent to the camps and died. It was an eerie experience which did evoke in me the thought of the horrible way in which my mother must have died. I could hardly stand it. I was grief stricken. I have always tried not to dwell on it and have been in denial. This brought it all home to me. Somehow, for Janet, however, it presented a kind of closure and peace.

In another synagogue, there was a heart-breaking exhibition of children's pencil or crayon drawings who had been sent to Theresienstadt and from there to concentration camps where they consequently died. The children were only allowed to draw "happy" scenes, such as landscapes with houses and pretty flowers, and none of the horrors which they must have been aware of. There were photographs of their teacher and photographs of the children whose drawings were exhibited. It broke my heart to think of what awaited these innocent children. The fine rain which came down that day was in keeping with this very sad experience.

The rest of our days were spent exploring this fabulous old city with its extraordinary baroque architecture which still remains, even though Prague was occupied by the Russians. At the time, a lot of restoration was going on. Unfortunately for us, the people were still very downcast from the former Russian oppression and not at all hospitable.

On another rainy day, we went to visit the castle which overlooks the city and dates back to the ninth century. During the following years, there have been many reconstructions. Since Charles IV of Bohemia who reigned during the 14th century, it was inhabited by kings, archbishops, and nobles. To this day, the president lives here at times. A flag is raised when he is in residence.

A tram took us up and we decided to stay for the afternoon concert which was to take place in the cathedral adjoining the castle. We purchased our tickets and then took a tour through St. Vitus Cathedral, its chapels and the rest of the castle.

Janet was taking photographs of the sculptures and stained glass windows. Unfortunately, for one moment she put down her backpack in the cathedral and when she went to pick it up, she saw that a zipper had been opened and her wallet with all her money and credit cards had been stolen. We could not believe that such a thing could happen in a place of worship. After reporting it to the police, Janet went to the British Consulate where an employee cancelled her credit cards. Luckily, I had enough money for both of us.

"Now," Janet said, "We will go and do whatever you want, I am at your mercy." This was not always the case, even though we get along pretty well, we sometimes do fight "like sisters," she says. Each wanting her own way.

Every evening, while in Prague, after taking many photographs, we would go to some local Czech restaurant, where the "goulash" was the best we ever tasted, and the waiter elegantly would ignite the "crepes suzettes" next to our table. These wonderful meals cost next to nothing, contrary to the very expensive hotel accommodations. Interestingly, we passed a night club, which displayed a photograph of President Clinton playing the saxophone. To relax, we would take a swim at the Hilton pool and generally enjoyed this intriguing city. But the day spent in the Jewish quarter will stay forever in my memory. It is unconscionable to think that such atrocities could have been committed in our century.

    I am glad to have had the opportunity to visit one of the most beautiful cities in Europe. But I know that I would never want to return again, because of the painful memories evoked by the Holocaust.

Chapter XXXVII

Martinique Revisited

A lot of years had passed since I was last in Martinique, where I had met a young native who was faithfully waiting for me five consecutive winter vacations.

Now, it was eighteen years later. In the same hotel, where I had stayed before, I enquired from a waitress who had been the former owner's sister, and who recognized me, what had happened to Marco. She told me: "He still lives in the vicinity." I decided to leave a note for him at the local grocery store, Boa Boa.

I was very anxious to find out what had happened to my ex-lover. Anse Mitan is, after all, a small village and the locals all know each other by name. Sure enough, the grocery owner told me: "I know him; he comes by here from time to time. I will give him your message." I was not sure whether he would really get my note. I was so curious to find out whether in the meantime, he had gotten married and had many children.

Several days went by. Suddenly the phone rang in my small hotel room. "There is a gentleman by the name of Marco, waiting for you at the reception," the voice said.

"I'll be right down, give me ten minutes," I said.

I was so excited that I was literally shaking. So many years had gone by. What will he look like? I thought. When I saw him, I was startled to see a tall slim man with a beard and with dreadlocks, looking like a hippie.

I invited him to my balcony for a drink and the first thing I asked him was: "Are you married?"

"No," he said. "I am divorced and I have a seven-year-old son."

Unfortunately, my plans for that evening were to meet a nice English couple for dinner at *Hemingway's* restaurant and bar. But there was a little time left to spend with Marco. "It was good, our love-making," he suddenly said. "When can we make love again?"

I could not believe that at my age he still found me attractive and answered somewhat elusively that I did want to meet him again, but that I had to go see my friends, as arranged.

"When do you want to see me again? It's up to you," he said.

"How about Wednesday?" I said, "because tomorrow we are renting a car to tour the island."

"I'll walk you to the restaurant along the beach," he said.

For a moment, I thought of cancelling my dinner plans since we had such a short time together after so many years. But then I decided against it. I did not want to be so easily available even though I knew my friends would have understood.

I thought later that he had held back about his marriage, when I asked him about his divorced wife, he had said. "I pick up my son from school every day at 4 p.m. and keep him till 7 p.m. Then I bring him to his mother."

"Do you stay there?" I asked.

"No," he said. "I detest her."

"How old is she?" I asked.

"She is younger that I am, but I like older women, they have more experience," he said.

"Do you live alone?" I asked.

"Yes," he said, "in my cabin in the country."

He walked me to the restaurant to meet my friends and we said good-bye.

Wednesday came, but my gut feeling told me: He is not going to show up. All kinds of crazy thoughts went through my mind: perhaps he had become gay; perhaps I had embarrassed him because of the fact that I had reminded him that he had told me in the past that he loved me; perhaps I talked too much about the "good old days." I was at a loss. I was right; he did not show up. I was extremely disappointed. I had wanted to see him again and to hear all about his life.

The rest of my days were spent having my usual morning cappuccino at the hotel on the beach where I used to stay long ago. I was extremely flattered that Josephine, the hotel owner's sister, had recognized me.

"You haven't changed," she had said. "I knew you right away."

We talked about how Martinique had changed.

"Chickens used to wake me up in the morning," I told her. There were no more chickens. Instead, a lot of petty bourgeois French groups from Brittany were staying in various small cottages in the back of the renovated hotel.

Other than that, actually Anse Mitan had not changed that much. The new restaurant, *Hemingway's* has a grassy field that serves as a parking lot, where two cows are grazing day and night. I found this wonderful. The village has a few new snack bars on the beach, but it still remains very primitive and the beach is still wonderful with its palm trees providing shade when the sun gets too hot.

The ferry still runs every hour or so to the main town, Fort de France, which is a bustling busy French city, somehow like a little Paris, with almost all the same type of shops. The large cruise ships stop there every day and many American tourists are milling around, desperately looking for a McDonald's; they are in luck: there is one there now. Except for the fact that I found a fairly clean bathroom there, why they would want to go there, when there are local cafés, where they can have a drink for half the price, is beyond me. (I must say that my skirt got soaked on the boat coming over and I used their hand dryers to dry it!) I had a great time shopping for food in one of the stores I recognized from Paris; it carries all the marvelous French cheeses, gourmet foods and my favorite bread, the baguette. I stopped for coffee and felt as if I were in Paris. I took some photographs of the beautiful library, the beheaded sculpture of Josephine because while married to Napoleon, she refused to abolish slavery; the natives simply knocked her head off. It got very hot, however, and in the end I couldn't wait to get the boat back to my hotel, to put on my bathing suit and jump into the blue sea. I never saw the sea to be that blue anywhere, certainly not on the French Riviera.

In the evening, I often went to *Hemingway's*. Michael, the restaurant's owner, who was over six feet tall, and who was originally from Texas, had a strange, almost Australian sounding accent, having lived all over the world. I was happy that he took a liking to me, because he was glad that I was an American. There are very few American tourists in Martinique because unless you speak French, it is not an island to visit; hardly anyone speaks English. The restaurant serves a wonderful buffet and the place attracts boat people cruising the Caribbean who stop there for lunch or dinner, since the restaurant has tables right on the sand, with a wonderful view of Fort de France.

Before I left Martinique, Michael gave me a huge bottle of the most delicious rum and six glasses as a souvenir.

At the end of my two weeks, Jean Claude, the owner of my hotel, said to me: "There was a local with dread locks asking for your room. I didn't want to send him up because why would you want to see him? So I sent him away." How little he knew. I was terribly upset.

Thus ended my fantasy of once again seeing my ex-lover.

Chapter XXXVIII

Edinburgh

It is now the summer of 1995, I have come full cycle. I am in Edinburgh, sitting in the dining room of the famous Hotel Balmoral, situated on the far side of Princess Street, Edinburgh's main street. My friend Janet and I are enjoying a great dinner here. The Balmoral is where the Queen stays when she is in residence in Scotland. It is a strange coincidence that I am here now when the city is celebrating the 50th anniversary of V. J. Day, the day the war ended in Japan at the end of World War II.

Sitting here brings back memories of exactly fifty years ago, when as a young girl, I stayed in this same hotel with my lover Badger, to celebrate the end of the war. How different things were for me then. I was in love and my whole life was before me. I felt protected by this man who had been my lover for two years. Despite feeling euphoric because it was the end of the war and we had escaped death, I was also sad because I knew that soon he and I were going to be separated, that he was going back home to America; that things were going to change drastically in my life too. But meanwhile we were celebrating here in Edinburgh.

Everything seems somewhat familiar and yet changed. The hotel's entrance is reminiscent of New York's Plaza Hotel. The porters are immaculately dressed with white gloves, as they push the guests' luggage around in the lobby. The hotel still serves afternoon tea with the traditional crumpets, strawberry jam and clotted cream, as well as watercress sandwiches; someone still plays the piano at tea time. But the one change we see is that the once sedate cocktail lounge now features a rock band, which plays at night to a rowdy young crowd that hangs out there in the evening.

Above Princess Street, which fifty years ago, was like our elegant Fifth Avenue, stands the castle high up like a giant, overlooking the whole city. But, unfortunately, now Princess Street is lined with a McDonald's, a Burger King, and a Pizza Hut. On the other hand, the adjoining gardens below the castle are well kept and flowers are blooming because of Scotland's wet climate. I watch as children are lolling around and tourists are enjoying themselves in these gardens which are open to the public.

Despite the many changes, Edinburgh is still a vibrant city, especially during the art festival when the city becomes one big party. I am happy to be here at this time when streets are packed with actors and tourists sightseeing, stopping and listening to the many happenings. On one side of the street, musicians are playing classical music; on the other side, a group of German musicians are playing 30's music; they attract a particularly large crowd. Somehow it all works. When they stop, they sell their tapes. A clown on stilts throws me a kiss when I photograph him. On one side of the street, where there is a red light, a man totally dressed in red is directing traffic; even his face is painted red. On the opposite side, facing him, another man is dressed in green with a green face. Kids in the streets are carrying banners advertising plays that can be seen all day long in various places.

Janet and I have seen six plays in five days: a Scottish play, brilliantly produced, which takes place on a farm at the turn of the century, showing how the farm hands were oppressed and taken advantage of by the owners, the gentry. Here I was unable to understand the Scottish brogue and in the first act could only understand one word: "Canada." Another play, taking place in England, was performed with a cockney accent, and again I had trouble understanding, but nevertheless, was at least able to follow the plot. The other plays, thank goodness, I understood more or less. We had to stand in long lines in order to get tickets for the best plays, but everyone was so friendly and we exchanged information about which plays to see, so it didn't matter.

We are staying in a bed and breakfast, a little way outside the center of town, where the landlady has taken great pains to make us feel at home. She suggested we buy a bus pass, and after two days, we did feel quite at home in this, one of the friendliest cities I have ever visited. She explained all the bus routes to us and the bus drivers were most patient with the many questions the tourists constantly asked. They were never disgruntled and they never lost their patience: "Just take your time, dearie," they would say with a smile.

We visited a contemporary museum, an exquisite architectural building, a little bit out of town, surrounded by acres of land, where we saw a wonderful exhibition that had originated in London's Tate Gallery.

For a change of pace, we took a bus to Glasgow, where one could see the city from an open-air bus.

Our entire trip was a sheer delight, even more so because we had travelled from London by train and we were thus able to see the countryside from our window; the golden fields bordered, at times, by the sea; the little villages with their church steeples, and often harbors with boats that seem to be dancing up and down in the breeze.

Now, one week later, during our train trip back to London, my thoughts wander back to my youth and I begin to get very sad. How little we know when we are young and how little I knew what was in store for me in the following fifty years.

"But one thing is sure," I say to Janet: "There won't be fifty more years."

"That goes for both of us," she says.

Author with Janet in front of her house in England. Ca 1999

Chapter XXXIX

Reminiscences About Travels

As is often the case, while travelling, one meets a lot of people who one becomes very friendly with and with whom one shares a lot of experiences. I find myself very often, getting into deep conversations while sitting in a plane next to someone, sharing intimate details with them. When the plane lands and the anxiety about flying disappears, one says good-bye, and even though, one sometimes exchanges telephone numbers, the whole incident seems to be forgotten. Somehow it is like that when meeting most people during travels.

My own experience with Claudette, despite travelling under extremely difficult circumstances from Avignon to Cadaquès and sharing a room for a week, could not have been more pleasant. We much enjoyed each others' company and had a lot of fun. However, when Claudette's vacation was over and she had to go back home to Rennes to continue her studies, we never saw each other again, but exchanged Christmas cards for a while. I always have fond memories of her and think back to the days when I was much more adventurous than later on in life.

The same was true with my relationship with Thierry on the Riviera. We met under extraordinary circumstances, in the middle of a revolution in Peru, where a curfew was imposed on us and we could not leave the hotel after 8 p.m. It was a night to remember with shooting taking place in the street outside the balcony of my window, and like in a wartime situation, we became close. So much so that he wanted to meet me the following year on the Riviera. Obviously, as we found out while travelling through the south of France, it was mostly a sexual attraction and once that wore out, there was not much that we had to say to each other. However, sometimes the opposite can also happen; this was the case when I met Mont in Barcelona. We had instant rapport, had much in common, and it turned into a relationship where for the past sixteen years, we have seen each other every year, either in Barcelona or in New York. To this day, we are still very close friends; we are in constant touch either by letter or telephone. It is hard to understand why this happens. Maybe that's why in life one has only a handful of very close friends.